Jambalaya

15th Anniversary Edition

Published by
**The Junior League
of New Orleans, Inc.**

The Junior League of New Orleans Publications
4319 Carondelet St.
New Orleans, La. 70115

1st Printing	August 1980	20,000
2nd Printing	December 1980	20,000
Revised Edition	October 1981	20,000
World's Fair Edition	July 1983	20,000
World's Fair Edition	March 1984	88,000
6th Printing	November 1994	12,000
7th Printing	October 1996	10,000
8th Printing	September 1998	5,000
9th Printing	December 1999	5,000
10th Printing	February 2001	10,000
11th Printing	July 2003	10,000

ISBN 0-9604774-3-8
Library of Congress Catalog #81-82780

WIMMER
COOKBOOKS

ConsolidatedGraphics

1-800-548-2537

CONTENTS

Brunch

Beignets and Cafe au Lait

Ask any native of the Crescent City what they most associate with home, and you can bet beignets and cafe au lait--our own very special version of donuts and coffee--will be on the list, near the top!

Beignets (pronounced ben-yays) are a bit like donuts with a French twist. They're rectangles, not rings, or a chewy dough that are deep fried to puff up into pillows, and then sprinkled with confectioners' sugar. Delicious! But what makes them really special is the experience of eating them, always accompanied by a fragrant cup of dark-roasted coffee and chicory, at a traditional New Orleans beignet cafe.

The most famous of these, Cafe du Monde and Morning Call, stood as arch rivals in the heart of the French Quarter for a hundred years. Then, in the 1970's, the latter moved out to the suburbs, where it does a thriving business. Cafe du Monde remains in its Decatur Street location directly across from Jackson Square just yards from the Mississippi River. There, the warm sweet smell of the frying beignets and the rich aroma of the coffee create an atmosphere like nowhere else in the world. Waiters in crisp white shirts and funny paper hats take your order from memory and entertain you with local lore. In the French Quarter, the sounds of jazz band on a nearby street or the deep echo of a riverboat's horn heighten this uniquely New Orleans experience.

A stop at Cafe du Monde or Morning Call is appropriate any time of the day, or night--both are open around the clock. Coffee and beignets are as perfect for breakfast as they are for dessert. A terrific time to visit is after-hours, particularly during Carnival season: even in thc smallest hours of the morning, you'll find Mardi Gras ball-goers and debutantes in formal white gowns ending their evening at the Cafe du Monde.

While most locals don't need to make their own beignets, if you're from out of town, it's a perfect way to bring a taste of New Orleans to your table. Jambalaya has a great Beignet recipe on page 19.

Scramble Jambalaya

4 tablespoons butter
¾ cup chopped onion
1½ cups chopped ham
2½ cups cooked rice
2 eggs
¼ cup finely chopped bell pepper

⅓ cup Parmesan cheese
½ teaspoon salt
¼ teaspoon black pepper
¾ cup grated cheddar cheese
1 tablespoon minced fresh parsley

Melt butter in an ovenproof skillet. Add onion and sauté until transparent. Remove from heat. Gently toss in ham and rice with a fork until well blended. In a small bowl, beat eggs and next 4 ingredients. Return skillet to heat and stir in egg mixture, cooking until done. Sprinkle with cheese and parsley. Place under a broiler until cheese melts. Yields 4 servings.

Egg Brunch

Sauce
4 slices bacon, diced
½ pound chipped beef, coarsely
    shredded
4 tablespoons butter

1 (8-ounce) can sliced mushrooms
½ cup all-purpose flour
¼ teaspoon black pepper
4 cups milk

Egg Mixture
16 eggs
¼ teaspoon salt

1 cup evaporated milk
4 tablespoons butter

In a large skillet, sauté bacon. Remove from heat. Add beef, butter, and most of mushrooms, reserving some mushrooms for garnish. Stir until butter melts. Sprinkle flour and pepper over mixture. Return to heat and gradually stir in milk. Cook, stirring constantly, until thick and smooth. To prepare egg mixture, beat eggs, salt, and milk in a large bowl. Melt butter in a large skillet. Add egg mixture and cook until done. Place half of egg mixture in a 9X13-inch baking dish. Top with half of sauce. Add remainder of egg mixture and cover with rest of sauce. Sprinkle reserved mushrooms over top. Cover with foil. Bake at 275° for 60 minutes. Yields 10 to 12 servings.

Baked Artichoke Heart and Shrimp Omelet

6 eggs
½ teaspoon salt
⅛ teaspoon cayenne pepper
2 tablespoons olive oil
¾ cup chopped green onions

1 (14-ounce) can artichoke hearts,
  drained and quartered
1 cup cooked and peeled shrimp
1 tablespoon butter
¾ cup grated Jarlsberg cheese
¼ cup Parmesan cheese

Beat eggs, salt, and cayenne pepper in a bowl. Heat oil in a skillet. Add onions and sauté until softened. Add artichokes and cook 2 to 3 minutes. Remove from heat and stir in shrimp. Pour artichoke mixture into egg mixture and blend well. Grease a 1½-quart baking dish with butter. Pour mixture into dish. Sprinkle cheeses evenly over top. Bake at 400° in upper portion of oven for 15 to 20 minutes or until omelet is firm and a knife inserted in the center comes out clean. Yields 4 servings.

Crawfish Omelet

¾ cup crawfish tails, boiled and
  seasoned (about 2 pounds whole)
3 tablespoons minced green onions
3 tablespoons butter
1 tablespoon chopped fresh parsley

1 teaspoon Worcestershire sauce
⅛ teaspoon cayenne pepper
⅛ teaspoon salt
1 (3-egg) basic omelet

Peel crawfish, reserving as much fat as possible. Coarsely chop crawfish. Lightly sauté onions in butter in a small skillet. Stir in crawfish, fat, and parsley. Season with Worcestershire sauce, cayenne pepper, and salt. Keep filling warm while preparing omelet. Spread filling over half of set omelet and fold. Serve immediately. Yields 1 serving.

Maple Syrup Souffléed Omelet

3 eggs, separated
6 tablespoons maple syrup, divided
½ teaspoon vanilla
pinch of salt

3 tablespoons butter
¼ cup blanched almonds
4 slices bacon, cooked and
    crumbled

Beat egg yolks until frothy. Add 3 tablespoons syrup, vanilla, and salt. In a separate bowl, beat egg whites until stiff peaks form. Fold white into yolk mixture. Melt butter in a 12-inch ovenproof skillet. Sprinkle with almonds. Pour in egg mixture and cook over low heat for 8 minutes. Transfer pan to oven and bake at 350° for 8 to 10 minutes. To serve, fold omelet and transfer to a hot serving dish. Pour remaining 3 tablespoons syrup over top. Garnish with bacon and serve immediately. Yields 2 servings.

Crabmeat Quiche

1 (10-inch) pastry shell
3 eggs
1 cup heavy cream
1 tablespoon tomato paste
½ teaspoon salt
⅛ teaspoon cayenne pepper

4 tablespoons butter
⅓ cup chopped green onions
½ cup chopped fresh mushrooms
1 cup fresh crabmeat
2 tablespoons dry vermouth
½ cup grated cheddar cheese

Prick pastry shell and bake at 425° for 12 minutes. In a bowl, beat eggs and cream. Add tomato paste, salt, and cayenne pepper. Mix well. Melt butter in a skillet. Add onions and mushrooms and sauté 5 minutes. Stir in crabmeat and vermouth and cook over low heat for several minutes. Add crabmeat mixture to egg mixture and stir until combined. Pour into pastry shell and bake at 375° for 35 minutes. Sprinkle with cheese and bake 10 minutes longer, or until a knife inserted in the center comes out clean. Yields 6 to 8 servings.

Spinach Quiche

1 (10-inch) pastry shell
¾ cup chopped white onion
⅓ cup chopped green onions
¼ cup chopped fresh parsley
2 tablespoons butter, melted
1 (10-ounce) package frozen
   chopped spinach, cooked and
   well drained
2 tablespoons all-purpose flour
1 teaspoon salt

¼ teaspoon black pepper
¼ teaspoon nutmeg
⅛ teaspoon cayenne pepper
1 tablespoon Worcestershire sauce
2 eggs, beaten
1 cup grated Swiss, Jarlsberg, or
   Gruyére cheese
⅓ cup Parmesan cheese
1¼ cups milk

Prick pastry shell and bake at 400° for 8 minutes. Sauté onions and parsley in butter. Add spinach and cook 2 minutes. Add flour and next 5 ingredients. Mix well. In a bowl, combine egg and remaining 3 ingredients. Add to spinach mixture. Pour into pastry shell and bake at 350° for 45 to 60 minutes or until a knife inserted in the center comes out clean. Yields 4 to 6 servings.

Apple Sausage Quiche

½ pound ground pork sausage
⅓ cup chopped onion
¼ teaspoon dried thyme
1¼ cups peeled and diced apple
1 tablespoon lemon juice

1 tablespoon packed brown sugar
3 eggs
1¼ cups light cream
½ cup grated cheddar cheese
1 (10-inch) pastry shell

Cook sausage in a skillet. Transfer sausage, using a slotted spoon, onto paper towels to drain. Add onion and thyme to skillet and sauté in remaining sausage drippings. In a bowl, toss apple, lemon juice, and sugar. In a separate bowl, beat eggs. Add apple mixture, sausage, onion mixture, cream, and cheese. Pour into pastry shell. Bake at 350° for 50 minutes or until a knife inserted in the center comes out clean. Yields 6 to 8 servings.

Artichoke Quiche

1 (9-inch) pastry shell
⅓ cup chopped green onions
2 tablespoons butter, melted
2 eggs
1 tablespoon all-purpose flour
⅔ cup light cream

1 (14-ounce) can artichoke hearts,
   drained and coarsely chopped
1 cup grated hot pepper cheese
1 cup grated cheddar cheese,
   divided

Prick pastry shell and bake at 400° for 12 minutes. Sauté onions in butter. In a large bowl, beat eggs, flour, and cream. Stir in onion mixture, artichokes, pepper cheese, and all but 3 tablespoons cheddar cheese. Pour into pastry shell. Bake at 350° for 35 minutes. Sprinkle remaining 3 tablespoons cheddar cheese over top. Bake 10 more minutes, or until a knife inserted in the center comes out clean. Yields 6 servings.

Mushroom Quiche

Shell and Filling
1 (9-inch) pastry shell
4 slices bacon, cooked and
   crumbled
1 cup water
1½ teaspoons salt

½ cup sliced white onion
¾ cup grated Swiss cheese
2 cups sliced fresh mushrooms
2 tablespoons butter

Custard
1 tablespoon butter
1 tablespoon all-purpose flour
1 cup milk, warmed
2 eggs, well beaten

½ teaspoon salt
⅛ teaspoon cayenne pepper
⅛ teaspoon nutmeg

Prick pastry shell and bake at 425° for 12 minutes. Sprinkle bacon over bottom of shell. Combine water and salt in a saucepan and bring to a boil. Add onion and cook until softened. Drain onion and place over bacon. Sprinkle cheese on top. Sauté mushrooms in butter. Drain mushrooms and distribute over cheese. To prepare custard, melt butter in a saucepan over low heat. Remove from heat and stir in flour until smooth. Return pan to heat and cook 3 minutes. Whisk in milk and cook slowly until slightly thickened. Cool 5 minutes. Stir in egg and remaining 3 ingredients. Pour mixture into pastry shell. Bake at 350° for 40 minutes or until a knife inserted in the center comes out clean. Yields 6 servings.

Sausage Quiche

1 (10-inch) pastry shell
1½ cups grated Swiss cheese
1½ cups grated cheddar cheese
½ cup Parmesan cheese
1 pound ground hot sausage,
  browned and drained

½ cup grated onion
3 eggs
½ cup light cream
1 cup sour cream

Prick pastry shell and bake at 425° for 12 minutes. Combine Swiss cheese and next 4 ingredients in a large bowl. In a small bowl, beat eggs and creams. Add to cheese mixture. Pour into pastry shell. Bake at 375° for 50 to 60 minutes or until a knife inserted in the center comes out clean. Yields 6 servings.

Brie Quiche

1 (9-inch) pastry shell
8 ounces Brie cheese, rind removed,
  softened
1 (8-ounce) package cream cheese,
  softened

4 tablespoons butter, softened
6 tablespoons heavy cream
4 eggs, beaten
4 dashes Tabasco sauce
1 tablespoon minced chives

Prick pastry shell and bake at 400° for 12 minutes. Blend Brie cheese and next 3 ingredients. Add egg and mix well. Stir in Tabasco sauce and chives. Pour into pastry shell. Bake at 375° in upper third of oven for 25 to 30 minutes or until quiche puffs and top browns. Yields 6 to 8 servings.

Baked Zucchini Pie

1¼ pounds zucchini, grated
2 teaspoons salt, divided
¾ cup Parmesan cheese, divided
4 egg yolks, lightly beaten
½ cup grated onion
1 cup mashed potato

1 tablespoon olive oil
¼ teaspoon minced garlic
¼ teaspoon black pepper
¼ teaspoon nutmeg
4 egg whites, stiffly beaten

Place zucchini in a bowl. Sprinkle with 1½ teaspoons salt and let stand 15 minutes. Drain well. Add remaining ½ teaspoon salt, ½ cup cheese, and next 7 ingredients. Fold in egg white until thoroughly combined. Pour into a lightly greased 10-inch pie plate. Sprinkle with remaining ¼ cup cheese. Bake at 350° for 30 minutes or until a knife inserted in the center comes out clean. Yields 8 servings.

Black Olive and Tomato Pie

1 (9-inch) pastry shell
2 medium tomatoes
¾ teaspoon salt, divided
¼ cup all-purpose flour
¼ teaspoon black pepper
2 tablespoons olive oil
½ cup sliced black olives

1 cup minced green onions, divided
3 ounces provolone cheese, thinly
  sliced
2 eggs, lightly beaten
1 cup grated cheddar cheese
1 cup heavy cream

Prick pastry shell and bake at 425° for 12 minutes. Cut each tomato into 7 (½-inch thick) slices. Place slices on paper towels and sprinkle with ¼ teaspoon salt. Let stand 15 minutes, turning once. Combine flour, remaining ½ teaspoon salt, and pepper in a shallow dish. Dip tomato slices in flour mixture. Heat oil in a skillet. Sauté tomato slices in oil. Arrange olives and all but 2 tablespoons green onions in the bottom of pastry shell. Cover with provolone cheese and top with tomato slices. In a bowl, combine egg, cheddar cheese, and cream. Pour over tomato slices. Bake at 375° for 45 minutes or until a knife inserted in the center comes out clean. Sprinkle with remaining 2 tablespoons onions. Cool 5 minutes before cutting. Yields 6 servings.

Sunday Brunch Delight

If desired, substitute diced ham or crawfish for shrimp.

3 tablespoons butter
3 tablespoons all-purpose flour
1½ cups milk
½ teaspoon salt
½ teaspoon curry powder
1 tablespoon minced onion
¼ teaspoon celery seed

1 cup cooked shrimp
5 eggs
1 cup grated cheddar cheese
5 slices buttered toast or English
  muffins
fresh parsley for garnish

Melt butter in a saucepan. Blend in flour. Add milk and next 4 ingredients. Bring to a boil over low heat, stirring constantly. Cook until thickened. Stir in shrimp. Pour into a greased shallow baking dish. Break eggs and drop on top. Sprinkle with cheese. Bake at 350° for 15 to 20 minutes or until eggs reach desired degree of doneness and cheese is lightly browned. Serve on toast and garnish with parsley. Yields 4 servings.

Fancy Egg Scramble

Cheese Sauce
2 tablespoons butter
2 tablespoons all-purpose flour
½ teaspoon salt

⅛ teaspoon black pepper
2 cups milk
1 cup grated cheddar cheese

Filling
1 cup diced Canadian bacon, ham,
  or cooked bacon
¼ cup chopped green onions
5 tablespoons butter, divided
12 eggs, beaten

1 (8-ounce) can sliced mushrooms,
  drained
2 cups Cheese Sauce
2¼ cups breadcrumbs
⅛ teaspoon paprika

Melt butter in a saucepan. Gradually stir in flour. Add salt and pepper. Slowly stir in milk and cook until sauce thickens. Add cheese and stir until melted. Remove from heat. To prepare filling, sauté bacon and onions in 3 tablespoons butter until onions soften. Add egg and cook, over low heat, until set. Remove from heat and stir in mushrooms and cheese sauce. Pour into a greased 7X11 inch baking dish. Melt remaining 2 tablespoons butter and mix with breadcrumbs and paprika. Sprinkle over egg mixture. Bake, uncovered, at 350° for 30 minutes. Yields 8 servings.

West Indian Eggs

1½ cups tomato sauce
¼ cup minced green onions
¼ cup minced bell pepper
2 tablespoons all-purpose flour
1 cup grated cheddar cheese,
  divided
2 dashes Tabasco sauce

1 teaspoon lemon juice
⅛ teaspoon dried tarragon
2 cups peeled and cubed avocado
12 eggs
⅔ cup light cream
½ teaspoon salt
4 tablespoons butter

Combine tomato sauce and next 3 ingredients in a saucepan. Bring to a boil. Cook and stir 2 to 3 minutes. Stir in ⅔ cup cheese and next 3 ingredients. Remove from heat and add avocado. DO NOT COOK, but keep warm. Adjust seasonings as needed. In a large bowl, beat eggs, cream, and salt. Melt butter in a large skillet. Add egg mixture and cook until set. Transfer egg mixture to a warmed serving platter. Spoon tomato sauce over top. Sprinkle with remaining ⅓ cup cheese. Serve immediately. Yields 8 servings.

Eggs Caviar

10 hard-cooked eggs, peeled and
  halved lengthwise
6 ounces blue cheese, softened
1/3 cup black caviar
1 tablespoon chopped chives

1 1/2 teaspoons minced fresh parsley
1/8 teaspoon cayenne pepper
1/2 cup mayonnaise
1 tablespoon lemon juice
5 black olives, sliced

Remove egg yolks and mash, reserving whites. In a bowl, mash cheese. Mix in caviar and next 5 ingredients. Blend in yolk. Spoon mixture into egg white shells. Garnish each with an olive slice. Yields 20 stuffed eggs.

Creole Scramble

1 tablespoon olive oil
1/2 pound smoked sausage, thinly
  sliced
1/2 teaspoon finely chopped garlic
1/8 teaspoon cayenne pepper
1/2 cup sliced green onions

3/4 cup peeled and quartered fresh
  tomato
1/2 cup thinly sliced bell pepper
1/3 cup cold water
1/8 teaspoon black pepper
6 eggs, lightly beaten

Heat oil in a skillet. Add sausage and next 3 ingredients. Cook, stirring frequently, until sausage is lightly browned. Add tomato and next 3 ingredients. Cook quickly until most of liquid evaporates but bell pepper is still crisp. Add egg. Cook and stir over low heat until soft and creamy. Serve immediately. Yields 4 servings.

Spanish Eggs

6 slices bacon
1 cup small corn chips
1 cup chopped onion
1/2 cup thinly sliced bell pepper
1/4 teaspoon salt

1/4 teaspoon cayenne pepper
8 eggs, beaten
1 (15-ounce) can chili, heated
1 cup grated sharp cheddar cheese

Cook bacon in a skillet until crisp. Transfer bacon, using a slotted spoon, onto paper towels to drain. Remove all but 3 tablespoons bacon fat from skillet. Add corn chips to skillet and cook and stir 2 minutes. Add onion and bell pepper and sauté until onion turns transparent. Crumble bacon into a bowl. Mix in salt, cayenne pepper, and egg. Pour into skillet and cook over medium-low heat, stirring constantly, until egg sets. Place mixture in a 1-quart casserole dish. Pour chili over top and sprinkle with cheese. Serve immediately. Yields 6 servings.

Bacon Cheese Soufflé

6 slices bacon	¼ teaspoon paprika
⅓ cup chopped white onion	1½ cups grated Swiss cheese
5 eggs, separated	¼ teaspoon salt
3 tablespoons all-purpose flour	1 cup grated cheddar cheese
2 dashes Tabasco sauce	1 tablespoon chopped fresh parsley
1¼ cups milk	

Cook bacon in a skillet until crisp. Transfer bacon, using a slotted spoon, onto paper towels to drain. Remove all but 2 tablespoons bacon fat from skillet. Add onion and sauté. In a large bowl, combine egg yolks and next 4 ingredients. Beat until smooth. Stir in Swiss cheese. In a small bowl, beat egg whites and salt until stiff, but not dry. Fold egg white into yolk mixture. Pour over onion in skillet and cover. Cook over low heat for 12 to 15 minutes, or until almost set. Crumble bacon over top and sprinkle with cheddar cheese. Cover and cook 5 minutes longer or until firmly set. Sprinkle with parsley and serve immediately. Yields 6 servings.

Sausage and Egg Puff

1 pound ground hot sausage	½ teaspoon salt
2 slices white bread, cubed	1 drop Tabasco sauce
1 cup grated sharp cheddar cheese	1 teaspoon dry mustard
6 eggs	1 teaspoon Worcestershire sauce
1⅔ cups milk	

Brown sausage in a skillet, stirring to crumble into small pieces. Drain. In a 2-quart casserole dish, layer sausage, bread, and cheese. In a bowl, beat eggs and remaining 5 ingredients. Pour over layers in casserole dish. Cover and refrigerate 12 hours or overnight. Remove from refrigerator 60 minutes before cooking. Bake, uncovered, at 350° for 45 minutes or until golden on top and firm. Yields 6 servings.

Souffléed Cheese Toast

6 slices white bread, crusts removed
2½ tablespoons butter, softened
6 slices ham
18 spears asparagus, cooked
4 eggs, separated
1 teaspoon dry mustard

¼ teaspoon Worcestershire sauce
⅛ teaspoon cayenne pepper
1 cup grated sharp cheddar cheese
¼ teaspoon salt
thinly sliced pimiento strips for
   garnish

Toast bread and lightly butter one side. Place buttered-side up on a greased baking sheet. Top each slice with 1 ham slice and 3 asparagus spears. In a bowl, beat egg yolks and next 3 ingredients. Stir in cheese. In a separate bowl, beat egg whites and salt until stiff. Fold a small amount of egg white into yolk mixture. Fold in remaining egg white. Spoon mixture over asparagus. Bake at 375° for 10 minutes or until puffed and lightly browned. Garnish with pimiento. Yields 6 servings.

Cheese Soufflé

6 tablespoons butter
6 tablespoons all-purpose flour
2 cups milk
¾ teaspoon salt
¼ teaspoon white pepper
10 drops Tabasco sauce

¼ teaspoon dry mustard
¼ teaspoon nutmeg
2 cups grated sharp cheddar cheese
8 egg yolks, well beaten
8 egg whites, stiffly beaten

Melt butter in the top of a double boiler. Stir in flour. Slowly add milk. Cook and stir until thickened. Add salt and next 5 ingredients. Stir until cheese melts. Stir 2 tablespoons of cheese mixture into egg yolk. Pour yolk mixture into cheese mixture. Whisk over double boiler for 30 seconds. Remove from heat and cool slightly. Fold in egg white. Pour into a 3-quart ungreased soufflé dish. Place in a pan of warm water. Starting 1 inch from the edge, make a ½ inch deep cut around the entire surface of soufflé. Bake at 325° for 55 minutes or until set in the middle and golden on top. Serve immediately. Yields 6 to 8 servings.

Deviled Eggs with Béchamel Sauce

Prepare deviled eggs ahead and refrigerate until ready to serve. If desired, prepare sauce ahead and freeze until needed.

Deviled Eggs

18 hard-cooked eggs, halved
   lengthwise
¾ cup mayonnaise

¼ cup hot mustard
4 dashes Tabasco sauce
½ teaspoon white pepper

Béchamel Sauce

4 tablespoons butter
6 tablespoons all-purpose flour
½ teaspoon salt
2 cups chicken broth
1¼ cups half-and-half
2 teaspoons lemon juice

16 ripe olives, chopped
16 pimiento-stuffed olives, chopped
½ teaspoon paprika
1 cup grated cheddar cheese
1½ tablespoons minced fresh
   parsley

Remove egg yolks and mash, reserving whites. Add mayonnaise and next 3 ingredients. Mix well. Spoon mixture into egg white shells. Place in a shallow baking dish. To prepare sauce, melt butter in the top of a double boiler. Blend in flour and salt. Slowly add broth and half-and-half. Cook and stir until thickened. Add lemon juice and next 4 ingredients. Stir until cheese melts. Spoon sauce over eggs. Sprinkle with parsley. Bake at 350° for 15 minutes. Yields 12 to 14 servings.

Broiled Cheese Muffins

2 cups grated cheddar cheese
4 hard-cooked eggs, chopped
½ cup mayonnaise
1 (2-ounce) jar diced pimiento,
   drained
1 tablespoon chopped celery

1 tablespoon chopped green onions
1 teaspoon horseradish
¼ teaspoon salt
3 dashes Tabasco sauce
4 English muffins, split
1 tablespoon chopped fresh parsley

Combine cheese and next 8 ingredients in a large bowl. Blend well and spread over muffin halves. Sprinkle with parsley. Broil on a baking sheet for 7 minutes or until golden brown. Yields 4 servings.

Swiss Toast

½ cup chopped white onion
3 sticks butter, softened, divided
1½ pounds fresh mushrooms, sliced
½ cup white wine
2 cups half-and-half
¾ cup all-purpose flour
1 teaspoon lemon juice
½ teaspoon salt

⅛ teaspoon white pepper
12 slices bread, toasted
24 slices ham
24 slices Swiss cheese
paprika
chopped fresh parsley and thinly
    sliced pimiento strips for garnish

Sauté onion in 1 stick of butter in a saucepan. Add mushrooms and wine. Cover and cook 10 to 15 minutes. Remove mushrooms with a slotted spoon and reserve. Add half-and-half to saucepan and remove from heat. In a small bowl, blend flour and another stick of butter. Add to saucepan and cook over low heat, stirring frequently, for 5 minutes or until smooth and thick. Stir in reserved mushrooms, lemon juice, salt, and pepper. Butter bread with remaining stick of butter. Place bread, buttered-side up, on 2 jelly-roll pans. Cover each piece with a slice of ham. Spoon mushroom mixture over top and cover with another slice of ham and 2 slices of cheese. Sprinkle with paprika. Bake at 375° for 7 minutes or until cheese melts. Garnish with parsley and pimiento. Yields 10 to 12 servings.

Beignets

Refrigerate any unused dough for up to 1 week.

1 package dry yeast
½ cup warm water
½ cup evaporated milk
1 egg, beaten
1 teaspoon vanilla
2 tablespoons vegetable oil

¼ cup sugar
1 teaspoon salt
3 cups all-purpose flour
oil for deep-frying
powdered sugar

Dissolve yeast in warm water in a large mixing bowl. Add milk and next 5 ingredients. Vigorously beat in flour. Dough will be very sticky. Work a fourth of the dough at a time. Place dough on a heavily floured surface. Use a well-floured rolling pin to roll dough to about ⅛-inch thickness. Cut into 2-inch squares. Drop beignets, a few at a time, into 370° oil. As beignets rise to the surface and puff, turn over to brown other side. When uniformly browned, remove from oil and drain on paper towels. Dust with powdered sugar and serve warm. Yields 4 dozen.

Eggs In Tomatoes Florentine

Spinach Mixture
2 (10-ounce) packages frozen
   chopped spinach, thawed
1 cup sour cream
½ teaspoon garlic salt
½ teaspoon celery salt
2 teaspoons Worcestershire sauce

2 teaspoons chives
¼ teaspoon black pepper
⅛ teaspoon cayenne pepper
¼ teaspoon nutmeg
½ cup Parmesan cheese

Tomatoes
6 (3-inch diameter) ripe, firm
   tomatoes
1 teaspoon salt
4 tablespoons butter, divided
2 tablespoons finely chopped green
   onions

6 eggs
¼ cup seasoned bread crumbs
¼ cup Parmesan cheese
6 slices bacon, cooked and crumbles

Squeeze moisture out of spinach. Combine spinach and next 9 ingredients in a saucepan. Cook over low heat until warm. To prepare tomatoes, slice the top off each tomato. Scoop out and discard pulp. Sprinkle inside of tomatoes with salt and invert on a rack for 20 minutes to drain. Place tomatoes, right-side up, in a lightly greased 10X12 inch casserole dish. Put 1 teaspoon butter in each tomato. Top with 1 teaspoon of onions. Break an egg into each tomato. Bake at 400° for 10 minutes. Line a separate greased 10X12 inch shallow baking dish with spinach mixture. Transfer tomatoes to dish. Loosely cover with foil and bake 15 minutes or until egg whites set. Melt remaining 2 tablespoons butter. Top each tomato with 2 teaspoons breadcrumbs, 2 teaspoons cheese, and 1 teaspoon melted butter. Broil until crumbs are lightly browned. Remove from oven and sprinkle with bacon. Yields 6 servings.

Hors D'Oeuvres & Appetizers

Mardi Gras Party

If you've been in New Orleans during the Carnival season you know what a truly unparalleled experience it is. Parades. Costumes. Parties. An endless revel that begins days before Fat Tuesday and builds to the frenzy that is Mardi Gras Day. It's an event like no other!

What makes Mardi Gras so special is the merriment and conviviality of it all. It's the ultimate social whirl: a festive free-for-all, where friends and families head for the streets, joining the crowds in laughter and drinking, all the while shouting at the passing floats the mantra, "Hey mister, throw me something!" It goes on for days, as parade after parade snakes through the streets of the city and suburbs alike.

And as if this were not enough fun, New Orleanians have found yet another way to add to the revelry: the parade party. There are no formal customs to be observed, but every parade party follows the same basic pattern. Among every group of friends are at least one or two who live on or near the streets where Mardi Gras parades pass. By virtue of that fact, they become parade party hosts for Mardi Gras, opening their doors to friends and acquaintances who wander in when in need of food, drink, or respite from the merrymaking on the street.

While the hedonistic atmosphere of Mardi Gras in New Orleans can never be duplicated, you can certainly throw a Mardi Gras-style party anywhere. In fact, transplanted New Orleanians do it every year, wherever they may be. Here a few tips on what you'll need:

Start off with plenty of decorations in purple, green and gold, the Mardi Gras colors; and a record of Mardi Gras tunes or good New Orleans Dixieland Jazz is a must! As for food, at a true Mardi Gras open house you'll be sure to find Red Beans and Rice (try our recipe on p. 48) and plenty of King Cake (You can make your own with our recipe on p.196). A big pot of Jambalaya is also a staple at most parade parties (we've got several: Shrimp and Sausage on p. 77 is a popular favorite). And you can't go wrong with a Glazed Party Ham (p. 132) served with party rolls and our spicy Creole Mayonnaise (p. 68). Of course, you'll have to have a few bowls of chips around; you can serve them with our Classic Spinach Dip (p.36).

Spicy Stuffed Mushrooms Jambalaya

1 pound large fresh mushrooms,
  washed and drained
2 tablespoons butter
1/2 cup finely chopped yellow onion
1/2 cup finely diced pepperoni
1/4 cup finely chopped bell pepper
1/4 teaspoon pressed garlic

2 cups finely crushed buttery
  cracker crumbs
3 tablespoons Parmesan cheese
1 tablespoon chopped fresh parsley
1/2 teaspoon seasoned salt
1/4 teaspoon dried oregano
1/8 teaspoon black pepper
1 cup chicken broth

Remove and chop mushroom stems, reserving mushroom caps. Melt butter in a skillet. Add onion and sauté 5 minutes. Add mushroom stems, pepperoni, bell pepper, and garlic. Cook 10 minutes or until vegetables are tender but not brown. Mix in cracker crumbs and next 5 ingredients. Stir in broth. Spoon stuffing mixture into mushroom caps, rounding tops. Place mushrooms in a shallow pan with about 1/4-inch water. Bake at 325° for 25 minutes. Serve immediately. Yields 12 servings.

Shrimp Meunière

1 stick butter
1 cup finely chopped green onions
1/2 cup finely chopped celery, inner
  stalks
1/4 cup finely chopped fresh parsley
1/3 cup finely chopped bell pepper
1 tablespoon garlic purée
1 teaspoon salt

1 teaspoon black pepper
1 tablespoon Worcestershire sauce
1 tablespoon cornstarch
1/4 cup dry white wine
3 pounds raw shrimp, peeled and
  deveined
toast points or saffron rice

Slowly melt butter in a large, covered skillet. Add green onions and next 7 ingredients. Blend thoroughly. Cover and simmer 30 minutes, stirring occasionally. Dissolve cornstarch in wine. Blend into vegetable mixture. Add shrimp. Cover and simmer 5 to 10 minutes. Serve immediately over toast points as an appetizer, or over saffron rice as an entrée. To reheat, place in top of a double boiler and heat slowly. Yields 8 appetizer servings, 6 entrée servings.

Shrimp Dip Delight

1 pound raw shrimp
1 (8-ounce) package cream cheese, softened
½ cup finely chopped green onions
½ cup chopped celery
3 tablespoons lemon juice
2 tablespoons chopped fresh parsley
½ teaspoon salt
⅛ teaspoon cayenne pepper
½ cup mayonnaise

Boil, peel, devein, and chop shrimp. Blend cream cheese and remaining 7 ingredients in a bowl. Fold in shrimp. Cover and refrigerate. Serve with crackers or fresh celery and carrot sticks. Yields 6 servings.

Seafood Glacé

2 (¼-ounce) packages unflavored gelatin
½ cup cold water
2 (10-ounce) cans consommé
1 tablespoon lemon juice
2 tablespoons finely chopped green onions
2 tablespoons finely chopped fresh parsley
¼ teaspoon Tabasco sauce
36 boiled shrimp or crawfish, or ½ pound fresh crabmeat
36 crackers
mayonnaise

Sprinkle gelatin over water and stir. Heat consommé until hot but not boiling. Stir in gelatin mixture, lemon juice, and next 3 ingredients. Divide shrimp among 36 greased small muffin tins or egg holders. Pour consommé mixture over shrimp. Cover and refrigerate 6 to 8 hours. Spread crackers with a thin layer of mayonnaise. Unmold consommé mixture and serve on crackers. Yields 3 dozen.

Shrimp Appetizer

6 pounds raw shrimp, unshelled
2 bay leaves
1 tablespoon celery seed
¾ cup salt
1 teaspoon cayenne pepper
2 cups oil
½ cup ketchup
3 tablespoons lemon juice
¼ cup apple cider vinegar
1 tablespoon Worcestershire sauce
1 (5-ounce) jar horseradish
1 (5-ounce) jar hot Creole mustard
1 cup thinly sliced yellow onion
salt and pepper to taste

Place shrimp in a large pot. Cover with water. Add bay leaves and next 3 ingredients. Bring to a boil and cook 5 minutes or until shrimp are pink. Drain and peel shrimp. Combine oil and next 7 ingredients. Add shrimp. Season with salt and pepper. Cover and refrigerate overnight. Serve with toothpicks or on crackers. Yields 12 to 14 servings.

Caponata

Caponata will keep several months under refrigeration, but will not freeze well.

2 pounds eggplant, peeled and cut
    into ½-inch cubes
1½ tablespoons salt
½ cup olive oil
1 cup chopped yellow onion
1½ cups finely chopped celery
¾ teaspoon minced garlic
2 teaspoons sugar
½ cup wine vinegar
1 cup sliced pimiento-stuffed olives

1 cup sliced black olives
¼ cup capers
½ cup vodka
3 cups canned Italian plum
    tomatoes, partially drained and
    chopped
¼ cup tomato paste
6 finely chopped anchovies
1 teaspoon black pepper
½ teaspoon Tabasco sauce

Sprinkle eggplant with salt and let stand in a colander for 60 minutes. Drain well on paper towels. Heat oil in a large saucepan. Add onion, celery, and garlic and sauté 10 minutes. Remove vegetables. Add eggplant to saucepan and sauté 15 minutes or until lightly browned. Add more oil if needed. Dissolve sugar in vinegar. Return vegetables to saucepan. Stir in sugar mixture, pimiento stuffed olives, and remaining 8 ingredients. Bring to a boil. Reduce heat and simmer 45 minutes, stirring frequently. Refrigerate at least 4 days before serving. Serve with crackers or melba toast. Yields 8 cups.

Crabmeat Stuffed Mushrooms

12 large fresh mushrooms, washed
1 cup finely chopped yellow onion
6 tablespoons butter, divided
1 tablespoon all-purpose flour
½ cup crabmeat

2 tablespoons sherry
1 tablespoon chopped fresh parsley
½ teaspoon salt
¼ teaspoon black pepper
½ cup corn flake crumbs

Remove and finely chop mushroom stems, reserving mushroom caps. Sauté onion in 3 tablespoons butter for 5 minutes or until golden. Add mushroom stems and cook 5 minutes. Stir in flour and next 5 ingredients. Sauté 2 to 3 minutes, stirring gently. Remove from heat. Stuff mixture into mushroom caps and place on a well-greased baking pan. Sprinkle with corn flake crumbs and top each cap with a pat of remaining butter. Bake at 350° for 20 minutes. Serve immediately. Yields 12 mushrooms.

Marinated Crab Claws

1 (0.6-ounce) package dry Italian
   salad dressing mix
3/4 cup olive oil
1/4 cup champagne vinegar
1/2 teaspoon dried oregano
1 tablespoon lemon juice
1/2 teaspoon finely minced garlic

1/4 cup dried parsley
1/4 teaspoon salt
1/2 teaspoon black pepper
1/4 cup Parmesan cheese
1 tablespoon white wine
1 tablespoon Worcestershire sauce
1 (16-ounce) can crab claws

Combine dressing mix, oil, and vinegar. Add oregano and next 8 ingredients. Place marinade mixture and crab claws in a large zip-top plastic bag and seal. Place bag in a shallow dish and refrigerate overnight, turning several times to redistribute marinade. Yields 6 to 8 servings.

Molded Crabmeat or Shrimp Ring

1 (10¾-ounce) can condensed
   cream of mushroom soup
2 (3-ounce) packages cream cheese,
   softened
2 tablespoons unflavored gelatin
6 tablespoons white wine
1 cup finely chopped green onions
1 cup finely chopped celery
1 pound white crabmeat, or 4
   pounds raw shrimp, cooked,
   peeled, and deveined

1 cup mayonnaise
1/2 teaspoon Tabasco sauce
2 teaspoons salt
2 tablespoons lemon juice
2 tablespoons Worcestershire sauce
1/2 teaspoon black pepper
1 (2-ounce) jar pimiento, or 1/4 cup
   sliced pimiento-stuffed olives

Warm soup in the top of a double boiler. Whisk in cream cheese until well blended. Dissolve gelatin in wine and add to soup mixture. Blend and remove from heat. Add onions and next 8 ingredients. Pour into a well-greased 8-inch mold. Cover and refrigerate overnight. Unmold and garnish with pimiento. Serve with melba toast or crackers. Yields 12 servings.

Hot Crabmeat

1½ sticks butter, divided
1 cup finely chopped yellow onion
½ cup finely chopped green onions
¾ teaspoon pressed garlic
½ cup finely chopped fresh parsley
¼ cup all-purpose flour
1 cup milk
1 cup white wine
1 pound crabmeat
1½ cups croutons
½ cup French dressing

Melt 1 stick butter in a small skillet. Add yellow onion and next 3 ingredients and sauté until tender. Drain on a paper towel. Melt remaining ½ stick butter in the top of a double boiler. Gradually stir in flour. Slowly add milk and cook 15 minutes or until mixture thickens. Slowly fold in wine with a whisk. Add sautéed vegetables. Gently fold in crabmeat. Keep hot over double boiler until ready to serve. Soak croutons in dressing for 20 minutes. Just prior to serving, fold croutons into crabmeat mixture and transfer to a chafing dish. Yields 25 servings.

Crawfish or Shrimp Mousse

2 (10¾-ounce) cans tomato soup
1 (8-ounce) package cream cheese
3 tablespoons unflavored gelatin
⅔ cup cold water
1 pound crawfish tails, coarsely chopped, or 2 cups cooked, peeled, and chopped shrimp
1 cup mayonnaise
1½ cups finely chopped celery
½ cup finely chopped green onions
½ cup finely chopped bell pepper
1 teaspoon Worcestershire sauce
¾ teaspoon Tabasco sauce
½ teaspoon salt
1 tablespoon lemon juice

Heat soup in a large saucepan. Whisk in cream cheese until smooth. Dissolve gelatin in cold water and add to saucepan. Mix well and remove from heat to cool. Add crawfish and remaining 8 ingredients. Pour into a well-greased 1-quart fish mold, or a 9-inch spring mold. Cover and refrigerate overnight. Unmold and serve with melba toast or crackers. Yields 12 appetizer servings, 8 salad servings.

Caviar Mold

1 cup finely chopped green onions	¼ teaspoon white pepper
1¼ sticks butter, softened, divided	2 tablespoons mayonnaise
5 hard-cooked eggs, finely grated	lettuce or fresh parsley for garnish
½ teaspoon salt	½ cup sour cream
¼ teaspoon cayenne pepper	1 (2-ounce) jar black caviar

Sauté onions in 2 tablespoons butter for 5 minutes or until soft. Drain and cool for 15 minutes on paper towels. Combine onions, remaining stick butter, egg, and next 4 ingredients in a bowl. Pour mixture into a lightly greased 2-cup mold. Cover and refrigerate overnight. Garnish a serving platter with lettuce or parsley. Unmold mixture onto platter. Spread sour cream over top and sides. Top with caviar. Serve with crackers or melba toast. Yields 12 to 16 servings.

Oysters Dunbar

If desired, prepare dish ahead of time up to point of baking. Just prior to serving, proceed with baking and broiling instructions.

2 artichokes, boiled	⅛ teaspoon black pepper
3½ dozen oysters	½ teaspoon dried thyme
2 cups oyster liquid	¼ teaspoon Tabasco sauce
1 stick butter	1 teaspoon Worcestershire sauce
2 tablespoons all-purpose flour	½ cup breadcrumbs
½ cup finely chopped green onions	¼ cup Parmesan cheese
½ teaspoon minced garlic	6-8 thin slices lemon
¼ teaspoon salt	

Separate artichoke leaves from hearts. Reserve 24 leaves. Scrape remaining leaves and mash pulp with a fork. Coarsely chop hearts. Boil oysters in oyster liquid for 3 to 5 minutes or until edges curl. Drain, reserving 2 cups liquid. Melt butter in a saucepan. Add flour and cook and stir until brown. Add onions and garlic and cook 3 minutes. Stir in reserved liquid and simmer 15 minutes. Add salt and next 4 ingredients. Mix in artichoke pulp and hearts and oysters. Simmer 10 minutes. Spoon mixture into individual ramekins and sprinkle with breadcrumbs and cheese. Bake at 350° for 15 minutes. Broil 3 to 5 minutes. Garnish each ramekin with a lemon slice and surround with artichoke leaves for dipping. Yields 6 servings.

Oysters Espagñole

Sauce Espagñole
2 tablespoons all-purpose flour
2 tablespoons butter
1 cup beef broth, heated
3 tablespoons tomato paste
2 tablespoons lemon juice

2 tablespoons sherry
2 tablespoons browning and
    seasoning sauce
¼ teaspoon Tabasco sauce

Blender Hollandaise
2 sticks butter
2 egg yolks
2 tablespoons lemon juice

¼ teaspoon salt
¼ teaspoon Tabasco sauce

Oysters Espagñole
2½ cups sliced fresh mushrooms
2 tablespoons butter
6 tablespoons chopped green onions
4 dozen oysters, well drained

Sauce Espagñole
Blender Hollandaise
toast points
¼ cup finely chopped fresh parsley

To make Sauce Espagñole, cook flour in butter in a saucepan for 10 minutes or until dark brown. Add broth and next 5 ingredients. Stir until thick and smooth. Makes 2 cups. To prepare Blender Hollandaise, heat butter until melted and remove from heat. Place yolks and next 3 ingredients in a blender. Turn blender on and off several times. Slowly add butter in a steady stream, turning switch on and off until all butter is absorbed. Makes 1 cup. To prepare Oysters Espagñole, sauté mushrooms in butter in a Dutch oven. Add onions and simmer 10 minutes. Add oysters, stirring constantly. When edges of oysters curl, remove excess liquid. Slowly stir in sauces. Blend and heat thoroughly. Serve immediately over toast points and garnish with parsley. Yields 4 to 6 servings.

For variety, serve over prepared tournedos.

Oysters Ellis

If desired, substitute 1 tablespoon Pickapeppa Sauce for 1 tablespoon browning and seasoning sauce.

6 tablespoons butter, divided
3 tablespoons all-purpose flour
1 cup beef broth, heated
3 tablespoons tomato paste
2 tablespoons sherry
2 tablespoons lemon juice
2 tablespoons browning and
   seasoning sauce

¾ teaspoon Tabasco sauce
¼ teaspoon black pepper
4 ounces fresh mushrooms, sliced
6 tablespoons minced green onions
¼ cup finely chopped fresh parsley
4 dozen oysters, well drained
toast points

Heat 3 tablespoons butter in a skillet. Gradually add flour. Cook and stir 10 minutes or until brown. Add broth and next 6 ingredients. Blend sauce until smooth. Sauté mushrooms in remaining 3 tablespoons butter in a large saucepan. Add onions and parsley and cook 5 minutes. Add oysters, stirring constantly. Spoon off and reserve excess liquid. Slowly add sauce to oyster mixture. Stir until well heated. If sauce is too thick, add some of reserved oyster liquid. Serve immediately over toast points. Yields 6 servings.

Brandy Cheese

Brandy Cheese stores in refrigerator up to 2 weeks, but does not freeze well.

8 ounces sharp cheddar cheese,
   grated
1 (8-ounce) package cream cheese,
   softened
3 tablespoons grated yellow onion
1 teaspoon Worcestershire sauce

4 dashes Tabasco sauce
¼ teaspoon salt
⅛ teaspoon white pepper
⅓ cup brandy
½ cup finely chopped pecans
¼ cup chopped fresh parsley

Blend cheeses in a bowl. Fold in onion and next 5 ingredients. Blend well. Add pecans and parsley. Spoon into a 2-cup crock or bowl and refrigerate overnight. Serve with crackers. Yields 8 servings.

Boursin Cheese

2 tablespoons butter, softened
½ teaspoon minced garlic
¼ teaspoon dried dill
⅛ teaspoon dried thyme
2 tablespoons finely chopped fresh
  parsley

1 tablespoon frozen or freeze-dried
  chives
salt to taste
1 (8-ounce) package cream cheese,
  softened
freshly ground black pepper

Using a wooden spoon, combine butter and next 6 ingredients in a small bowl. Blend in cream cheese until smooth. Chill. Mold into desired shape and sprinkle all sides with pepper. Cover and refrigerate. Yields 6 to 8 servings.

Cheese Drops

Cheese Drops freeze well.

2 cups all-purpose flour
1 teaspoon cayenne pepper
½ teaspoon salt
2 sticks butter, softened

8 ounces sharp cheddar cheese,
  grated, room temperature
1 cup chopped pecans
2 teaspoons caraway seed

Sift together flour, cayenne pepper, and salt. Cream butter and cheese in a large bowl. Add flour mixture. By hand, fold in pecans and caraway seed. Drop by half teaspoons onto an ungreased baking sheet. Bake at 350° for 15 to 18 minutes. Yields 5 dozen drops.

Cheese Straws

6-8 tablespoons butter, melted
2 cups extra sharp cheddar cheese,
  grated, room temperature
1 cup sifted flour

2 teaspoons baking powder
1 teaspoon salt
½-1 teaspoon cayenne pepper
pecan halves (optional)

Cream 6 tablespoons butter and cheese. Add flour and next 3 ingredients. If dough is too dry, add more butter. Press 1 teaspoon of dough into straws by using a cookie gun or rolling into small balls. Press a pecan half into the center of each ball. Bake on a greased baking sheet at 325° until crisp, dried out, and starting to brown. Yields 50 to 75 straws.

Curried Cheese Pâté

2 (8-ounce) packages cream cheese, softened
2 cups sharp cheddar cheese, grated, room temperature
6 tablespoons sherry
2 tablespoons Worcestershire sauce
1 teaspoon curry
½ teaspoon salt
1 (8-ounce) jar chutney
½ cup chopped peanuts
½ cup chopped green onions
½ cup grated coconut

Blend cream cheese and next 5 ingredients. Line an 8-inch cake pan with plastic wrap, or lightly grease an 8-inch spring mold. Fill with cheese mixture. Cover and chill 4 hours or up to 3 days, or freeze. If frozen, thaw before garnishing. Unmold pâté onto a large platter. Garnish in layers with chutney, peanuts, onions, and coconut. Serve with crackers. Yields 24 servings.

Liver Pâté

Pâté can be frozen, but may be somewhat dry when thawed. If so, mash in a small amount of brandy with a fork.

1 pound chicken livers
½ teaspoon salt
2 sticks butter, cut into pieces
2 tablespoons grated yellow onion
½ teaspoon ground cloves
1 teaspoon nutmeg
1 teaspoon white or black pepper
¼ teaspoon cayenne pepper
3-4 tablespoons brandy
½ cup sour cream (optional)
1 (2-ounce) jar caviar (optional)

Place livers in a saucepan. Add water until just covered. Add salt and bring to a boil. Simmer 15 minutes. Drain and partially cool. Place livers in a food processor fitted with a metal blade. Add butter and next 6 ingredients. Blend until smooth. Spoon mixture into a 2-cup crock. Cover and refrigerate. Spread with sour cream and caviar. Serve with melba toast. Yields 12 servings.

Marbleheat Pâté

2½ sticks butter, divided
1½ cups coarsely chopped green
  onions
1 pound chicken livers
½ cup brandy
1½ teaspoons salt

½ teaspoon dried thyme
1 teaspoon dried basil
1 teaspoon garlic salt
1 teaspoon black pepper
1 teaspoon nutmeg
10 black olives, sliced

Melt 1 stick butter in a skillet. Add onions and sauté 5 minutes. Add livers and cook 5 minutes or until lightly browned. Add remaining 1½ sticks butter, brandy, and next 6 ingredients. Cook 2 minutes. Blend mixture in a food processor or blender. Mixture will be liquid. Line a 4-cup mold with wax paper or foil. Place olive slices on bottom of mold. Add liquid and refrigerate until set. Unmold and serve with melba toast or crackers. Yields 12 servings.

Hot Asparagus Roll-Ups

Roll-ups can be made ahead and frozen before dipping in butter.

20 slices thin white bread, crusts
  trimmed
3 ounces blue cheese, softened
1 (8-ounce) package cream cheese,
  softened
1 egg, beaten

¼ teaspoon garlic salt
⅛ teaspoon cayenne pepper
½ cup finely chopped green onions
20 canned asparagus spears
1½ sticks butter, melted
½ cup finely chopped fresh parsley

Flatten bread slices with a rolling pin. Combine blue cheese and next 4 ingredients. Fold in onions. Spread mixture evenly over bread slices. Roll an asparagus spear in each slice of bread, using some of cheese mixture to seal edge. Roll in butter and place on an ungreased baking sheet. Bake at 400° for 15 to 20 minutes or until lightly browned. Garnish with parsley. Yields 20 roll-ups.

Artichoke Balls

1 (6-ounce) jar marinated artichoke
  hearts
2 eggs
1 tablespoon garlic juice
1 tablespoon Worcestershire sauce
½-1 teaspoon liquid smoke
½ teaspoon Tabasco sauce

1 (14-ounce) can water-packed
  artichoke hearts, drained, finely
  chopped
1½ cups Italian-seasoned
  breadcrumbs
1 (3-ounce) can Parmesan or
  Romano cheese

Drain and finely chop marinated artichoke hearts, reserving marinade. Beat eggs and reserved marinade in a large bowl. Blend in garlic juice and next 3 ingredients. Add marinated and water-packed artichokes and breadcrumbs. Form into small balls. Roll each ball in cheese. Refrigerate up to 1 week. Serve at room temperature, or bake at 300° on a lightly greased baking sheet for 7 to 10 minutes. Serve immediately. Yields 60 to 80 balls.

Mushroom Strudel

1 pound fresh mushrooms, minced
1½ sticks butter, divided
1 tablespoon vegetable oil
½ cup minced yellow onion
1 cup minced green onions
¼ teaspoon Tabasco sauce

½ cup sour cream
2 tablespoons minced fresh dill, or 1
  tablespoon dried
½ teaspoon salt
¼ teaspoon black pepper
6-8 sheets phyllo dough

Place mushrooms, a handful at a time, in a cheesecloth and squeeze out moisture. Heat 3 tablespoons butter and oil in a skillet. Add mushrooms and onions and sauté 15 minutes or until moisture evaporates. Remove from heat and stir in Tabasco sauce and next 4 ingredients. Cool. Place phyllo sheets under a damp cloth while working to keep moist. Melt remaining butter. Place one phyllo sheet on wax paper and brush lightly with butter. Place a second sheet of dough directly over the first and brush with butter. Spread a 1-inch wide strip of mushroom mixture along the edge of the long side of the dough. Roll up sheets in jelly roll fashion. Repeat procedure with remaining sheets of dough. Place rolls, seam-side down, on a greased baking sheet. Brush with butter. Bake at 350° for 45 minutes or until crisp and golden. Cool 5 minutes before cutting on an angle into 1-inch slices. Yields 4 dozen slices.

Bacon Stuffed Mushrooms

The cream cheese mixture can be made several hours ahead, but stuff and bake mushrooms just prior to serving.

24 fresh mushrooms, washed and
 drained
¼ pound bacon, cooked and
 crumbled, divided
1 (8-ounce) package cream cheese,
 softened

½ teaspoon salt
¼ teaspoon pressed garlic
⅓ cup finely chopped yellow onion
1 tablespoon soy sauce
¼ cup finely chopped fresh parsley

Remove and chop mushroom stems, reserving mushroom caps. Blend mushroom stems, half the bacon, and next 5 ingredients until creamy. Stuff mushroom caps with mixture and place in a shallow pan. Bake at 375° for 8 to 10 minutes. Remove from oven and sprinkle with remaining bacon and parsley. Serve immediately. Yields 2 dozen mushrooms.

Green Chili Squares

2 (9-inch) pastry shells
6 eggs
2 cups hot milk
¼ cup all-purpose flour
3 cups grated Swiss cheese
1 cup Parmesan cheese

1 (4-ounce) can chopped green chili
 peppers, drained
½ teaspoon salt
¼ teaspoon black pepper
½ cup chopped onion

Press pastry shells into a 12X15 inch jelly-roll pan and trim edges. Bake at 425° for 15 minutes. In a large bowl, beat eggs and milk. Add flour and remaining 6 ingredients. Pour into crust and bake at 325° for 30 to 40 minutes or until a knife inserted in the center comes out clean. Cut into small squares. Yields 4 dozen squares.

Sausage Hors D'Oeuvres

Meatballs can be made ahead and frozen.

1 pound ground hot sausage
1 pound ground mild sausage
¼ cup dry sherry

1 cup sour cream
1 (8-ounce) jar chutney, finely
  chopped

Blend sausages in a bowl. Roll into 1-inch balls and brown in a skillet. Remove balls with a slotted spoon. Drain grease, reserving crusty bits in skillet. Add sherry, sour cream, and chutney and cook and stir over low heat. Add balls and cook until hot. Transfer to a chafing dish and serve with toothpicks. Yields 6 dozen balls.

Spinach Dip

1 (10-ounce) package frozen
  chopped spinach, thawed and
  drained
1 teaspoon salt
¼ teaspoon black pepper
½ teaspoon celery salt
⅛ teaspoon nutmeg

¼ teaspoon garlic salt
⅛ teaspoon Tabasco sauce
1 cup sour cream
½ cup mayonnaise
½ cup finely chopped fresh parsley
½ cup minced yellow onion
1 teaspoon lemon juice

Combine all ingredients. Cover and refrigerate overnight. Serve with fresh vegetables. Yields 2 cups.

Soups & Gumbos

If it's Monday, it must be Red Beans and Rice

In New Orleans, some things never change. Red beans and rice on Mondays is one of those things. In local kitchens, neighborhood diners and four-star restaurants alike, that simmered, spicy and oh-so-savory dish is a staple on the menu at the start of every week.

The dish is Creole in heritage and made its way to New Orleans via Africa and the Caribbean, where rice and bean dishes were and still are very popular. It caught on here, as most traditions do, because it met a specific need. In the days before electric washing machines and clothes dryers, Monday was wash day. That meant the women of the house didn't have have much time as usual to cook for the family. Red beans -- technically they're kidney beans -- required little preparation and even less maintenance. Chop a few vegetables here; throw in a few spices and a ham hock there; put it all together in a large pot with beans and plenty of water and let it simmer all day. In fact, the longer it cooks, the better it tastes.

There are other advantages to red beans and rice, which have helped ensure its popularity for generations. For one, though it may taste rich, it's actually quite inexpensive to prepare. Back in the days after the Civil War, money in these parts was tight, so a dish like red beans and rice was a natural. Besides that, when mixed with rice -- they're always served together -- red beans provide a complete protein. That means they make a stand-alone meal that's not only great tasting but nutritious as well.

There are subtle variations on the theme of beans and rice. But unlike gumbo and jambalaya -- both of which can be prepared in several different ways, Red Beans and Rice follow the same basic recipe every time. Beans are slow cooked for several hours in water with herbs, spices and meat -- which may be added merely for flavoring or as an actual accompaniment. With salad and a little French bread, you've got the city's signature dish. And by the way, though Monday is the traditional day for red beans repast, people in New Orleans enjoy them any day of the week, and so can you!

For a great Jambalaya recipe for Red Beans and Rice, see p. 48.

Jambalaya Seafood Gumbo

6 tablespoons vegetable oil, divided
2 pounds okra, thinly sliced
1 tablespoon all-purpose flour
2 cups finely chopped onion
½ cup finely chopped celery
⅔ cup finely chopped bell pepper
1 cup finely chopped green onions
2 cloves garlic, pressed
1 (6-ounce) can tomato paste
3 large bay leaves
¼ teaspoon dried thyme
1 tablespoon salt
½ teaspoon Tabasco sauce
¼ teaspoon cayenne pepper
½ teaspoon black pepper
1 tablespoon Worcestershire sauce
1 (16-ounce) can whole tomatoes, chopped, undrained
7 cups water
2½ pounds raw shrimp, peeled and deveined
1 pound claw crabmeat
2 dozen oysters with liquid
2 tablespoons chopped fresh parsley
4-5 cups steamed rice

Heat 4 tablespoons oil in a large, non-iron skillet. Add okra and cook, stirring often for 40 to 50 minutes or until no longer stringy. Add more oil if needed to prevent burning. In a 5-quart kettle, heat remaining 2 tablespoons oil. Gradually add flour. Cook and stir until mixture turns dark brown. Add onion and celery and cook until tender. Add bell pepper, green onions, and garlic and cook 3 minutes. Stir in tomato paste and next 7 ingredients. Mix in tomatoes. Add cooked okra. Slowly stir in water. Bring to a boil. Reduce heat, cover, and simmer 30 minutes. Add shrimp and crabmeat. Simmer, covered, for 10 minutes. Add oysters and oyster liquid and parsley. Cook 10 minutes longer. Remove bay leaves. Thin with extra water if too thick. Serve over rice. Yields 10 servings.

Cream of Artichoke Soup

6 small artichokes, or 4 large
1⅓ cups chopped onion
1 tablespoon butter
4 cups chicken broth
1 teaspoon salt
¼ teaspoon dried thyme
¼ teaspoon black pepper
2 tablespoons lemon juice
¼ teaspoon Tabasco sauce
1 cup light cream
1 cup heavy cream

Scrape artichoke leaves and chop hearts to equal 3 cups. Reserve ½ cup sliced heart for garnish. In a saucepan, sauté onion in butter for 5 minutes. Add scraped and chopped artichoke, broth, and next 3 ingredients. Cover and simmer 15 minutes. Cool slightly and purée. Season with lemon juice and Tabasco sauce. Stir in creams. Refrigerate several hours or overnight. Serve cold or heat to just boiling. Garnish with sliced artichoke heart. Yields 6 servings.

Curried Tomato Bisque

2 tablespoons butter
1½ cups chopped onion
1½ cloves garlic, pressed
1-2 tablespoons curry powder
5 cups cored and quartered ripe
   tomato, or canned plum tomatoes
½ bay leaf

½ teaspoon dried thyme
½ cup dry rice
2 cups chicken broth
⅛ teaspoon Tabasco sauce
1½ teaspoons salt
2 cups milk
1 cup heavy cream

Melt butter in a large pot. Add onion and garlic and sauté until tender. Sprinkle with curry powder and cook 3 minutes, stirring often. Add tomato and next 6 ingredients. Cover and simmer 45 minutes, stirring occasionally. Remove bay leaf and purée. Blend in milk and cream. Serve hot or cold. Yields 10 to 12 servings.

Golden Cauliflower Soup

5-6 cups cauliflower florets
2 teaspoons salt, divided
3 cups water
1 cup finely chopped green onions,
   plus extra for garnish
1 stick butter
2 tablespoons all-purpose flour
2 cups whole milk, or 1 cup milk
   and 1 cup half-and-half, warmed

8 ounces cheddar cheese, grated,
   plus extra for garnish
3 cups chicken broth
⅛ teaspoon white pepper
⅛ teaspoon Tabasco sauce
1 tablespoon Worcestershire sauce
2 tablespoons lemon juice
paprika

Combine cauliflower, 1 teaspoon salt, and water in a saucepan. Cover and cook until tender. Drain. In a skillet, sauté onions in butter for 7 minutes. Add flour and cook 2 minutes, stirring often. Slowly add milk, stirring constantly. Stir in cheese and cook until melted. Purée cauliflower and return to saucepan. Add broth to cauliflower. Stir in cheese mixture. Add remaining 1 teaspoon salt, white pepper, and next 3 ingredients. Serve hot or cold. If serving cold, use water or broth to thin soup if too thick. Garnish with cheese, green onions, and paprika. Yields 6 servings

Cream of Carrot Soup

1 pound carrots, sliced
1 cup chopped onion
4 cups chicken broth
1 bay leaf
⅛ teaspoon dried thyme

½ teaspoon salt
⅛ teaspoon black pepper
⅛ teaspoon Tabasco sauce
1 cup heavy cream

Combine carrot and next 4 ingredients in a 2-quart saucepan. Cover and cook 20 minutes or until carrot is tender. Remove bay leaf and purée mixture. Season with salt, pepper, and Tabasco sauce. Stir in cream. Serve hot or cold. Yields 6 servings.

Pecan Soup

2 cups pecan halves
6 cups beef broth
1 stick butter
2 tablespoons finely chopped green onions
1 clove garlic, pressed
1 tablespoon cornstarch
¼ cup water

2 tablespoons tomato paste
1 egg yolk
¼ cup heavy cream, room temperature
½ teaspoon salt
¼ teaspoon white pepper
⅛ teaspoon nutmeg

Grind pecans with broth in a blender. Melt butter in a 3-quart saucepan. Add onions and sauté 5 minutes or until soft but not brown. Add garlic and cook 1 minute. Dissolve cornstarch in water. Slowly add cornstarch, pecan mixture, and tomato paste to saucepan. Cook 30 minutes. Beat egg yolk into heavy cream and slowly whisk into soup. Do not boil. Season with salt, pepper, and nutmeg. Serve hot or cold. Yields 8 servings.

Harvest Pumpkin Soup

6 cups puréed pumpkin
3 cups chicken broth
2 cups mashed potato
1 cup finely chopped onion
1 cup finely chopped celery

½ teaspoon nutmeg, plus extra for garnish
1 teaspoon salt
⅛ teaspoon white pepper
2 cups heavy cream
chopped fresh parsley or chives

Combine pumpkin and next 7 ingredients in a large saucepan. Simmer 15 minutes. Cool slightly and purée. Stir in cream. Serve hot or cold. Garnish with nutmeg, parsley, or chives. Yields 8 servings.

Garden Patch Chowder

For best flavor, prepare soup ahead and chill until ready to serve.

3/4-1 pound Polish sausage
2 cups water
1 1/2 cups peeled and diced potato
1 cup thinly sliced carrot
1 cup thinly sliced celery
1/3 cup chopped onion
1/2 teaspoon salt

1 1/2 teaspoons black pepper
1 stick butter
1/4 cup all-purpose flour
1 cup milk, warmed
1/2 cup chicken broth, warmed
8 ounces cheddar cheese, grated
1/8-1/4 teaspoon dried dill

Cook sausage and drain. Cut into 1/4-inch slices. Bring water to a boil in a 2-quart saucepan. Add potato and next 5 ingredients. Cover and simmer 15 minutes or until vegetables are tender. In a separate 4-quart saucepan, melt butter. Stir in flour and cook and stir until smooth. Remove from heat and slowly stir in milk and broth. Return to heat and bring to a boil, stirring constantly. Boil and stir 1 minute. Add cheese and stir until melted. Add undrained vegetables, dill, and sausage. Heat thoroughly before serving. Yields 4 servings.

Lentil Soup

This soup freezes well.

1 pound dried lentils
6 cups beef broth
2 cups water
1 pound smoked sausage or ham,
   cut into bite-size pieces
1 cup chopped celery
1 cup chopped green onions
2/3 cup chopped onion

1 cup chopped carrot
2 tablespoons chopped fresh parsley
1 clove garlic, pressed
1 bay leaf
1/2 teaspoon dried thyme
1/4 cup dry sherry
salt and pepper to taste
Tabasco sauce to taste

Rinse lentils and drain. Place lentils, broth, and water in a large saucepan. Cover and simmer 60 minutes. Sauté sausage in a skillet. Remove with a slotted spoon and add to lentil mixture. Add celery and next 5 ingredients to skillet drippings. Sauté until tender. Add vegetables to lentil mixture. Stir in bay leaf and thyme. Cover and simmer 60 minutes, stirring occasionally. Add water as needed for desired consistency. Remove from heat and stir in sherry, salt, pepper, and Tabasco sauce. Yields 8 servings.

Cream of Eggplant Soup

If desired, prepare in advance and refrigerate up to 4 days.

2 small eggplants (about 2 pounds),
   peeled and sliced
4 tablespoons butter
1½ cups finely chopped onion
1½ cups finely chopped celery
1½ cups peeled and diced potato
1 teaspoon curry powder

¼ teaspoon dried thyme
¼-½ teaspoon dried basil
1 teaspoon salt
4 cups chicken broth
1½ cups half-and-half
¼ teaspoon black pepper
Tabasco sauce to taste

Cover eggplant with cold salted water and soak 10 minutes. Rinse, drain, and dice. Melt butter in a large saucepan. Add eggplant, onion, celery, and potato and sauté 20 minutes. Cover tightly and cook 40 minutes or until vegetables are tender. Stir frequently. Stir in curry powder and next 3 ingredients. Cook 10 minutes. Add broth, cover, and cook 40 minutes, stirring occasionally. Cool slightly and purée. Stir in half-and-half. Add pepper and Tabasco sauce. Thin with milk or water if too thick. Yields 8 servings.

Broccoli and Cheese Soup

2 (10-ounce) packages frozen
   chopped broccoli
3½ cups chicken broth, divided
2 tablespoons butter
10 large fresh mushrooms, sliced
⅔ cup finely chopped celery
⅓ cup chopped green onions

1 tablespoon finely chopped fresh
   parsley
2 teaspoons garlic salt
1½ cups grated mild cheddar cheese
½ cup sour cream
½ teaspoon Tabasco sauce

Cook broccoli according to package directions. Drain and purée with 1¾ cups broth. Place purée and remaining 1¾ cups broth in a saucepan and simmer. Melt butter in a skillet. Add mushrooms and next 3 ingredients and sauté until tender. Season with garlic salt. Add vegetables to saucepan. Cover and cook 30 minutes. Stir in cheese and sour cream. Season with Tabasco sauce and serve hot. Yields 6 servings.

Broccoli Bisque

½ cup chopped onion
1 stick butter
2 (10-ounce) packages frozen
  chopped broccoli, thawed
2 cups chicken broth

¾ teaspoon dried basil
1 teaspoon salt
¼ teaspoon black pepper
1 tablespoon lemon juice
1 cup light cream

In a saucepan, sauté onion in butter for 5 minutes. Add broccoli and next 4 ingredients. Cover and simmer 15 minutes. Purée until smooth. Add lemon juice and cream. Serve hot or cold. Yields 6 servings.

Cold Zucchini Soup

1½ pounds zucchini, peeled and
  sliced
⅔ cup chopped yellow onion
¼ cup chopped bell pepper
2½ cups chicken broth

1 cup heavy cream
½ teaspoon dried dill
salt to taste
Tabasco sauce to taste

Combine zucchini and next 3 ingredients in a 3-quart saucepan. Cover and simmer 30 minutes. Cool and purée. Blend in cream and dill. Season with salt and Tabasco sauce. Chill before serving. Yields 6 servings.

Chilled Avocado Cucumber Soup

2 cups peeled, seeded, and coarsely
  chopped cucumber
1 large avocado, peeled and
  coarsely chopped
2 small green onion bulbs, chopped
2 cups chicken broth
1 cup sour cream

1 tablespoon lemon juice
salt to taste
Tabasco sauce to taste
thinly sliced cucumber or avocado,
  or chopped fresh chives for
  garnish

Purée cucumber, avocado, and onions in a blender or food processor. With machine running, add broth, sour cream, and lemon juice. Season with salt and Tabasco sauce. Chill and garnish before serving. Yields 4 servings.

Cold Squash Soup

1 pound yellow squash, thinly sliced
²/₃ cup chopped onion
1½ cups chicken broth, divided
½ cup sour cream
¼ teaspoon salt

⅛ teaspoon white pepper
¼ teaspoon Worcestershire sauce
3 drops Tabasco sauce
bacon bits, dill, or caraway seed for
    garnish

Combine squash, onion, and 1 cup broth in a saucepan. Cover and simmer 30 minutes. Purée and transfer to a bowl. Stir in remaining ½ cup broth, sour cream, and next 4 ingredients. Chill and garnish before serving. Yields 4 servings.

Spinach Soup

3 (10-ounce) packages frozen
    spinach
5 tablespoons butter
²/₃ cup chopped yellow onion

3 (10½-ounce) cans chicken broth
2 (8-ounce) packages cream cheese,
    cubed
Tabasco sauce to taste

Cook spinach in a large saucepan according to package directions. Drain well and return to saucepan. In a small skillet, melt butter. Add onion and sauté until tender. Add onion, broth, and cheese to spinach. Purée. Season with Tabasco sauce. Serve hot or cold. Yields 6 servings.

Turnip Soup

For a richer soup, substitute heavy cream for half-and-half.

1 tablespoon butter
½ cup chopped onion
3½ cups chicken broth
1 cup water
2 pounds turnips, peeled and cubed
1 teaspoon dried basil
2½ teaspoons salt

⅛ teaspoon black pepper
2½ teaspoons sugar
2 tablespoons chopped fresh parsley
1 bay leaf
1 tablespoon lemon juice
1 cup half-and-half
chopped fresh parsley

Melt butter in a large saucepan. Add onion and cook until soft. Add broth and next 9 ingredients. Cover and simmer 60 minutes. Remove bay leaf and purée. Return to saucepan and add half-and-half. Cook until heated through. Garnish with parsley. Yields 6 servings.

Oyster and Artichoke Soup

4 artichokes, cooked
1 stick butter
½ cup finely chopped green onions
1 outer stalk celery with leaves,
    finely chopped
1 medium carrot, chopped
1 tablespoon finely chopped fresh
    parsley
2 cloves garlic, pressed
½ teaspoon dried thyme
1 bay leaf
3 tablespoons all-purpose flour

4 cups chicken broth, warmed
¼ teaspoon anise seed
¼ teaspoon cayenne pepper
1 teaspoon salt
1 teaspoon Worcestershire sauce
4 cups oysters with liquid
½ cup vermouth
¼ cup dry white wine
¼ cup half-and-half
1 teaspoon lemon juice
zest of 1 lemon

Scrape artichoke leaves and chop hearts. Melt butter in a 4-quart saucepan. Add onions and next 6 ingredients. Sauté until celery and carrot are tender. Add artichoke scrapings and hearts. Stir well. Slowly stir in flour, but do not brown. Gradually add broth. Add anise seed and next 3 ingredients. Simmer 15 minutes. Drain oysters, reserving liquid. Chop oysters and add with reserved liquid to artichoke mixture. Cook over low heat for 10 minutes. Add vermouth and remaining 4 ingredients. Remove bay leaf. Purée until smooth. Refrigerate until ready to serve. Heat before serving. Yields 10 servings.

Crabmeat Bisque Cardinale

6 tablespoons butter
3 tablespoons grated onion
6 tablespoons all-purpose flour
½ teaspoon dry mustard
4 cups half-and-half, warmed
2 cups whole milk, warmed
2 tablespoons ketchup
1½ teaspoons tomato paste

2 teaspoons chopped fresh parsley
1 pound crabmeat
2 tablespoons dry sherry
2 teaspoons Worcestershire sauce
¼ teaspoon Tabasco sauce
2 teaspoons salt
white pepper to taste

Melt butter in a pot. Add onion and sauté 5 minutes. Stir in flour and cook 2 minutes. Add mustard and mix well. Lower heat and whisk in half-and-half, milk, and ketchup. In a small bowl, combine ¼ cup milk mixture and tomato paste. Stir until smooth. Add tomato paste mixture, parsley, and remaining 6 ingredients to pot. Refrigerate overnight. Serve hot or cold. Yields 8 servings.

Cream of Crawfish Soup

If desired, add extra sherry to each serving.

1½ sticks butter, divided
2 tablespoons finely chopped green onions
1 pound cooked crawfish tails with fat, minced
¼ teaspoon dried tarragon
½ teaspoon salt
¼ teaspoon cayenne pepper
¾ cup dry sherry

¼ cup brandy
1 cup finely chopped white onion
½ cup all-purpose flour
6 cups fish broth, or 3 cups clam juice and 3 cups water, warmed
4 cups milk
1 cup heavy cream
3 egg yolks
¼ cup fresh or frozen chives

Melt 4 tablespoons butter in a skillet. Stir in green onions and next 4 ingredients. Cook and stir 5 minutes. Add sherry and bring to a boil. Cook until reduced by half. Heat brandy, flame, and add to skillet. Cook and stir 3 minutes. In a Dutch oven, sauté white onion in remaining stick of butter until tender. Stir in flour and cook 3 minutes. Remove from heat and stir in broth and milk. Add crawfish mixture and simmer 30 minutes. If preparing in advance, soup can be frozen at this point. In a small bowl, whisk cream into egg yolks. Add a little hot soup to cream mixture and then slowly stir mixture into soup. Heat thoroughly and garnish with chives. Yields 8 servings.

Creole Crab Bisque

This soup freezes well.

1½ sticks butter
¾ cup all-purpose flour
3 tablespoons tomato paste
1½ cups finely chopped yellow onion
1 cup finely chopped celery
½ cup finely chopped green onions
4 cloves garlic, pressed
⅔ cup finely chopped bell pepper
3 tablespoons finely chopped fresh parsley

2 quarts chicken broth
1 tablespoon Worcestershire sauce
1 bay leaf
1 teaspoon dried thyme
1 teaspoon salt
⅛ teaspoon white pepper
⅛ teaspoon cayenne pepper
½ teaspoon ketchup
1 pound crabmeat

Melt butter in a large pot. Add flour and cook and stir 20 to 30 minutes or until golden brown. Add tomato paste and next 5 ingredients. Cook until tender. Add parsley. Slowly stir in broth. Add Worcestershire sauce and remaining 7 ingredients. Cover and simmer 40 minutes, stirring occasionally. Remove bay leaf. Yields 8 servings.

Crawfish Gumbo

This gumbo is best prepared ahead and reheated when ready to serve. Freezes well.

½ cup vegetable oil
½ cup all-purpose flour
1½ cups chopped onion
1 (8-ounce) can tomato sauce
6 cups hot water
¾ cup chopped bell pepper
2 large cloves garlic, pressed

1 tablespoon salt
¾ teaspoon cayenne pepper
2 pounds peeled crawfish, tails, and fat
¼ cup chopped green onion tops
¼ cup chopped fresh parsley
3 cups steamed rice

Heat oil in a Dutch oven. Gradually add flour and cook and stir 40 minutes or until dark brown. Add onion and cook until tender. Add tomato sauce. Cook over low heat for 15 minutes. Slowly add water, stirring until smooth. Add bell pepper and next 3 ingredients. Bring to a boil. Reduce heat and simmer 40 minutes. Add crawfish and onion tops. Simmer 15 minutes. Stir in parsley. Serve over rice. Yields 6 servings.

Red Beans and Rice

1 pound dried red beans, rinsed and drained
8 cups water
1 ham bone
2 pounds smoked sausage, cut into 1-inch pieces
3 cloves garlic, pressed
1½ cups chopped yellow onion
¾ cup chopped green onions

1½ cups chopped celery
⅔ cup chopped bell pepper
1 bay leaf
1 teaspoon Worcestershire sauce
¼ teaspoon Tabasco sauce
1 tablespoon minced fresh parsley
1½ teaspoons salt
3 cups steamed rice

Combine beans, water, and ham bone in a large saucepan. Bring to a boil. Reduce heat and simmer 40 minutes. Add sausage and cover. Cook 60 minutes, stirring occasionally. Add garlic and next 5 ingredients. Cover and cook 1 hour, 30 minutes or until beans are soft. Add Worcestershire sauce and next 3 ingredients. Simmer 5 minutes. Remove bay leaf. Serve over rice. Yields 6 servings.

Shrimp Bisque

Shrimp Broth

2 pounds raw shrimp
8 cups water
1 carrot, cut into thirds
1 onion, quartered
2 cloves
1 outer stalk celery with leaves

1 sprig fresh parsley
½ lemon
1 teaspoon salt
¼ teaspoon cayenne pepper
½ cup dry white wine

Bisque

3 tablespoons butter
½ cup finely chopped carrot
⅔ cup finely chopped onion
½ cup finely chopped celery
1 tablespoon finely chopped fresh
　parsley
½ bay leaf
¼ teaspoon dried thyme

½ teaspoon dried tarragon
2 tablespoons tomato paste
1 cup dry white wine
½ cup dry rice
6 cups Shrimp Broth
½ cup heavy cream
¾ teaspoon salt
¼ cup Madeira

Prepare broth by peeling and deveining shrimp, reserving heads and shells. Set shrimp aside. Combine heads and shells, water, and next 9 ingredients in a large pot. Cook 60 minutes, skimming foam off top. Strain. To make bisque, melt butter in a skillet. Add carrot and next 6 ingredients. Cover and cook 10 minutes. Stir in shrimp, tomato paste, and wine. Cover and cook 5 minutes. For garnish, remove 10 to 12 shrimp and coarsely chop. Combine rice and broth in a 3-quart sauce-pan. Cover and cook 20 minutes. Add shrimp mixture, cover, and cook 10 minutes. Remove bay leaf and purée. Stir in cream, salt, and Madeira. Heat thoroughly and garnish with chopped shrimp. Yields 8 servings.

Oyster Soup

3 tablespoons butter
¼ cup finely chopped celery
¼ cup finely chopped green onions
2 tablespoons all-purpose flour

2 cups oysters with liquid
1 teaspoon salt
¼ teaspoon white pepper
2 cups milk, warmed

Melt butter in the top of a double boiler. Add celery and onions and sauté. Stir in flour and cook 2 minutes. Add oysters and oyster liquid and cook just until edges curl. Add salt, pepper, and milk and cook until heated. Yields 4 servings.

Duck Gumbo

Duck Broth
4 ducks, cleaned and washed
2 tablespoons salt
1 teaspoon black pepper

3 onions, quartered
3 stalks celery
2 bay leaves

Gumbo
⅔ cup vegetable oil
⅔ cup all-purpose flour
2 cups chopped onion
1 cup chopped bell pepper
1½ cups chopped celery
½ teaspoon salt
¼ teaspoon black pepper
¼ teaspoon white pepper

1½ pounds smoked sausage, sliced
3 quarts Duck Broth
1 teaspoon Tabasco sauce
½ cup chopped fresh parsley
½ cup chopped green onion tops
24 oysters, well drained
1 tablespoon filé powder
3 cups steamed rice

Prepare broth by placing ducks in a large pot. Cover with water. Add salt and next 4 ingredients. Bring to a boil. Reduce heat and simmer 60 minutes or until tender. Remove ducks. Discard skin and bones and cube meat. Strain broth and reserve. To make gumbo, heat oil in a Dutch oven. Gradually add flour and cook and stir until dark brown. Add onion, bell pepper, and celery. Cook 10 to 15 minutes or until tender. Add salt, black pepper, white pepper, and duck meat. Cook 10 minutes, stirring often. In a separate skillet, cook sausage 5 minutes. Drain and add to Dutch oven. Slowly mix in broth. Bring to a boil. Reduce heat and simmer 60 minutes. Add Tabasco sauce, parsley, and onion tops and cook 5 minutes. Stir in oysters and cook 10 minutes. Skim fat and thicken with filé powder. Serve over rice. Yields 8 to 10 servings.

Turkey Corn Chowder

5 ears fresh corn
1 turkey carcass
2 onions, halved
3 stalks celery with leaves, cut into
　　thirds
2 carrots, cut into thirds
1 bay leaf
$\frac{1}{8}$ teaspoon dried thyme
$\frac{1}{8}$ teaspoon dried basil

$\frac{1}{8}$ teaspoon dried rosemary
12 cups water
1 tablespoon salt
1 teaspoon black pepper
1 teaspoon Worcestershire sauce
$\frac{1}{4}$ teaspoon Tabasco sauce
$\frac{1}{4}$ teaspoon curry powder
$\frac{1}{4}$ cup dry sherry
1 cup heavy cream

Cut kernels from corn cobs to measure 3 cups and reserve. Combine corn cobs, turkey carcass, and next 8 ingredients in an 8-quart pot. Bring to a boil. Reduce heat, cover, and simmer 1 hour, 30 minutes, stirring occasionally. Strain and return broth to pot. Purée onion, celery, carrot, 1 cup corn kernels, and 2 cups broth. Add puréed mixture and remaining 2 cups corn to pot. Cook 1 hour, 30 minutes. Add salt and remaining 6 ingredients. Yields 10 servings.

Chicken, Sausage, and Oyster Gumbo

1 (3-pound) chicken, cut into pieces
4 cups water
$\frac{1}{4}$ cup vegetable oil
$\frac{1}{4}$ cup all-purpose flour
$1\frac{1}{2}$ cups chopped yellow onion
$1\frac{1}{2}$ cups chopped celery
$\frac{1}{2}$ cup chopped bell pepper
$\frac{1}{2}$ cup chopped green onions
3 cloves garlic, pressed
$\frac{1}{4}$ cup chopped fresh parsley

1 bay leaf
$\frac{1}{2}$ teaspoon dried thyme
$\frac{3}{4}$ pound sausage, preferably
　　andouille, sliced
salt and pepper to taste
cayenne pepper to taste
Worcestershire sauce to taste
1 cup oysters with liquid
3 cups steamed rice
1 tablespoon filé powder

Cook chicken in water until tender, skimming fat and foam off top. Strain broth and reserve. Discard skin and bones of chicken and chop meat. Heat oil in a Dutch oven. Gradually add flour and cook and stir until dark brown. Add yellow onion and next 7 ingredients. Cook until tender, stirring often. Slowly stir in reserved broth. Add chicken meat. In a skillet, sauté sausage and drain. Add to gumbo. Cover and simmer 60 minutes, stirring occasionally. Add salt, black pepper, cayenne pepper, and Worcestershire sauce. Add oysters and oyster liquid and heat just until edges of oysters curl. Remove bay leaf and serve over rice. Sprinkle $\frac{1}{2}$ teaspoon filé powder over each serving. Yields 6 servings.

Creole Chicken Gumbo

Broth

3½-4 pounds chicken pieces
12 cups water
2 outer stalks celery with leaves
1 carrot, cut into thirds

1 medium onion, quartered
1 bay leaf
1 teaspoon salt

Gumbo

⅓ cup vegetable oil
½ cup all-purpose flour
1 pound okra, cut into ¼-inch pieces
1 cup chopped onion
¾ cup chopped celery
½ cup chopped bell pepper
½ cup chopped green onions
2 cloves garlic, pressed
¼ cup chopped fresh parsley
1 bay leaf
¾ teaspoon dried thyme

½ teaspoon dried marjoram
½ teaspoon dried basil
1 (16-ounce) can whole tomatoes, undrained
½ pound ham, cubed
1 pound hot smoked sausage, sliced
salt and pepper to taste
1 teaspoon Worcestershire sauce
cayenne pepper to taste
Tabasco sauce to taste
4 cups steamed rice

Combine all broth ingredients in a large pot. Bring to a boil. Reduce heat and simmer 25 minutes, skimming fat and foam off top. Remove chicken meat from bones and reserve. Return bones to broth and continue to simmer. To prepare gumbo, heat oil in a separate large, non-iron, pot. Gradually add flour and cook and stir until medium brown. Add okra and next 3 ingredients. Cook and stir until okra is no longer stringy. Add reserved chicken meat, green onions and next 8 ingredients. Strain broth and slowly stir into okra mixture. Cook sausage in a skillet, drain, and add to gumbo. Simmer 1 hour, 30 minutes, stirring occasionally. Season with salt, pepper, and next 3 ingredients. Serve over rice. Yields 8 servings.

Salads, Dressings & Sauces

Rémoulade

A well-known fact in the famous kitchens of New Orleans is that you can't have good Creole cooking without good sauces. Among the savory sauces that top our delicate fish dishes and form the base of our hearty etouffes, none is more famous than the rémoulade.

If you haven't heard of rémoulade -- that's rem-uh-lod -- don't feel badly. It's a specialty unique to New Orleans, perfected over generations in the city's finest old French restaurants. Not surprisingly, rémoulade sauce has its roots in French cooking. It's a highly seasoned blend of mustard, flour, oil, vinegar and other herbs and spices, with a thick texture and a reddish color. It is served chilled, with seafood, cold meats, poultry, or vegetable salads, but is most famous for its pairing with shrimp.

Shrimp Rémoulade is one of the most delectable appetizers you'll find on a Crescent City menu. On a recent trip to New Orleans, President Bill Clinton reportedly was treated to a meal that began with Crawfish Rémoulade, a spin-off of the classic shrimp dish. So impressed was the President, that he declared the lunch one of the finest he had ever eaten.

This issue of Jambalaya features our own recipe for rémoulade, of which we are quite proud. You can find it on page 65. Perhaps the most essential ingredient in the recipe is the Creole mustard, that hot 'n spicy brown condiment that closely resembles its French cousin country Dijon. If you can't find Creole mustard or happen to run out, you can substitute country Dijon. Just make sure you use one or the other, and never, ever, plain yellow mustard!

Jambalaya Rice Salad

2 cups dry rice
4 cups salted water
1 cup mayonnaise
2 tablespoons prepared yellow
   mustard

3 tablespoons French dressing
1 clove garlic, pressed
1 cup diced celery
2½ cups diced tomato
½ cup chopped bell pepper

Cook rice in water and cool. In a small bowl, combine mayonnaise and next 3 ingredients. Place rice in a salad bowl. Add mayonnaise mixture and top with celery, tomato, and bell pepper. Chill before serving. Yields 8 to 10 servings.

Layer Salad Supreme

Prepare this salad up to 48 hours in advance.

1 (10-ounce) package fresh spinach,
   stems removed
salt
black pepper
1 tablespoon sugar
6 strips bacon, cooked and
   crumbled
3 hard-cooked eggs, sliced
grated lettuce to cover
salt
black pepper

1 teaspoon sugar
1 cup sliced raw mushrooms
½ cup chopped green onions
1 (10-ounce) package frozen peas,
   thawed
salt
black pepper
1 teaspoon sugar
½ cup chopped pecans
1 cup mayonnaise
1 cup grated Swiss cheese
1 teaspoon paprika

Layer ingredients in order listed in a 11X13 inch casserole dish. Refrigerate overnight. Yields 10 to 12 servings.

Spinach and Bacon Salad

Salad
2 (10-ounce) packages fresh
   spinach, stems removed

½ pound bacon, cooked and
   crumbled
½ cup sliced Bermuda onion

Dressing
2 tablespoons sugar
1 teaspoon salt
1 teaspoon dry mustard
⅓ cup cider vinegar

1 cup vegetable oil
1 tablespoon poppy seed
1½ cups cottage cheese

Tear spinach into bite-size pieces in a salad bowl. Add bacon and onion. To make dressing, combine sugar and next 4 ingredients. Shake well. Add poppy seed and shake again. Add cottage cheese and shake well. Pour over salad and toss. Serve immediately. Yields 8 servings.

Korean Spinach Salad

Dressing
¼ cup vegetable oil
¼ cup sugar
3 tablespoons ketchup
¼ cup red wine vinegar

½ teaspoon Worcestershire sauce
1 tablespoon grated onion
salt to taste

Salad
1 (10-ounce) package fresh spinach,
   stems removed
½ cup alfalfa sprouts
1 (8-ounce) can sliced water
   chestnuts, drained

3 hard-cooked eggs, diced
3 slices bacon, cooked and
   crumbled

Mix together all dressing ingredients and chill. Refrigerate up to 2 weeks. To make salad, combine spinach and remaining 4 ingredients in a salad bowl. Toss with dressing. Yields 6 servings.

Cranberry Apple Salad

2 (16-ounce) cans whole berry
  cranberry sauce
2 cups boiling water
2 (3-ounce) packages raspberry-
  flavored gelatin

2 tablespoons lemon juice
½ teaspoon salt
1 cup mayonnaise
2 cups peeled and diced apple
½ cup chopped walnuts

Melt cranberry sauce in a saucepan. Drain, reserving liquid and berries. Combine reserved liquid, boiling water, and gelatin and stir until gelatin dissolves. Add lemon juice and salt. Chill until mixture mounds slightly on a spoon. Beat in mayonnaise until smooth. Fold in reserved berries, apple, and walnuts. Pour into a greased 2-quart mold. Refrigerate overnight. Yields 10 to 12 servings.

Frozen Fruit Salad

Salad
1 cup sugar
½ cup lemon juice
½ cup Royal Ann pitted cherries,
  drained
½ cup mandarin orange sections,
  drained
1½ cups sliced canned peaches,
  drained

1 cup crushed pineapple, drained,
  juice reserved
1½ cups sliced banana
1 cup mayonnaise
1 cup heavy cream, whipped
½ cup pecans

Dressing
1 cup sugar
2 tablespoons all-purpose flour
2 eggs

½ cup lemon juice
½ cup pineapple juice
½ cup orange juice

Combine sugar and lemon juice in a large bowl. Mix well. Add cherries and next 4 ingredients. In a separate bowl, blend mayonnaise and cream. Mix cream mixture and pecans into fruit. Pour into a greased 2½-quart mold. Freeze up to 2 weeks. To prepare dressing, mix sugar and flour in a saucepan. Whisk in eggs. Add juices and cook, stirring often, over low heat until thick. Chill. When ready to serve, unmold frozen salad and serve with dressing. Yields 8 servings.

Wilted Greens with Warm Vinaigrette

2 heads lettuce, torn into bite-size
    pieces
2 tomatoes, cut into bite-size pieces
1¼ cups chopped green onions
¾ cup grated carrot
¾ cup chopped celery
½ cup sugar

½ cup vinegar
½ cup water
½ cup bacon drippings
8 slices bacon, cooked and
    crumbled
4 hard-cooked eggs, sliced

Toss together lettuce and next 4 ingredients in a salad bowl. Let stand at room temperature for 60 minutes. Combine sugar and next 3 ingredients in a saucepan. Simmer 10 minutes. Pour over salad. Top with bacon and egg. Serve immediately. Yields 8 to 10 servings.

Chicken Salad

3 cups diced cooked chicken
1 cup finely chopped celery
1 cup sliced Thompson seedless
    grapes
½ cup slivered almonds, toasted

2 tablespoons minced fresh parsley
1 teaspoon salt
1 cup mayonnaise
½ cup heavy cream, whipped

Combine all ingredients and chill until ready to serve. Serve on lettuce. Yields 6 servings.

Curried Chicken Salad

Salad
2 cups diced cooked chicken
¼ cup sliced water chestnuts
8 ounces Thompson seedless grapes,
    halved

½ cup coarsely chopped celery
½ cup slivered almonds, toasted
1 (8-ounce) can pineapple chunks,
    drained

Dressing
¾ cup mayonnaise
1 teaspoon curry powder

2 teaspoons soy sauce
2 teaspoons lemon juice

Combine all salad ingredients in a bowl. Mix together all dressing ingredients and add to salad. Chill. Serve on lettuce or in a scooped-out pineapple half. Yields 4 to 6 servings.

Sour Cream Potato Salad

4 hard-cooked eggs, halved
²/₃ cup mayonnaise
³/₄ cup sour cream
1½ teaspoons prepared mustard
    with horseradish
½ pound bacon, cooked and
    crumbled

⅓ cup chopped green onions
1 cup chopped celery
7 cups cubed potato, cooked
⅓ cup Italian salad dressing
salt to taste

Remove egg yolks and place in a small bowl, reserving egg whites. Mash yolks. Blend in mayonnaise, sour cream, and mustard. In a separate bowl, chop egg whites. Mix in bacon and next 4 ingredients. Fold in mayonnaise mixture and season with salt. Yields 8 to 10 servings.

Tuna Fish Salad

Dressing
³/₄ cup mayonnaise
½ teaspoon lemon juice
1 teaspoon soy sauce

⅛ teaspoon curry powder
⅛ teaspoon nutmeg

Salad
1 (9½-ounce) can water-packed
    tuna, drained
½ (10-ounce) package frozen peas,
    thawed
1 (6-ounce) jar pearl onions, drained
    and halved
²/₃ cup chopped celery

⅓ cup sliced water chestnuts,
    drained
1 (2-ounce) bag slivered almonds,
    toasted
½ teaspoon salt
1 cup chow mein noodles

Mix together all dressing ingredients. To prepare salad, combine tuna and next 6 ingredients in a bowl. Add dressing and mix well. Top with noodles. Yields 4 servings.

Seafood Salad

Use shrimp, crawfish, crabmeat, tuna, or a combination. For best flavor, prepare salad ahead.

2 pounds cooked seafood
½ cup French dressing
1½ tablespoons finely grated onion
½ cup finely grated bell pepper
½ cup finely grated celery
1 teaspoon salt

½ teaspoon black pepper
1 teaspoon Tabasco sauce
1 teaspoon Worcestershire sauce
1 cup mayonnaise
2 eggs, hard cooked and chopped

Combine seafood and next 8 ingredients in a large bowl. Mix well and refrigerate 30 minutes. Fold in mayonnaise and egg. Yields 6 to 8 servings.

Haitian Avocado and Shrimp

1 (14-ounce) can hearts of palm
1 teaspoon prepared yellow mustard
1½ teaspoons salt
¼ teaspoon black pepper
½ teaspoon garlic salt
3 tablespoons red wine vinegar

¼ cup minced onion
⅓ cup olive oil
1 tablespoon lemon juice
1½ cups cooked shrimp
4 avocados, peeled and halved

Slice hearts of palm into ¼-inch rounds. In a bowl, combine mustard and next 7 ingredients. Add hearts of palm and shrimp. Spoon mixture into avocado halves and chill. Yields 8 salad servings, 4 entrée servings.

Avocado Stuffed with Crabmeat

1½ cups mayonnaise
1 tablespoon lemon juice
2 tablespoons capers, drained
1 tablespoon chopped fresh parsley
3 tablespoons ketchup
2 tablespoons chopped green onions

2 teaspoons dried dill
⅛ teaspoon black pepper
⅛ teaspoon salt
3 cups crabmeat
4 avocados, peeled and halved

Combine mayonnaise and next 8 ingredients. Refrigerate 24 hours. Spoon crabmeat into avocado halves. Top with dressing. Yields 8 servings.

Walnut Shrimp Salad

1 tablespoon butter
1 tablespoon soy sauce
1 cup walnut halves
1 cup diagonally sliced celery
½ cup sliced green onions
1 (8-ounce) can sliced water
   chestnuts, drained

1 (11-ounce) can mandarin orange
   sections, drained
3 cups cooked shrimp
½ cup bottled sweet and spicy salad
   dressing
crisp salad greens

Melt butter in a saucepan. Add soy sauce and walnuts. Stir over low heat 10 minutes or until walnuts are lightly toasted. Cool. Combine walnut mixture, celery, and remaining 6 ingredients in a salad bowl and toss. Refrigerate until ready to serve. Yields 4 to 6 servings.

Cold Crabmeat Salad

¼ cup mayonnaise
1 tablespoon lemon juice
½ teaspoon dry mustard
1 teaspoon Worcestershire sauce
½ teaspoon Tabasco sauce
⅛ teaspoon garlic salt

1½ cups coarsely chopped celery
2 green onions, finely chopped
2 tablespoons chopped fresh parsley
6 pimiento-stuffed olives, chopped
1 pound crabmeat

Combine mayonnaise and next 9 ingredients. Pour over crabmeat. Refrigerate until ready to serve. Yields 6 servings.

Crabmeat Mousse

1 (8-ounce) package cream cheese,
   softened
1½ cups mayonnaise
1½ pounds white crabmeat
1 (2-ounce) bottle capers, drained
½ cup finely chopped celery
¼ cup minced fresh parsley

1 teaspoon garlic salt
½ teaspoon paprika
¼ teaspoon Tabasco sauce
1 teaspoon Worcestershire sauce
2 teaspoons unflavored gelatin
1 cup water

Blend cream cheese and mayonnaise in a bowl. Add crabmeat and next 7 ingredients. Soften gelatin in water and heat until dissolved. Cool and add to crabmeat mixture. Pour into a 6-cup mold. Refrigerate until set. Yields 8 servings.

Gazpacho Mold

2 tablespoons unflavored gelatin
4 cups spicy tomato juice, divided
1 tablespoon lemon juice
½ cup finely chopped celery
½ cup finely chopped onion

¼ cup finely chopped bell pepper
1 hard-cooked egg, finely chopped
½ teaspoon salt
¼ teaspoon black pepper

Dissolve gelatin in 2 cups tomato juice in a large bowl. In a saucepan, heat remaining 2 cups tomato juice and add to gelatin mixture. Add lemon juice and remaining 6 ingredients. Pour into a greased 5-cup mold. Refrigerate until set. Yields 8 to 10 servings.

Cold Artichokes

Artichokes
5 artichokes
2 lemons, sliced

2 cloves garlic, sliced
1 teaspoon salt

Dressing
½ cup vegetable oil
2 tablespoons lemon juice
2 tablespoons red wine vinegar
1 tablespoon brown mustard
2 cloves garlic

2 green onions
1 small bell pepper, sliced
1 teaspoon salt
½ teaspoon black pepper

Combine artichokes and next 3 ingredients in a saucepan. Add water to cover and cook 45 minutes or until a leaf easily pulls free. Remove and chill artichokes. To prepare dressing, blend oil and remaining 8 ingredients. Let stand at least 30 minutes. Just before serving, blend again. Serve dressing with artichokes. Yields 5 servings.

Vegetable Aspic

2 tablespoons unflavored gelatin
1/2 cup cold water
1/2 cup boiling consommé
2 cups cold consommé
3/4 cup tomato juice
4 teaspoons Worcestershire sauce
3 tablespoons lemon juice

1 teaspoon Tabasco sauce
1 1/2 teaspoons celery salt
1/8 teaspoon paprika
1 cup chopped celery
1 (8 1/2-ounce) can artichoke hearts,
    quartered, drained
1 (10 1/2-ounce) can asparagus tips,
    drained

Soften gelatin in cold water. Add boiling consommé and stir to dissolve. Cool. Add cold consommé and next 6 ingredients. Chill until almost set, stirring occasionally. Fold in celery, artichoke heats, and asparagus. Pour into a 5-cup wet and chilled mold. Refrigerate until set. Serve with mayonnaise. Yields 10 to 12 servings.

Tomato Aspic with Cream Cheese

4 cups tomato juice
2 cloves garlic, pressed
1/2 teaspoon dry mustard
2 1/2 teaspoons salt
2 1/2 teaspoons sugar
1/3 cup lemon juice
1 teaspoon paprika
1 bay leaf

1/8 teaspoon cayenne pepper
3 tablespoons unflavored gelatin
3/4 cup bouillon
2 (3-ounce) packages cream cheese,
    softened
3 tablespoon grated onion
1/2 teaspoon Tabasco sauce

Combine tomato juice and next 8 ingredients in a saucepan. Bring to a boil. Cook 3 minutes and remove from heat. Soften gelatin in bouillon. Add gelatin mixture to saucepan and stir to dissolve. Remove bay leaf. Pour into a 1 1/2-quart mold and refrigerate. Combine cream cheese, onion, and Tabasco sauce and roll into small balls. Chill. When aspic starts to gel, arrange cheese balls in mold. Refrigerate until set. Unmold and serve with mayonnaise. Yields 10 to 12 servings.

Feta Cheese Dressing

2 cups crumbled feta cheese
2 cups mayonnaise
2 small cloves garlic, minced
1/2 cup red wine vinegar
1 teaspoon dried basil
1 teaspoon dried oregano

1 tablespoon Worcestershire sauce
2 tablespoons olive oil
freshly ground black pepper to taste
2 tablespoons minced green onion
  tops

Blend all ingredients until smooth. Stores well in refrigerator. Yields 4 cups.

Italian Cheese Dressing

1/2 cup vegetable oil
1/4 cup tarragon vinegar
1/2 cup mayonnaise

1/2 cup grated Romano cheese
1/4 teaspoon salt
freshly ground black pepper to taste

Whisk together all ingredients. Refrigerate. Mix before serving. Yields 1 1/2 cups.

For a different flavor, use a Romano and Parmesan cheese mixture.

Green Goddess Dressing

1 clove garlic, pressed
1 cup sour cream
1 cup anchovies, or 2 tablespoons
  anchovy paste
3 tablespoons finely chopped green
  onion tops

1 tablespoon lemon juice
3 tablespoons cider vinegar
1 cup mayonnaise
1/3 cup finely chopped fresh parsley
salt and pepper to taste

Process all ingredients in a blender and chill. Stores well in refrigerator. Yields 2 cups.

Mint Dressing

⅓ cup lemon juice
¼ cup dry sherry
8 sprigs fresh mint, chopped

2 tablespoons honey
1 teaspoon celery seed

Combine all ingredients. Serve over fruit salad. Yields 1 cup.

Celery Seed Dressing

1 cup sugar
1 teaspoon salt
1 teaspoon paprika
1 teaspoon grated onion

⅓ cup ketchup
1 cup vegetable oil
⅓ cup cider vinegar
½ teaspoon celery seed

Combine sugar and next 4 ingredients in a blender. Blend at medium speed and slowly add oil and vinegar, alternately. Add celery seed. Serve on grapefruit sections or molded fruit salad. Stores well in refrigerator. Yields 2 cups.

Rémoulade Sauce

2 large cloves garlic, pressed
1 hard-cooked egg
3 anchovies
salt and pepper to taste
¾ cup olive oil
¼ cup vinegar
1 tablespoon lemon juice

½ cup ketchup
2 tablespoons Worcestershire sauce
2½ tablespoons Creole mustard
2 teaspoons dry mustard
2 teaspoons Dijon mustard
1 tablespoon paprika

In a food processor with a metal blade, blend garlic, egg, and anchovies until smooth. Transfer to a bowl. Stir in salt, pepper, and remaining 9 ingredients. Chill. Stores well in refrigerator. Yields 2 cups.

Lemon Butter Sauce

3 tablespoons lemon juice
1 tablespoon Dijon mustard
1 egg yolk

¼ teaspoon salt
⅛ teaspoon white pepper
¾ cup vegetable oil, warmed

Combine lemon juice and next 4 ingredients in a bowl. Add oil in a slow, steady stream, whisking until thickened. Serve over vegetables, meat, fish, or chicken. Yields 1 cup.

Hollandaise Sauce

This recipe doubles well.

3 egg yolks
2 tablespoons lemon juice
1 stick butter, cut into pieces

⅛ teaspoon cayenne pepper
⅛ teaspoon salt

Combine all ingredients in the top of a double boiler. Stir constantly over low heat with a wooden spoon for 5 to 8 minutes or until creamy. Do not allow water in double boiler to come to a boil. Remove from heat when thickened. Cover and set entire double boiler on side until ready to serve. Sauce thickens as it sits. Yields ¾ cup.

Béarnaise Sauce

⅓ cup coarsely chopped green
   onions
1 tablespoon black pepper
1 cup dry vermouth or dry white
   wine

¾ cup cider vinegar
1½ tablespoons tarragon
1 tablespoon fresh parsley
2 tablespoons chervil (optional)
¾ cup Hollandaise Sauce (page 66)

Combine green onions and next 6 ingredients in a blender or food processor. Blend on high speed for 30 seconds. Pour into a saucepan and bring to a boil. Cook 30 minutes or until liquid evaporates. Cool. Beat 1 teaspoon of essence into Hollandaise Sauce. Refrigerate or freeze remaining essence for up to several weeks. Yields ¾ cup.

Marchand De Vin Sauce

Flavor improves the longer the broth mixture simmers. For a thicker sauce, blend 1 tablespoon softened butter and 1 tablespoon flour. Add to sauce and simmer several minutes.

6 tablespoons butter, divided
¼ cup all-purpose flour
3 cups beef broth, divided
½ cup chopped onion
¼ cup chopped celery
¼ cup chopped ham
2 tablespoons chopped fresh parsley

1 tablespoon chopped garlic
2 bay leaves
¾ teaspoon dried thyme
4 ounces mushrooms, coarsely
   chopped
½ cup Madeira or red wine
¼ teaspoon lemon juice

Melt 4 tablespoons butter in a large skillet. Gradually add flour and cook and stir until dark brown. Combine 1 cup broth and next 5 ingredients in a blender or food processor. Blend 30 seconds. Add to skillet. Stir in remaining 2 cups broth, bay leaves, and thyme. Simmer at least 30 minutes. Sauté mushrooms in remaining 2 tablespoons butter in a separate skillet. Add mushrooms to broth mixture and simmer 10 minutes, stirring occasionally. Add Madeira and simmer 5 minutes. Stir in lemon juice and remove bay leaves. Blend well. Yields 4 cups.

Rockefeller Sauce

3 (10-ounce) packages fresh spinach
1 bunch green onions
leaves from ½ bunch celery
1 whole bulb garlic, separated and
   peeled
1 bunch fresh parsley

4 cups water
1 cup Parmesan cheese
1 cup breadcrumbs
4 sticks butter, melted
1 jigger Pernod (anise liqueur)

Combine spinach and next 5 ingredients in a large saucepan. Bring to a boil and cook 20 minutes. Drain and chop in a food processor. Return mixture to saucepan. Mix in cheese, breadcrumbs, and butter. Add Pernod and stir. Serve over oysters. Yields enough sauce for 5 dozen oysters.

Secret Mayonnaise

4 cups mayonnaise
1 tablespoon vinegar
2 tablespoons lemon juice
1 teaspoon salt
1 teaspoon black pepper
¼ teaspoon cayenne pepper
1 tablespoon horseradish

1 tablespoon prepared yellow
  mustard
1 tablespoon Worcestershire sauce
¼ teaspoon dried basil
¼ teaspoon dried thyme
1 clove garlic, pressed
1 tablespoon grated onion

Combine all ingredients in a bowl and mix well. Cover and refrigerate. Yields 1 quart.

Creole Mayonnaise

1½ cups vegetable oil, divided
1 egg
3 tablespoons chopped onion
1 tablespoon Creole mustard
3 tablespoons vinegar or lemon juice

¼ teaspoon paprika
Tabasco sauce to taste
1 teaspoon prepared yellow mustard
1 teaspoon salt

Place ¼ cup oil in a blender or food processor. Add egg and next 7 ingredients. Blend on high speed until smooth. Immediately add remaining 1¼ cups oil in a slow steady stream. Yields 2 cups.

Sweet Hot Mustard

4 ounces dry mustard
1 cup cider vinegar or tarragon
  vinegar

3 eggs
1 cup sugar

Combine mustard and vinegar in a bowl. Cover and refrigerate overnight. The next day, beat eggs. Combine egg and sugar in the top of a double boiler. Stir in mustard mixture. Cook, stirring occasionally, for 10 minutes or until mixture thickens. Store in refrigerator. Yields 2 cups.

French Butter Pecan Sauce

1 stick butter, melted
2 tablespoons chives
1/2 teaspoon salt
1/4 teaspoon black pepper

1/4 teaspoon dried marjoram
3 tablespoons lemon juice
1/2 cup chopped pecans

Combine all ingredients and heat thoroughly. Serve over cooked vegetables or fish. Yields 1 cup.

Sour Cream Cheese Sauce

1/2 cup mayonnaise
1/2 cup sour cream
1/2 teaspoon Worcestershire sauce
1/4 teaspoon salt

white pepper to taste
1/2 cup grated cheddar or Parmesan cheese
1/2 cup finely chopped green onions

Combine mayonnaise and next 4 ingredients in a bowl. In a separate bowl, combine cheese and onions. Add cream mixture to cheese mixture. Blend well. Pour over warm vegetables and bake at 350° for 2 minutes. Yields 1 3/4 cups.

White Wine Sauce

1/4 cup white wine vinegar
1/4 cup dry white wine
1/4 cup minced green onions
1 tablespoon heavy cream
1 1/2 sticks butter, cut into 6 pieces

1/4 teaspoon salt
1/4 teaspoon black pepper
1/2 teaspoon lemon juice
1/8 teaspoon celery salt

Combine vinegar, wine, and onions in a small saucepan. Simmer until mixture is almost a glaze. Remove from heat and add cream. Return to low heat and whisk in butter, 1 piece at a time. Add each piece of butter before previous one has completely melted. Do not allow sauce to get too hot or it will break down. Add salt and remaining 3 ingredients. Pour over warm seafood and serve immediately. Yields 1 cup.

Barbecue Sauce

2 sticks butter
¾ cup chopped onion
½ cup packed light brown sugar
¼ teaspoon cayenne pepper
1 cup vegetable oil
1 teaspoon dry mustard

½ cup Worcestershire sauce
1½ cups ketchup
2 tablespoons chili sauce
2 cloves garlic, minced
¼ cup lemon juice
3 drops Tabasco sauce

Melt butter in a large saucepan. Add onion and sauté 3 minutes or until transparent. Stir in sugar and remaining 9 ingredients. Simmer 15 minutes, stirring frequently. Stores well in refrigerator. Yields 3½ cups.

Tartar Sauce

1 cup mayonnaise
½ teaspoon dry mustard
4 teaspoons finely chopped green
   onions
1 tablespoon chopped sweet pickle,
   drained

½ clove garlic, minced
1 teaspoon capers (optional)
1 teaspoon tarragon vinegar or
   lemon juice
salt to taste
cayenne pepper to taste

Combine all ingredients. Stores well in refrigerator. Yields 1¼ cups.

Orange Jezebel Sauce

Serve with cheese and crackers, as a condiment with meats, or as a dip for egg rolls and wontons.

1 (18-ounce) jar apple jelly
1 (18-ounce) jar pineapple or
   apricot preserves
3 tablespoons dry mustard
¼ cup horseradish

¾ teaspoon orange zest
½ teaspoon black pepper
¼ teaspoon poppy seed or mustard
   seed

Combine all ingredients. Stir well, cover, and chill. Stores well in refrigerator. Yields 5 cups.

Tomato Relish

6 pounds ripe tomatoes (about 12
   large)
3 cups finely chopped onion
1 cup finely chopped bell pepper
1 cup cider vinegar

2 cups sugar
1 teaspoon cinnamon
2 teaspoons salt
½ teaspoon ground cloves
cayenne pepper to taste

Peel, chop, and drain tomatoes. Combine tomato and remaining 8 ingredients in a saucepan. Bring to a boil. Reduce heat and simmer 2 hours, stirring occasionally. Seal in sterile jars. Yields 5 pints.

Bread and Butter Pickles

12 medium cucumbers, peeled and
   sliced
6 medium yellow onions, thinly
   sliced
1 cup salt
2½ cups cider vinegar

2 cups sugar
2 teaspoons mustard seed
2 teaspoons turmeric
2 teaspoons celery seed
¼ teaspoon ground cloves

Layer cucumber, onion, and salt in a large bowl. Cover with cold water and let stand 2 hours. Drain well. In a large saucepan, combine vinegar and remaining 5 ingredients. Bring to a boil. Add cucumber and onion and boil 10 minutes. Seal in sterile jars. Yields 6 pints.

Yellow Squash Pickles

25 yellow squash, sliced
8 cups chopped onion
2 cups chopped bell pepper
½ cup salt
5 cups sugar

5 cups cider vinegar
2 tablespoons mustard seed
½ tablespoon ground cloves
1 teaspoon turmeric

Combine squash and next 3 ingredients in a large stainless steel bowl. Let stand 3 hours. Drain. In a large stainless steel or enamel saucepan, combine sugar and remaining 4 ingredients. Bring to a boil. Add vegetables and return to a boil. Seal in sterile jars. Place in a hot water bath for 5 minutes. Yields 8 pints.

Pickled Okra

Small pods of okra work best. Alum is available at drug stores.

7 pounds okra, unwashed
6 tablespoons alum
4 quarts water
16 green chili peppers
48 cloves garlic
1 gallon cider vinegar

1 (1 pound) package light brown
  sugar
1 cup salt
1 teaspoon peppercorns
1 teaspoon mustard seed
1 teaspoon pickling spice

Trim okra stems without exposing seeds. Combine okra, alum, and water and let stand 2 hours. Rinse well in cold water and drain. Arrange okra among 16 sterile pint jars. Place 1 chili pepper and 3 cloves garlic in each jar. In a large saucepan, combine vinegar and remaining 5 ingredients. Boil 10 minutes. Divide among jars and seal. Turn jars regularly. Allow to set several days before eating. Yields 16 pints.

Captain's Relish

3 heads cabbage, grated
3 large Bermuda onions, grated
3 large bell peppers, grated
2 large heads cauliflower, separated
  into florets or thinly sliced
¾ cup salt
1 gallon boiling water

3 cups sugar
1 cup minus 1 tablespoon all-
  purpose flour
1 teaspoon turmeric
9 tablespoons dry mustard
2 tablespoons salt
3 quarts cider vinegar

Combine cabbage and next 3 ingredients in a 5-quart saucepan. Cover with salt. Pour boiling water over vegetables and let soak 60 minutes. Drain and cover with ice water. Let stand 30 minutes and drain. Combine sugar and remaining 5 ingredients in a separate large saucepan. Boil 5 minutes. Add vegetables and simmer 30 minutes. Seal in sterile jars. Yields 12 pints.

Apple Butter

2½ pounds tart cooking apples,
   peeled, cored, and quartered
3 cups water
1 cup apple juice
1 cup honey
1 cup sugar

2½ tablespoons lemon juice
¾ teaspoon ground cloves
1 teaspoon ground allspice
1 teaspoon cinnamon
½ teaspoon nutmeg
½ teaspoon lemon zest

Combine apple and water in an enamel or stainless steel saucepan. Bring to a boil and cook 30 minutes or until tender. Purée and return to saucepan. Add apple juice and remaining 8 ingredients. Mix well and bring to a boil. Reduce heat and simmer 1 hour, 30 minutes or until thickened, stirring occasionally. Seal in sterile jars and store in a cool, dark place. Yields 2 pints.

Cranberry Relish

2 pounds fresh cranberries
6½ cups sugar
1 pound raisins
2 large oranges, unpeeled, finely
   chopped

1 tablespoon lemon juice, or
   chopped lemon rind
1 cup cider vinegar
½ teaspoon ground cloves
2 teaspoons cinnamon

Combine all ingredients in a large saucepan. Cook over low heat for 30 minutes or until cranberries pop. Seal in sterile jars. Yields 5 pints.

Pear Chutney

1 lemon, seeded and chopped
1 clove garlic, minced
5 cups peeled and chopped cooking
   pears
1 (1 pound) package dark brown
   sugar
1 cup raisins
2 ounces crystallized ginger

1½ teaspoons salt
2 cups cider vinegar
⅓ cup chopped onion
1 tablespoon mustard seed
¼ teaspoon cinnamon
⅛ teaspoon ground allspice
¼ teaspoon cayenne pepper

Combine all ingredients in a large saucepan. Cook 45 minutes or until fruit is tender and syrup is thick. Seal in sterile jars. Yields 2½ pints.

Hot Pepper Jelly

Protect hands by wearing rubber gloves when preparing peppers.

1⅓ cups seeded and finely chopped
green chili pepper
2½ cups seeded and finely chopped
bell pepper

3 cups cider vinegar
13 cups sugar
4 (3-ounce) packages liquid pectin
green or red food coloring

Combine peppers, vinegar, and sugar in a large saucepan. Bring to a boil and cook 1 minute. Reduce heat and cook 5 minutes. Remove from heat and add pectin. Stir well. Mix in a few drops of food coloring. Seal in sterile jars. Yields 7 pints.

Parsley Jelly

1½ cups packed flat-leaf parsley,
leaves only
3½ cups boiling water
2 tablespoons lemon juice

1 (1¾-ounce) package dry pectin
4 cups sugar
green food coloring

Chop parsley and place in a large bowl. Pour boiling water over parsley. Cool, cover, and refrigerate overnight. Strain liquid through a cheesecloth. Combine 3 cups liquid, lemon juice, and pectin in a large saucepan. Bring to a boil, stirring occasionally. Immediately stir in sugar. Add food coloring. Cook and stir until mixture returns to a rolling boil that cannot be stirred down. Boil 1 minute. Remove from heat. Skim foam with a metal spoon. Seal in hot sterile jars. Serve with lamb, pork, or game. Yields 3 pints.
For mint jelly, substitute mint leaves for parsley.

Crawfish & Seafood

It wouldn't be Friday without seafood

If it's Friday in New Orleans, you'll find seafood on the menu, whether you're dining at the finest Creole restaurant in the French Quarter, a neighborhood joint with formica table tops, or the home of a close friend. Like many culinary traditions in the Crescent City, the serving of seafood on Friday is well established and widely followed. And like other customs here, it has its roots in the city's Catholic heritage.

The tradition goes back to the earliest days of New Orleans. The city was predominantly Catholic and in the Catholic church Friday was a day of fast in which eating meat was forbidden. In other parts of the country, that might have been quite a sacrifice. But as they always seem to do, New Orleanians found in it an excuse for festivity, and with the rich bounty of fish and shellfish in the local waters, eating seafood on Fridays evolved into something that natives looked forward to. On Friday nights, many families would gather at neighborhood restaurants that served up heaping platters of spicy fried shrimp and trays of raw oysters on the half shell. Others would host down-home fish fries in their backyards. Some nuns, concerned that the spirit of sacrifice was being lost in the local translation, were heard to advise school children to eat scrambled eggs for their Friday meal instead!

In the mid-1960s, the Second Vatican Council loosened many of the rules which had governed the Catholic Church, among them the prohibition of eating meat on Fridays. From then on, Friday fasting was only required during the Lenten season. Nevertheless, the tradition remains alive and well in the Crescent City, and as they have done for years, most local menus still have seafood specials on Friday all year long.

Jambalaya features dozens of delicious and authentic Creole and Cajun seafood dishes to enjoy on Friday or any day of the week! See pages 77-98.

Shrimp and Sausage Jambalaya

Creole seasoning is a mixture of salt, cayenne pepper, black pepper, chili powder, and garlic powder.

1 pound smoked sausage, thinly
  sliced
3 tablespoons olive oil
²/₃ cup chopped bell pepper
2 cloves garlic, minced
¾ cup chopped fresh parsley
1 cup chopped celery
2 (14½-ounce) cans tomatoes,
  chopped, undrained
2 cups chicken broth

1 cup chopped green onions
1½ teaspoons thyme
2 bay leaves
2 teaspoons dried oregano
1 tablespoon Creole seasoning
½ teaspoon salt
¼ teaspoon cayenne pepper
¼ teaspoon black pepper
2 cups dry long-grain converted rice
3 pounds raw shrimp, peeled

Sauté sausage in a 4-quart saucepan. Remove with a slotted spoon and reserve. Add oil and next 4 ingredients to saucepan and sauté 5 minutes. Add tomato and next 9 ingredients. Wash and rinse rice 3 times and add to saucepan. Stir in sausage and cover. Cook over low heat, stirring occasionally, for 30 minutes or until most of liquid is absorbed. Add shrimp and cook until pink. Transfer mixture to an oblong baking dish. Bake at 350° for about 25 minutes. Yields 10 servings.

Shrimp Fettuccine

1 stick butter, divided
2 tablespoons vegetable oil
5 green onions, chopped
2 cups sliced mushrooms
2 cloves garlic, minced
1 pound raw shrimp, peeled

2 teaspoons salt
8 ounces fettuccine
¾ cup grated Romano cheese
¾ cup Parmesan cheese
1 cup heavy cream
¼ cup chopped fresh parsley

Heat 4 tablespoons butter and oil in a large skillet. Add onions, mushrooms, and garlic and sauté. Add shrimp and sauté until pink. Pour off excess liquid and season with salt. Cover and keep warm. Cook fettuccine in boiling salted water and drain. Melt remaining 4 tablespoons butter in a saucepan. Mix in fettuccine, cheeses, and cream. Combine with shrimp mixture. Sprinkle with parsley and toss. Serve immediately. Yields 4 to 6 servings.

Shrimp Clemenceau

2 cups peeled and cubed potato
4 sticks butter
2 cups small fresh mushroom caps
1½ teaspoons minced garlic
4 pounds raw shrimp, peeled and
   deveined

2 teaspoons lemon juice
2 tablespoons Worcestershire sauce
2 cups small green peas
2 teaspoons minced fresh parsley

Sauté potato until tender. In a separate large skillet, melt butter. Add mushrooms and garlic and sauté 3 to 5 minutes. Add potato, shrimp, lemon juice, and Worcestershire sauce. Sauté 6 to 8 minutes or until shrimp are pink. Add peas and parsley. Heat thoroughly. Yields 4 servings.

Shrimp and Rice Casserole

1 stick plus 3 tablespoons butter,
   divided
3 pounds raw shrimp, peeled
½ cup chopped bell pepper
1 cup chopped yellow onion
4 ounces fresh mushrooms, sliced
6 cups cooked rice
1 teaspoon dried thyme

1 teaspoon salt
½ teaspoon black pepper
2 teaspoons Worcestershire sauce
¼ teaspoon Tabasco sauce
1 tablespoon chopped chives
1 tablespoon chopped pimiento
½ cup dry breadcrumbs
½ cup heavy cream

Melt 1 stick butter in a large skillet. Add shrimp and next 3 ingredients. Sauté 3 to 5 minutes. Stir in rice and next 5 ingredients. Gently mix over low heat. Fold in chives and pimiento. Transfer mixture to a 3-quart casserole dish. Melt remaining 3 tablespoons butter and combine with breadcrumbs. Sprinkle over casserole. Pour cream around edge of casserole. Bake at 375° for 25 to 30 minutes. Yields 12 servings.

Shrimp Oriental Casserole

1 stick butter
½ cup all-purpose flour
½ cup chopped bell pepper
½ cup chopped celery
2 cups light cream
1 cup dry white wine
1 cup grated cheddar cheese
8 ounces fresh mushrooms, sliced

2 teaspoons salt
2 teaspoons soy sauce
½ teaspoon white pepper
2 tablespoons lemon juice
3 pounds shrimp, cooked, peeled, and deveined
3 cups steamed rice, or 6 patty shells

Melt butter in a large skillet. Blend in flour. Add bell pepper and celery. Cook 5 to 7 minutes or until soft but not brown. Gradually add cream and wine. Stir in cheese and next 5 ingredients. Simmer 2 minutes. Add shrimp. Pour into a 2-quart casserole dish. Bake at 350° for 20 to 25 minutes. Serve over rice. Yields 6 servings.

Shrimp and Chicken Curry

4 large chicken breasts, skinned and boned
4 tablespoons butter, divided
½ cup finely chopped yellow onion
1 small clove garlic, crushed
½ cup finely diced celery
2 tablespoons curry powder
1 tablespoon tomato paste

½ cup cubed banana
1 cup peeled and cubed apple
1 cup chicken broth
1 teaspoon salt, divided
½ teaspoon black pepper
1 pound raw shrimp, peeled and deveined
3 cups steamed rice

Cut chicken into 1-inch cubes. Melt 2 tablespoons butter in a large skillet. Add onion and garlic and cook briefly. Add celery and cook and stir 1 minute. Stir in curry powder. Mix in tomato paste, banana, and apple. Gradually pour in broth and blend well. Add ½ teaspoon salt and simmer 10 minutes. In a saucepan, melt remaining 2 tablespoons butter. Add chicken and sprinkle with remaining ½ teaspoon salt and pepper. Cook, stirring occasionally, 2 to 3 minutes. Add shrimp and simmer, stirring constantly, for 2 minutes. Transfer chicken and shrimp with a slotted spoon to a 1½-quart casserole dish. Pour curry sauce over top. Bake at 350° for 20 to 25 minutes. Serve over rice. Yields 6 servings.

Shrimp Dewey

4 tablespoons butter
1½ cups chopped green onions
¾ cup canned Italian tomatoes,
   liquid reserved
1½ pounds raw shrimp, peeled and
   deveined
1 cup sliced mushrooms
¼ cup chopped fresh parsley
3 tablespoons cornstarch

¼ cup water
⅓ cup white wine
1 cup sour cream
1½ teaspoons salt
¼ teaspoon dried basil
½ teaspoon dried oregano
¼ teaspoon black pepper
Tabasco sauce to taste
6 patty shells, heated

Melt butter in a large skillet. Add onions and sauté. Add tomatoes and ½ cup tomato liquid. Cook 5 minutes and mash well. Add shrimp and simmer 5 minutes. Stir in mushrooms and parsley and cook a few minutes. Dissolve cornstarch in water and slowly stir into shrimp mixture. Cook until thickened. Add wine and next 6 ingredients. Heat, but do not boil. Spoon into patty shells. Yields 6 servings.

Cold Shrimp Curry

4 tablespoons butter
1 cup peeled and chopped apple
2 cups chopped green onions
1 teaspoon crushed coriander seed
1 teaspoon ground ginger
1 tablespoon curry powder
1 teaspoon all-purpose flour
1 large orange, peeled and chopped

½ cup coconut liquid or coconut
   milk
1½ teaspoons sugar
2 cups mayonnaise
salt and pepper to taste
dash of cayenne pepper
2 tablespoons lemon juice
3 pounds cooked and peeled shrimp

Melt butter in a skillet. Add apple and onions and sauté 8 to 10 minutes or until softened. Add coriander seed and next 3 ingredients. Mix well. Add orange. Combine coconut liquid and sugar and stir until dissolved. Add coconut liquid to skillet, one teaspoon at a time, using just enough to form a smooth paste. Cool and mix paste with mayonnaise. Add salt, pepper, cayenne pepper, and lemon juice. Stir in shrimp and chill. Yields 8 servings.

Serve in scooped-out pineapple halves. Garnish with cubed pineapple and toasted, grated coconut.

Crab and Shrimp Étouffé

1½ sticks butter
1 cup finely chopped onion
¼ cup finely chopped bell pepper
¼ cup finely chopped celery
4 cloves garlic, minced
4 teaspoons cornstarch
1-1½ cups chicken broth, divided
½ cup white wine
4 teaspoons tomato paste

¼ cup finely chopped green onions
¼ cup finely chopped fresh parsley
1 tablespoon Worcestershire sauce
3 pounds raw shrimp, peeled and
    deveined
salt and pepper to taste
Tabasco sauce to taste
1 pound crabmeat
3 cups steamed rice

Melt butter in a Dutch oven. Add onion, bell pepper, and celery and cook until tender. Add garlic. Dissolve cornstarch in 1 cup broth and add to vegetables. Stir in wine. Add tomato paste and next 3 ingredients. Blend well. Add shrimp and cover. Simmer 10 minutes, stirring occasionally. If necessary, add more broth. Add salt, pepper, and Tabasco sauce. Gently stir in crabmeat and cook until thoroughly heated. Serve over rice. Yields 6 servings.

Shrimp and Spaghetti

2 sticks butter, divided
1 cup chopped onion
5 cloves garlic, minced
⅔ cup coarsely chopped celery
1 bell pepper, cut into strips
4 pounds raw shrimp, peeled and
    deveined
¼ cup dry white wine
¼ cup water

salt and pepper to taste
2 bay leaves
1 teaspoon dried thyme
Tabasco sauce to taste
1 pound thin spaghetti, cooked al
    dente
½ cup chopped fresh parsley
freshly grated Romano cheese

Melt 1½ sticks butter in a Dutch oven. Add onion and garlic and sauté until tender. Add celery and bell pepper and cook 2 minutes. Stir in shrimp and cook 5 minutes or until pink. Transfer mixture with a slotted spoon to a heated bowl and keep warm. Add wine and water to Dutch oven and boil 5 minutes. Reduce heat. Add salt, pepper, and next 3 ingredients. Simmer 20 minutes. Mix in remaining 4 tablespoons butter and shrimp mixture. Remove bay leaves and keep warm. Place hot, drained spaghetti in a large, heated shallow dish. Sprinkle parsley over shrimp mixture. Pour mixture over spaghetti. Toss well and sprinkle with cheese. Serve immediately. Yields 6 to 8 servings.

Shrimp Vermouth

2 sticks butter
2 cloves garlic, split
5 pounds raw shrimp, peeled and
    deveined
6 tablespoons chopped fresh parsley
1 teaspoon dried tarragon

1 cup dry vermouth
2 teaspoons salt
1/4 teaspoon cayenne pepper
1/2 teaspoon black pepper
1 teaspoon paprika
garlic bread or toast points

Heat butter in a large skillet. Add garlic and cook 2 minutes, mashing garlic with back of a wooden spoon. Discard garlic. Add shrimp and sauté 5 minutes or until pink. Transfer shrimp to a hot platter. Add parsley, tarragon, and vermouth to skillet. Increase heat and simmer 30 seconds. Add shrimp. Season with salt and next 3 ingredients. Serve on garlic bread. Yields 4 servings.

Shrimp Artichoke Casserole

1 (14-ounce) can artichoke hearts,
    drained and quartered
1 1/2 pounds cooked shrimp, peeled
    and deveined
1 stick butter, divided
1/2 pound fresh mushrooms, sliced
1/4 cup all-purpose flour
1 cup heavy cream

1/2 cup milk
1 teaspoon salt
1/2 teaspoon black pepper
1/4 cup dry sherry
1 tablespoon Worcestershire sauce
1/4 cup freshly grated Parmesan
    cheese
1/4 teaspoon paprika

Place artichoke hearts in the bottom of a well-greased 1 1/2-quart casserole dish. Cover with shrimp. Melt 4 tablespoons butter in a skillet. Add mushrooms and sauté 6 to 8 minutes. Pour over shrimp. Melt remaining 4 tablespoons butter in skillet. Blend in flour and cook over low heat for 3 to 5 minutes, stirring constantly. Gradually add cream and milk and cook until thickened. Add salt and next 3 ingredients. Stir until smooth. Pour over shrimp mixture. Top with cheese and paprika. Bake at 375° for 25 minutes or until lightly browned and bubbly. Yields 4 servings.

Shrimp Creole

1½ tablespoons bacon fat
1½ tablespoons all-purpose flour
½ cup finely chopped onion
⅓ cup finely chopped bell pepper
¼ cup finely chopped celery
1 (8-ounce) can tomato sauce
1 (14½-ounce) can Italian plum
 tomatoes with basil, undrained
1 clove garlic, minced
3 dashes Tabasco sauce

2 tablespoons Worcestershire sauce
1 teaspoon sugar
2 teaspoons salt
¼ teaspoon black pepper
2½ pounds raw shrimp, peeled and
 deveined
2 tablespoons chopped fresh parsley
¾ cup chopped green onions
2 cups steamed rice

Heat bacon fat in a large saucepan. Add flour and cook and stir until golden brown. Add onion, bell pepper, and celery and cook until tender. Pour in tomato sauce and tomatoes. Blend well. Add garlic and next 5 ingredients. Simmer 30 minutes, stirring occasionally. Add shrimp, parsley, and green onions. Cook 30 minutes. Serve over rice. Yields 4 servings.

Barbecued Shrimp

4 sticks butter
2 cups olive oil
¾ cup Worcestershire sauce
6 tablespoons black pepper
4 lemons, sliced
½ teaspoon Tabasco sauce

1 tablespoon Italian seasoning
3 cloves garlic, minced
1 teaspoon paprika
4 teaspoons salt
8 pounds raw, unpeeled jumbo
 shrimp

Heat butter and oil in a 2-quart saucepan. Add Worcestershire sauce and next 7 ingredients. Mix thoroughly and simmer 5 to 7 minutes. Divide shrimp between 2 Dutch ovens. Pour sauce over each. Cook 6 to 8 minutes or until shrimp start to turn pink. Bake at 450° for 10 minutes, stirring once. Serve with French bread. Yields 8 servings.

Shrimp Mousse with Horseradish Sauce

Mousse

1¼ pounds raw shrimp, peeled,
  divided
2 egg whites
1½ teaspoons salt
½ teaspoon black pepper

¼ teaspoon nutmeg
¼ teaspoon Tabasco sauce
2 cups heavy cream
2 tablespoons butter

Horseradish Sauce

1 tablespoon butter
1 tablespoon all-purpose flour
½ cup milk
1 whole clove

1 small bay leaf
2 egg yolks, lightly beaten
¼ cup heavy cream, lightly whipped
1½ teaspoons horseradish

Purée shrimp in a blender or food processor, reserving 6 for garnish. With machine running, add egg whites, one at a time. Add salt and next 3 ingredients. If using a blender, transfer purée to a bowl and work in cream with a wooden spoon. If using a food processor, add cream 1 tablespoon at a time. Pour mixture into a greased 1-quart mold and cover with greased wax paper. Set in a pan of hot water reaching halfway up sides of mold. Bake at 350° for 30 minutes. Sauté remaining 6 shrimp in butter until pink. Pour off excess butter and keep warm. At end of cooking time, remove mousse from oven˜and run a knife around inside of mold. Invert onto a warm serving platter and spoon on horseradish sauce. Garnish with shrimp and serve immediately. To prepare sauce, melt butter in a saucepan. Blend in flour. Slowly add milk and mix until smooth. Add clove and bay leaf. Cook over low heat, stirring constantly, until sauce thickens. Stir a few spoonfuls of hot sauce into egg yolk. Add egg mixture back to sauce and blend well. Add cream and horseradish. Heat thoroughly, but do not boil. Remove clove and bay leaf. Yields 4 to 6 servings.

Seafood Stuffed Eggplant

4 medium eggplants, halved
   lengthwise
6 tablespoons bacon fat
1 cup chopped onion
2 teaspoons minced green onions
2 cloves garlic, minced
½ cup minced celery
½ teaspoon dried oregano
1½ pounds raw shrimp, peeled and
   chopped
½ teaspoon salt
¼ teaspoon Tabasco sauce
1½ teaspoons Worcestershire sauce
¼ teaspoon black pepper
2 cups steamed rice
¼ cup lemon juice
¼ cup chopped fresh parsley
1 pound crabmeat
1 cup breadcrumbs
6 tablespoons butter, melted
½ cup Parmesan cheese

Boil eggplant in salted water for 10 minutes or until tender. Cool and scoop out pulp, leaving a ¼-inch thick shell. Finely chop pulp. In a Dutch oven, heat bacon fat. Add onion and next 4 ingredients and sauté 20 minutes. Reduce heat and add eggplant pulp. Cover and simmer about 15 minutes. Add shrimp and cook until pink. Remove from heat and stir in salt and next 5 ingredients. Gently fold in parsley and crabmeat. Arrange eggplant shells in lightly greased baking dishes. Spoon seafood mixture into shells. Combine breadcrumbs, butter, and cheese. Sprinkle over eggplant. Bake at 350° for 30 minutes or until hot and browned on top. Yields 8 servings.

Baked Oysters Italian

1¼ sticks butter
½ cup olive oil
½ cup chopped green onions
¼ cup chopped fresh parsley
2 tablespoons minced garlic
1⅓ cups seasoned breadcrumbs
½ cup Parmesan cheese
1 teaspoon salt
½ teaspoon black pepper
¼ teaspoon cayenne pepper
1 teaspoon dried basil
1 teaspoon dried oregano
8 cups oysters, drained on paper
   towels

Heat butter and oil in a large skillet. Add onions, parsley, and garlic and sauté. In a bowl, combine breadcrumbs and next 6 ingredients. Add to skillet and mix well. Remove from heat and gently stir in oysters. Place in a 2-quart baking dish. Bake at 425° for 15 minutes or until browned and crusty. Yields 6 servings.

Oyster and Artichoke Casserole

If desired, prepare dish ahead and bake just prior to serving.

6-8 artichokes, boiled (1 per person)
1 stick butter
2½ cups finely chopped green
  onions
½ cup finely chopped celery
1 (10¾-ounce) can condensed
  cream of mushroom soup
1 tablespoon Worcestershire sauce
1 teaspoon salt
¼ teaspoon Tabasco sauce
1 tablespoon lemon zest
¼ teaspoon black pepper
8 cups oysters, drained on paper
  towels
½ cup breadcrumbs
lemon slices for garnish
fresh parsley for garnish

Scrape artichoke leaves and mash scrapings with a fork. Keep artichoke hearts whole. Melt butter in a skillet. Add onions and celery and sauté. Reduce heat and add soup and next 5 ingredients. Simmer 10 minutes. Add artichoke scrapings and oysters and simmer 10 minutes. Arrange artichoke hearts in a 2-quart casserole dish. Pour oyster mixture over hearts and top with breadcrumbs. Bake at 350° for 30 minutes. Spoon off excess liquid if necessary. Broil 3 to 5 minutes or until breadcrumbs brown. Garnish with lemon slices and parsley. Yields 6 to 8 servings.

Oysters and Spaghetti

1 cup olive oil
4 cups sliced mushrooms
4 cups chopped green onions
1 clove garlic, minced
1 cup chopped fresh parsley
8 cups oysters, drained
2 (2-ounce) cans anchovies
1 teaspoon salt
1 teaspoon black pepper
2 sticks butter
1 (16-ounce) package vermicelli,
  cooked al dente
4 ounces Parmesan cheese, freshly
  grated

Heat oil in a Dutch oven. Add mushrooms, green onions, and garlic and sauté until tender. Stir in parsley, oysters, and anchovies. Cook until oysters begin to curl. Remove from heat and season with salt and pepper. Keep warm. Melt butter in a large saucepan. Add hot, drained vermicelli and cheese. Mix well. Add oyster mixture and toss thoroughly. Serve immediately. Yields 8 servings.

Oysters Dufossat

1½ cups breadcrumbs
½ teaspoon dry mustard
dash of cayenne pepper
½ teaspoon paprika
1 teaspoon salt
3 tablespoons Parmesan cheese

6 cups oysters, drained on paper
  towels
1 stick butter, melted
¼ teaspoon pressed garlic
8 slices bacon, cooked and
  crumbled
lemon wedges for garnish

Combine breadcrumbs and next 5 ingredients in a shallow dish. Roll oysters in mixture. Place in a single layer on a greased baking pan. Combine butter and garlic. Baste oysters with half of butter mixture. Broil until golden brown. Turn and baste with remaining butter mixture. Broil until top browns. Sprinkle bacon over top and garnish with lemon wedges. Yields 6 servings.

Oysters In Ramekins

This dish can be prepared up to a day ahead and refrigerated. When ready to serve, add cracker crumbs and bake.

2 sticks butter
½ cup all-purpose flour
¼ cup finely chopped celery
¼ cup finely chopped bell pepper
¼ cup minced fresh parsley
2 cups finely chopped onion

8 cups oysters, drained on paper
  towel, liquid reserved
salt and pepper to taste
¼ cup Worcestershire sauce
2 cups coarsely crushed cracker
  crumbs

Melt butter in a large saucepan. Slowly add flour and cook and stir until golden brown. Add celery and next 3 ingredients. Sauté until onion turns transparent. Stir in ½ cup oyster liquid, a little at a time, until sauce is smooth and the consistency of a thick gravy. Add oysters, salt, and pepper. Cook, stirring occasionally, until edges of oysters begin to curl. Remove from heat and add Worcestershire sauce. Divide among individual ramekins. Top with cracker crumbs. Bake at 350° for 10 to 15 minutes or until browned and bubbly. Yields 6 servings.

Oysters Rockefeller Casserole

3 sticks butter
1 teaspoon dried thyme
1²/₃ cups chopped green onions
1 cup chopped celery
1 large clove garlic, pressed
1 tablespoon Worcestershire sauce
1 teaspoon anchovy paste
1½ cups seasoned breadcrumbs
8 cups oysters, drained, liquid
    reserved

¾ cup chopped fresh parsley
½ cup Parmesan cheese
2 tablespoons Pernod (anise liqueur)
3 (10-ounce) packages frozen
    chopped spinach, cooked and
    drained
½ teaspoon salt
¼ teaspoon black pepper
¼ teaspoon cayenne pepper

Melt butter in a large skillet. Add thyme and next 3 ingredients. Sauté 5 minutes. Add Worcestershire sauce, anchovy paste, and breadcrumbs. Cook and stir 5 minutes or until breadcrumbs are toasted. Fold in oysters, ½ cup oyster liquid, and next 3 ingredients. Cook 3 minutes or until oysters curl. Add spinach and remaining 3 ingredients. Place in a 3-quart casserole dish and bake at 375° for 20 to 25 minutes. Serve in casserole dish or as an appetizer in individual ramekins. Yields 10 servings.

Spinach Crabmeat Casserole

1 stick butter
1 cup chopped yellow onion
¼ cup chopped green onions
2 (10-ounce) packages frozen
    chopped spinach, cooked and
    drained
2 cups sour cream
½ cup Parmesan cheese

1 (7-ounce) can artichoke hearts,
    drained
1 teaspoon salt
¼ teaspoon white pepper
1 teaspoon Worcestershire sauce
¼ teaspoon Tabasco sauce
1 pound crabmeat
1 cup boiled and peeled shrimp

Melt butter in a skillet. Add yellow and green onions and sauté 5 to 8 minutes. Add spinach, sour cream, and cheese. Reduce heat and simmer 2 to 3 minutes. Add artichoke hearts and next 4 ingredients. Simmer 3 minutes. Gently fold in crabmeat and shrimp until blended well. Pour mixture into a 2-quart casserole dish. Bake at 350° for 20 to 30 minutes. Yields 6 servings.

Soft Shell Crab Amandine

⅔ cup all-purpose flour
½ teaspoon salt
½ teaspoon black pepper
⅛ teaspoon garlic powder
½ teaspoon cayenne pepper
6 medium soft shell crabs, cleaned

1½ sticks butter
2 tablespoons vegetable oil
¾ cup sliced almonds
2 tablespoons lemon juice
3 tablespoons dry white wine
Worcestershire sauce to taste

Combine flour and next 4 ingredients. Dredge crabs in flour mixture. Heat butter and oil in a large skillet. When hot, add crabs, all at one time, being sure not to overcrowd. Cook 6 minutes. Turn and cook 4 to 5 minutes longer. Transfer to a heated platter and keep hot. Add almonds to skillet juices and sauté until lightly browned. Mix in lemon juice, wine, and Worcestershire sauce. Heat and pour over crabs. Yields 6 servings.

Crabmeat Caroline

2 tablespoons butter
2 tablespoons all-purpose flour
¼ cup minced green onions
¼ cup minced bell pepper
1 clove garlic, minced
⅛ teaspoon dried rosemary
1 tomato, peeled and chopped
¼ cup dry white wine
1 cup heavy cream

1 teaspoon salt
¼ teaspoon Tabasco sauce
⅓ cup grated Gruyère cheese
⅛ teaspoon dry mustard
1 pound crabmeat
3 tablespoons grated mozzarella
  cheese
3 tablespoons Parmesan cheese

Melt butter in a large skillet. Gradually blend in flour. Cook and stir 2 minutes. Add onions and next 4 ingredients. Sauté 2 to 3 minutes. Add wine and cook until vegetables are tender. Reduce heat and slowly blend in cream, salt, and Tabasco sauce. Remove from heat and stir in Gruyère cheese and mustard. Gently fold in crabmeat. Spoon into individual greased ramekins. Combine mozzarella and Parmesan cheeses and sprinkle on top. Bake at 350° for 10 to 15 minutes or until browned and bubbly. Yields 4 servings.

Stuffed Crabs

1¼ sticks butter, divided
¼ cup minced celery leaves
½ cup minced onion
2 cloves garlic, minced
1 pound crabmeat
¼ cup minced fresh parsley
1 teaspoon black pepper
1 teaspoon salt
3 bay leaves

2 teaspoons Worcestershire sauce
cayenne pepper to taste
¼ teaspoon Tabasco sauce
2 cups cubed French bread
1 cup chicken broth
2 eggs, beaten
8 crab shells
4 teaspoons breadcrumbs

Melt 6 tablespoons butter in a Dutch oven. Sauté celery leaves, onion, and garlic until tender. Add crabmeat and next 7 ingredients. Simmer 8 minutes. Remove bay leaves. Soak bread cubes in broth. Mix in eggs. Stir into crab mixture and cook 5 minutes or until thoroughly heated. Spoon mixture into crab shells. Sprinkle each shell with ½ teaspoon breadcrumbs and dot each with ½ teaspoon of remaining butter. Bake at 350° for 15 to 20 minutes. Yields 8 servings.

Crabmeat Casserole

1 stick butter
½ cup chopped green onions
½ cup chopped yellow onion
5 tablespoons all-purpose flour
1½ cups milk
½ cup dry sherry
1 (7-ounce) can mushrooms, drained
1 cup grated sharp cheddar cheese
2 bay leaves
3 lemons, seeded and sliced
1 teaspoon Worcestershire sauce

1 teaspoon seasoned salt
¼ teaspoon Tabasco sauce
1 teaspoon salt
¼ teaspoon black pepper
¼ cup chopped fresh parsley
1 (14-ounce) can artichoke hearts, drained
1 pound crabmeat
¼ cup seasoned breadcrumbs
½ cup freshly grated Parmesan cheese

Melt butter in a large skillet. Add green and yellow onions and sauté 3 minutes or until soft. Add flour and cook and stir until thick and bubbly. Add milk alternately with sherry and mushrooms. Simmer, stirring constantly. Add cheddar cheese and stir until melted. Add bay leaves and next 7 ingredients. Simmer 5 minutes. Remove from heat and discard bay leaves and lemon slices. Arrange artichoke hearts in the bottom of a 2-quart casserole dish. Cover with crabmeat. Pour cheese sauce over top. Gently blend, but do not stir. Top with breadcrumbs and Parmesan cheese. Bake at 350° for 30 minutes or until bubbly. Yields 6 servings.

Crawfish In Ramekins

1¾ sticks butter, divided
1 cup chopped onion
2 cloves garlic, minced
1 tablespoon ketchup
1 bay leaf
1 tablespoon Italian seasoning
1 pound crawfish tails
2 teaspoons lemon juice

¾ teaspoon salt
½ teaspoon black pepper
¼ teaspoon Tabasco sauce
2 tablespoons minced fresh parsley
2 tablespoons breadcrumbs
fresh parsley
lemon wedges
French bread, toasted

Melt 6 tablespoons butter in a large skillet. Add onion and garlic and sauté until tender. Stir in ketchup, bay leaf, and Italian seasoning. Add remaining 1 stick butter, crawfish tails, and next 5 ingredients. Heat thoroughly. Remove bay leaf. Spoon into individual ramekins and top with breadcrumbs. Broil until golden brown. Garnish with parsley and lemon wedges. Serve with French bread. Yields 4 servings.

Crawfish Étouffé

2 pounds crawfish tails
2 teaspoons salt
1 teaspoon black pepper
¼ teaspoon paprika
1 stick butter
1½ cups chopped yellow onion
1 clove garlic, minced
1½ teaspoons all-purpose flour

1¾ cups water
¼ cup brandy
¾ cup chopped green onions
2 tablespoons chopped fresh parsley
2 teaspoons lemon zest
2 teaspoons lemon juice
Tabasco sauce to taste
3 cups steamed rice

Season crawfish tails with salt, pepper, and paprika. Melt butter in a large skillet. Add crawfish and sauté 3 minutes. Add yellow onion and garlic and cook 10 minutes, stirring frequently. Sprinkle with flour and blend. Add water and next 6 ingredients. Simmer 10 minutes. Serve over rice. Yields 6 servings.

Crawfish Cardinale

If desired, substitute 1 cup clam juice plus ¼ cup water for chicken broth.

5 tablespoons butter
¼ cup minced onion
1 clove garlic, minced
5 tablespoons all-purpose flour
1 tablespoon tomato paste
1¼ cups chicken broth
1 teaspoon salt
pinch of dried thyme

¼ teaspoon nutmeg
½ teaspoon Tabasco sauce
1 bay leaf
1 cup light cream
2 tablespoons lemon juice
2 tablespoons brandy
1 pound crawfish tails

Melt butter in a large skillet. Add onion and garlic and sauté until tender but not browned. Blend in flour. Add tomato paste and cook 2 minutes. Gradually stir in broth. Add salt and next 4 ingredients. Mix well. Stir in cream, lemon juice, and brandy. Add crawfish tails. Remove bay leaf. Spoon into individual ramekins. Bake at 350° for 10 minutes or until bubbly. Yields 6 servings.

Spicy Fried Crawfish Tails

2½ teaspoons salt, divided
6 tablespoons all-purpose flour
1 teaspoon black pepper
2 tablespoons liquid crab boil
2 eggs, beaten

2 tablespoons milk
2 pounds crawfish tails
¼ teaspoon cayenne pepper
4 cups vegetable oil

Combine 2 teaspoons salt and next 4 ingredients in a bowl. Add milk, 1 teaspoon at a time, until a thick batter forms. Season crawfish with remaining ½ teaspoon salt and cayenne pepper. Add crawfish to batter and let stand at least 60 minutes. In a Dutch oven, heat oil to 375°. Drop crawfish into oil, a handful at a time, making sure to separate them as they cook. Fry 1 minute or until golden brown. Drain on a platter lined with paper towels. Keep warm in oven. When all crawfish are fried, serve immediately. Yields 6 servings.

Poached Fish Provençal

3 pounds white fish fillets, cut into
  2-inch pieces
salt and pepper to taste
1/4 cup olive oil
2 cups chopped onion
3/4 cup chopped green onions
1/4 cup chopped fresh parsley
1/2 cup tomato paste
3 cloves garlic, minced

1/8 teaspoon dried thyme
1/8 teaspoon dried basil
1 bay leaf
1 1/2 cups water
1 1/2 cups dry white wine
12 black olives, sliced
2 tablespoons capers
3 cups steamed rice
lemon wedges

Season fish with salt and pepper. Heat oil in a Dutch oven. Add onions and parsley and sauté until tender. Add tomato paste and cook, stirring frequently, until it loses its bright red color. Add garlic and next 4 ingredients. Season with salt and pepper. Cover and simmer 30 minutes. Add wine, olives, and fish. Cover and cook 10 to 15 minutes or until fish flakes easily with a fork. Remove bay leaf. Sprinkle with capers. Serve over rice and garnish with lemon wedges. Yields 6 servings.

Baked Fish Beatrice

2 pounds white fish fillets
salt and pepper to taste
1/2 cup thinly sliced onion
2 tablespoons butter

1 cup mayonnaise
1/4 cup prepared yellow mustard
2 tablespoons dry vermouth

Season fish liberally with salt and pepper in a shallow baking dish. Cover with onion and dot with butter. Bake at 350° for 20 minutes or until fish flakes easily with a fork. In a small bowl, mix mayonnaise, mustard, and vermouth. Pour over fish and broil 2 to 3 minutes or until browned and bubbly. Yields 4 servings.

Trout Nantua

Trout
5 tablespoons butter, divided
3 pounds trout fillets
salt and pepper to taste

1 cup sliced onion
¾ cup dry white wine

Sauce Nantua
6 tablespoons butter, divided
3 tablespoons all-purpose flour
1 cup finely chopped green onions
¼ cup finely chopped fresh parsley
⅓ cup chopped celery
1 pound crawfish tails

½ cup heavy cream
½ teaspoon Tabasco sauce
½ teaspoon salt
¼ cup freshly grated Parmesan
cheese

Grease a baking dish with 2 tablespoons butter. Season fillets with salt and pepper on both sides. Arrange in a single layer in dish. Spread onion over top and dot with remaining 3 tablespoons butter. Add wine and bake at 400° for 15 minutes or until fish flakes easily with a fork. To prepare sauce, melt 4 tablespoons butter in a large skillet. Gradually add flour. Cook and stir until light brown. Add green onions, parsley, and celery and sauté until tender. Add crawfish and cook until pink. Remove from heat. Drain fish juices from baking dish into crawfish mixture. Return skillet to heat and cook until sauce is thick and bubbly. Remove from heat and gradually stir in cream. Blend in Tabasco sauce and salt. Pour sauce over fish. Dot with remaining 2 tablespoons butter and sprinkle with cheese. Bake at 375° for 15 minutes. Brown under broiler. Yields 6 servings.
Substitute 1 pound crabmeat or 1 pound raw, peeled shrimp for crawfish.

Trout Florentine

Spinach Mixture
½ cup chopped green onions
3 tablespoons butter
salt and pepper to taste
2 cups cooked spinach, well drained

1 cup sour cream
⅛ teaspoon minced garlic
¼ teaspoon nutmeg
Tabasco sauce to taste

Trout
4 green onions, chopped
2 teaspoons salt
6 peppercorns
½ cup dry white wine
¼ cup lemon juice

3 pounds trout fillets
2 cups Hollandaise Sauce (page xxx)
½ cup grated Swiss cheese
¼ cup Parmesan cheese

Sauté onions in butter. Add salt, pepper, and next 5 ingredients. Mix well. Purée. Spread mixture in a greased baking dish. Place in a 150° oven to keep warm. To make trout, combine onions and next 4 ingredients. Add enough water to cover. Bring to a boil. Add trout and reduce heat. Simmer 5 minutes or until fish flakes easily with a fork. Transfer trout, using a slotted spoon, to spinach-filled dish. Spoon hollandaise sauce over top. Sprinkle with cheeses. Broil until golden brown. Yields 6 servings.

Trout Orleans

3 pounds trout fillets
salt and pepper to taste
garlic salt to taste
lemon juice to taste
1¼ sticks butter, divided

¼ cup finely chopped celery
¼ cup chopped green onions
½ cup sliced water chestnuts
1 pound crabmeat
¼ teaspoon dried tarragon

Season fillets generously with salt, pepper, garlic salt, and lemon juice. Heat 4 tablespoons butter in a skillet until bubbly. Add celery, onions, and water chestnuts and quickly sauté until crisp-tender. Add crabmeat and tarragon. Stir until thoroughly heated. Place fillets in a single layer in a baking dish. Dot with remaining 6 tablespoons butter. Broil 5 minutes, basting with butter in dish. Spoon crabmeat mixture over fillets. Baste again and broil 4 minutes longer or until fish flakes easily with a fork. Serve immediately. Yields 6 servings.

Trout Audubon

¾ cup all-purpose flour
3 tablespoons salt
2 tablespoons black pepper
dash of cayenne pepper
2 pounds trout fillets
1 cup milk
¾ cup fine breadcrumbs

2 sticks butter
1 cup sliced mushrooms
1 cup quartered artichoke hearts,
  drained
2 tablespoons minced fresh parsley
¼ cup dry white wine

Combine flour and next 3 ingredients. Dip fillets in milk and roll in flour mixture. Dip in milk again and coat with breadcrumbs. Melt butter in a large skillet over high heat. Add fillets and brown on both sides. Transfer to a heated platter. Reduce heat and add mushrooms, artichoke hearts, and parsley. Cook 3 minutes. Stir in wine. Spoon mushroom sauce over fish and serve immediately. Yields 4 servings.

Red Snapper Maison

Sauce Maison
4 tablespoons butter
¼ cup all-purpose flour
1 tablespoon chopped fresh parsley
1 green onion, chopped
2 cups chicken broth
½ cup sliced mushrooms

¼ cup lemon juice
⅛ teaspoon Tabasco sauce
⅛ teaspoon Worcestershire sauce
½ cup dry white wine
3 egg yolks, beaten

Red Snapper
1 stick butter
3 green onions, finely chopped
2 tablespoons chopped fresh parsley

1 stalk celery, finely chopped
3 pounds red snapper fillets
salt and pepper to taste

Heat butter in a saucepan until it starts to brown. Blend in flour. Add parsley and green onion and cook 1 minute. Slowly add broth. Cook and stir until thick and creamy. Blend in mushrooms and next 3 ingredients. Add wine. Slowly stir in egg yolk and cook until sauce starts to thicken. Keep warm. To prepare red snapper, melt butter in a saucepan. Add onions, parsley, and celery. Warm thoroughly, but do not brown. Season fillets lightly with salt and pepper. Place fillets in a single layer in a lightly greased baking pan. Brush with half the butter sauce. Broil 4 minutes without browning. Turn fish and brush with remaining butter sauce. Broil 2 minutes. Transfer to a heated platter. Spoon Sauce Maison over top and serve immediately. Yields 6 servings.

Cold Redfish with Sauce Verte

Decorate with flowers cut from lemon peel, using parsley for stems and leaves. Use a black olive slice over eye. Garnish platter with lettuce, cucumbers, cherry tomatoes, and lemon wedges.

Court-bouillon
2 cups white wine
2 tablespoons chopped fresh parsley
2 cups chopped green onions
1 tablespoon salt
1 teaspoon peppercorns
2 bay leaves

pinch of dried thyme
⅛ teaspoon Tabasco sauce
¼ cup lemon juice
1 (6 to 7-pound) redfish
salt and pepper to taste

Sauce Verte
1 cup plus 1 tablespoon water,
    divided
¼ cup chopped spinach
¼ cup chopped green onions
¼ cup chopped fresh parsley
¼ cup chopped watercress
1 tablespoon dried tarragon
2 tablespoons dried chervil

4 eggs
6 tablespoons white wine vinegar
2 teaspoons salt
½ teaspoon black pepper
3 cups vegetable oil
1½ tablespoons unflavored gelatin
½ cup white wine

Combine wine and next 8 ingredients in a fish poacher or roasting pan. Cover and simmer 30 minutes. Wash and dry redfish. Sprinkle inside and out with salt and pepper. Wrap in cheesecloth and secure with a string. Place in fish poacher and add enough water to cover. Simmer, covered, for 6 to 8 minutes per pound or until fish flakes easily with a fork. Lift fish out of liquid, remove cheesecloth, and place on a serving platter. Allow to cool until able to handle. Remove skin, row of bones along top and bottom, and any dark meat. Refrigerate. To prepare sauce, bring 1 cup water to a boil in a saucepan. Add spinach and onions and boil 1 minute. Add parsley and next 3 ingredients. Boil 1 minute. Drain through a fine strainer and turn out onto paper towels to dry. Process eggs and vinegar in a food processor or blender. Add vegetable mixture, salt, and pepper and process further. Transfer to a mixing bowl. Using an electric mixer on high speed, gradually add oil until mixture thickens. Refrigerate. Soften gelatin in wine in a small saucepan. Place over low heat. Add remaining 1 tablespoon water and stir until gelatin dissolves. Cool. Blend into chilled sauce. Spread some of sauce over fish. Refrigerate or serve immediately. Serve extra sauce on side. Yields 8 servings.

Notes and Other Recipes

Meat, Poultry & Game

Celebrate Christmas New Orleans Style

Inside the grand old homes that line the streets of New Orleans' historic neighborhoods, many traditions and memories of the customs of the past still linger. During the holidays, those remembrances come alive in many ways -- family rituals, festive gatherings and feasts like the Reveillon Dinner.

The Reveillon -- pronounced rev-ay-yawn -- was the traditional Christmas Eve feast, brought to New Orleans from the Old World by the city's French founding fathers. A gastronomic event around which the Christmas holiday was planned, it was a multi-course meal that began after midnight mass on Christmas Eve and lasted until the early hours of the morning when Papa Noel would deliver gifts to the children of the house.

Over time, the custom gradually gave way to more conventional celebrations of Christmas. But in recent years, restaurants around the city have resurrected the Reveillon Dinner, introducing it to visitors as well as to locals, whose ancestors would have known the tradition well. The rebirth of the Reveillon has been well received, and throughout the month of December you can find traditional meals on local menus. If you have the opportunity to partake in a Reveillon Dinner, it's an experience not to be missed. But wherever you live and however you celebrate your holidays, you can bring the spirit of the Reveillon into your festivities, using some of the traditional Creole recipes in Jambalaya.

A traditional Reveillon Dinner begins with an appetizer, usually oysters. Try the Oysters Dunbar (p. 28), a creamy oyster and artichoke dish, or the Oysters Ellis (p. 30), which has a pungent tomato-based sauce. A more old-fashioned first course and a lighter alternative is the Seafood Glace (p. 0). The second course usually showcases seafood as well. Cold Redfish with Sauce Verte (p. 97) is a nice choice. It's an elaborate dish that is as pleasing to the eye as to the palate. If you can't find redfish in your area, you can easily substitute any flaky fish like snapper, trout, mahi-mahi, drum or lemonfish.

Poultry or game is the traditional centerpiece of a Reveillon meal. Try Wild Duck with Mushroom Stuffing (p. 156), the Quail with Mushrooms (p. 154) or the exquisite Coq au Vin (p. 147). If you're partial to beef, the Stuffed Tenderloin of Beef with pine nuts and tawny port (p. 103) is a perfect holiday meal. Conclude your Reveillon Dinner with a rich, sumptuous dessert. Crêpes Suzette (p. 220) is a favorite, as is Orange Créme Brulee (p. 222), a classic dessert in Creole homes. Make sure not to forget plenty of coffee for after dinner and liqueurs make a nice final touch.

Sausage and Ham Jambalaya

2 cups sliced smoked sausage
1 cup finely chopped yellow onion
¾ cup diced bell pepper
1 large clove garlic
2 cups diced ham
½ cup dry white wine
1 (14½-ounce) can tomatoes,
   undrained

1 teaspoon salt
½ teaspoon dried thyme
¼ teaspoon dried basil
¼ teaspoon dried marjoram
¼ teaspoon paprika
¼ teaspoon Tabasco sauce
2 tablespoons chopped fresh parsley
1 cup long-grain converted rice

Sauté sausage in a Dutch oven for 10 minutes. Remove with a slotted spoon and drain on paper towels. Add onion, bell pepper, and garlic to sausage drippings and sauté 5 minutes or until tender. Stir in sausage, ham, and next 8 ingredients. Bring to a boil. Reduce heat and mix in parsley and rice. Cover and simmer 25 minutes. Yields 6 servings.

Individual Beef Wellington

If preparing a day ahead, cover with foil after decorating with dough pieces and refrigerate overnight. When ready to serve, bake as directed.

8 (5 to 6-ounce) beef fillets
2 tablespoons vegetable oil
1 teaspoon salt
½ teaspoon black pepper
3 tablespoons all-purpose flour

2 (6 count, 10-ounce) packages
   patty shells, thawed
4 ounces pâté de foie gras
1 egg white, beaten, room
   temperature

Place fillets in freezer for 20 minutes. Remove and brush with oil. Sear fillets 3 minutes on each side in a hot skillet. Sprinkle with salt and pepper and refrigerate 20 minutes. Lightly flour each patty shell. Using a floured rolling pin, roll each shell on wax paper to ⅛-inch thick. Shape pâté into 8 small, flat circles and place a circle on each of 8 flattened shells. Place a fillet on top of each circle. Fold dough around meat and pinch to seal. Place Wellingtons 1 inch apart on a baking sheet (avoid non-stick sheets), seam-side down. Make a small hole in the center of crust. Cut designs from remaining dough, moisten with water, and decorate top of crusts. Brush with egg white just before cooking. Bake at 450° in upper third of oven for 10 minutes for rare, 12 minutes for medium-rare, or 15 minutes for medium. If crusts are not browned, broil on a low rack for 2 to 3 minutes or until golden. Transfer to a heated platter and serve. Yields 8 servings.

Beef Wellington

Beef
1 (5-pound) beef tenderloin, well
trimmed
1 teaspoon salt

½ teaspoon black pepper
1 clove garlic, sliced lengthwise

Forcemeat
4 tablespoons unsalted butter
½ cup finely chopped yellow onion
1 cup finely chopped mushrooms
¼ cup brandy
½ pound ground pork
½ pound ground veal
1 egg, lightly beaten

¼ cup heavy cream
¼ cup finely chopped fresh parsley
½ teaspoon powdered thyme
½ teaspoon powdered rosemary
½ teaspoon dried basil
1½ teaspoons salt
½ teaspoon black pepper

Pastry
4 cups sifted flour
1 teaspoon salt
2 sticks unsalted butter, softened
⅔ cup vegetable shortening

⅔ cup ice water
3 tablespoons unsifted flour, divided
2 egg whites, lightly beaten

Rub tenderloin with salt, pepper, and garlic. Place on a rack in a large shallow roasting pan. Insert meat thermometer. Bake at 350° for 50 minutes or until thermometer registers 130°. Cool, cover, and refrigerate overnight. To prepare forcemeat, melt butter in a large skillet. Add onion and sauté 3 minutes. Squeeze mushrooms tightly in a towel to extract liquid. Reduce heat and stir in mushrooms and brandy. Simmer 3 minutes. Transfer to a bowl. Mix in pork and next 9 ingredients. Cover and refrigerate overnight.

To make pastry, combine sifted flour and salt. In a large bowl, cut flour mixture into butter and shortening until mixture resembles large breadcrumbs. Sprinkle water over mixture. Work in water quickly until dough forms a ball. Sprinkle with 2 tablespoons unsifted flour and wrap in wax paper. Refrigerate overnight. On day of serving, remove pastry from refrigerator 3 hours before rolling. Set 2 sheets of wax paper side by side and sprinkle with remaining 1 tablespoon unsifted flour. Rub rolling pin in flour. Roll out most of pastry, reserving a small amount for later. Roll large enough to enclose beef and trim to form a rectangle, allowing 1 inch for overlapping under tenderloin. Lay tenderloin along one edge of pastry. Tuck in tail of meat. Spread forcemeat evenly over beef. Lift pastry around beef, overlapping it under meat. Pinch edges to seal. Roll remaining dough and cut out designs. Moisten and place on pastry roll to decorate. Brush roll with egg white. Place on an ungreased baking sheet (avoid non-stick sheets). Bake at 425° for 40 minutes in the upper third of the oven. Transfer to a heated serving platter and cover loosely with foil. Let stand 20 minutes before carving in ¾-inch slices. Yields 10 servings.

Stuffed Tenderloin of Beef

1 (5-pound) beef tenderloin, well
   trimmed
1 teaspoon salt
1 teaspoon black pepper
1 tablespoon vegetable oil
2 coarsely chopped carrots
1 coarsely chopped yellow onion
1½ cups minced yellow onion
1 clove garlic, minced

18 black olives, finely chopped
½ cup chopped ham
4 ounces mushrooms, finely
   chopped
¼ cup minced fresh parsley
2 egg yolks, lightly beaten
2 tablespoons brandy
½ cup pine nuts (optional)
3 tablespoons tawny port

Without slicing all the way through, cut tenderloin into ¾-inch slices. Dry meat with paper towels and sprinkle with salt and pepper. Heat oil in a large, shallow roasting pan over high heat. Add carrot and coarsely chopped onion and sauté 2 minutes. Remove from heat and place tenderloin on top. Combine minced onion and next 8 ingredients in a bowl. Mix well. Spread mixture equally among tenderloin slices. Bake at 500° for 5 minutes. Reduce heat to 350° and cook 35 minutes. Transfer to a heated serving platter, cover loosely with foil, and let stand 20 minutes. Place pan on stove top and add port. Boil 3 minutes. Strain and serve with tenderloin. Yields 10 servings.

Fillet Flambé

6 tablespoons butter, divided
8 ounces mushrooms, thinly sliced
½ teaspoon salt
½ teaspoon black pepper
1 tablespoon brandy
1 tablespoon sherry

1 tablespoon Madeira
4 tablespoons unsalted butter,
   softened
1 tablespoon Dijon mustard
4 (5 to 6-ounce, 1 inch thick) beef
   fillets

Melt 3 tablespoons butter in a skillet. Add mushrooms and sauté 5 minutes. Add salt and pepper and remove from heat. In a small saucepan over low heat, warm brandy, sherry, and Madeira. Ignite and pour flaming liquid into skillet. Shake skillet until flames stop. Cream unsalted butter and mustard in a small bowl. Stir into skillet. Cook and stir mushroom sauce over low heat for 5 minutes or until slightly thickened. Keep sauce warm. Dry fillets with paper towels. Melt remaining 3 tablespoons butter in a large skillet over high heat. As butter starts to brown, add fillets and cook 3 minutes on each side for rare, 4 minutes per side for medium rare, or 5 minutes per side for medium. Transfer fillets to a heated platter. Pour sauce over meat and serve immediately. Yields 4 servings.

Fillet of Beef with Oyster Stuffing

1½ sticks butter, divided
1 cup finely chopped green onions
8 ounces mushrooms, finely
   chopped
1 pint oysters, drained and
   quartered
¾ cup dry breadcrumbs
1½ teaspoons minced fresh parsley

1 egg, lightly beaten
1 teaspoon salt
½ teaspoon black pepper
1 (5 to 6-pound) beef tenderloin,
   well trimmed
½ cup brandy
¼ cup dry mustard

Heat 4 tablespoons butter in a Dutch oven. Add onions and sauté 3 minutes. Add mushrooms and oysters and cook and stir 3 minutes. Remove from heat. Stir in breadcrumbs and next 4 ingredients. Cut tenderloin lengthwise without slicing all the way through. Stuff with oyster mixture and tightly tie closed using a thick string at 1 to 2-inch intervals. Melt remaining stick of butter in a saucepan. Add brandy and mustard. Cook, stirring constantly, for 3 minutes. Bake tenderloin at 500° for 5 minutes. Reduce heat to 350° and bake for 35 minutes, basting frequently with brandy sauce. Remove from oven, cover loosely with foil, and let stand 20 minutes. Carve in ¾-inch slices and arrange on a heated platter. Yields 8 to 10 servings.

Instead of cutting a lengthwise slit in tenderloin, cut a 1-inch wide, 2-inch deep, lengthwise wedge along top of tenderloin. Remove wedge, fill cavity with stuffing, and replace wedge.

Barbequed Beef

2 pounds boneless beef chuck roast
3 tablespoons vegetable oil
2½ cups water
2 cups finely chopped yellow onion
1½ cups finely chopped celery
¾ cup finely chopped bell pepper

3 cloves garlic, minced
¾ cup tomato paste
3 tablespoons Worcestershire sauce
3 tablespoons cider vinegar
2 teaspoons Tabasco sauce
2 teaspoons salt

Pat beef dry with paper towels. Heat oil in a Dutch oven. Add beef and brown on all sides. Mix in water and remaining 9 ingredients. Cover and simmer 3 to 4 hours or until beef shreds easily and liquid is absorbed. Stir occasionally with cooking. Serve on hot buttered buns. Yields 8 servings.

Filet De Boeuf En Gelée

Horseradish Sauce

1 cup sour cream
1 cup mayonnaise
⅓ cup horseradish
¼ cup minced parsley
1 teaspoon prepared yellow mustard

1 teaspoon lemon juice
1 teaspoon Worcestershire sauce
1 teaspoon coarse salt
½ teaspoon black pepper

Beef

1 (3-pound) beef tenderloin, well
   trimmed
1 tablespoon prepared yellow
   mustard

3 tablespoons Worcestershire sauce
1 teaspoon coarse salt

Gelée

1 tablespoon unflavored gelatin
¼ cup dry Madeira

2 cups beef consommé

Combine all horseradish sauce ingredients in a bowl 24 hours before serving and chill. To prepare beef, place tenderloin in a shallow roasting pan. Coat underside of tenderloin with mustard. Sprinkle Worcestershire sauce over top of meat. Cover tightly with foil and refrigerate 24 hours. Remove filet from refrigerator at least 60 minutes before cooking. Roast at 400° for 50 minutes. Remove from oven and sprinkle with salt. Transfer to a platter to cool. When cool, carve into ¼-inch slices and refrigerate. To make gelée, sprinkle gelatin over Madeira in a bowl. Do not stir. Soak 5 minutes or until gelatin absorbs all the wine. Heat consommé in a saucepan just to boiling point. Stir consommé into gelatin mixture until dissolved. Cool to room temperature or until gelée begins to thicken. Use a chilled spoon to spoon a small amount over beef. Chill beef until gelée is firm. Repeat, spooning and chilling, until all gelée is used. Refrigerate until ready to serve. Serve with horseradish sauce. Yields 10 servings.

Fillet of Beef with Green Peppercorn Sauce

1 tablespoon vegetable oil
2 carrots, coarsely chopped
1 medium-size yellow onion,
   coarsely chopped
1 (4-pound) beef tenderloin, well
   trimmed
7 tablespoons butter, divided
4 tablespoons all-purpose flour

1½ cups beef broth, divided
⅓ cup Madeira
3 tablespoons brandy
1 cup heavy cream
¼ cup green peppercorns, drained
1 teaspoon lemon juice
1 teaspoon salt
½ teaspoon Tabasco sauce

Heat oil over high heat in a large, shallow roasting pan. Add carrot and onion and sauté 2 minutes. Remove from heat and place tenderloin on vegetables. Roast at 500° for 5 minutes. Reduce heat to 350° and bake 40 minutes. Transfer meat to a carving board, cover loosely with foil, and let stand 20 minutes. Reserve pan drippings and discard vegetables. Melt 4 tablespoons butter in a Dutch oven. Gradually blend in flour and cook and stir until light brown. Remove from heat and slowly stir in ¾ cup broth. Over low heat, stir in remaining ¾ cup broth and Madeira. Simmer 15 minutes. Remove from heat. Add reserved drippings, brandy, and cream and bring to a boil. Cook and stir 2 minutes. Reduce heat and add remaining 3 tablespoons butter, peppercorns, and remaining 3 ingredients. Cook, stirring constantly, for 5 minutes. Carve tenderloin into ¾-inch slices. Arrange on a heated platter and spoon some sauce over top. Serve remaining sauce in a heated sauceboat. Yields 8 servings.

Basic Bolognese Sauce

1½ cups sliced hot sausage
1½ cups sliced Italian sausage
2 tablespoons butter
1½ cups chopped onion
1 cup chopped bell pepper
½ cup chopped fresh parsley
2 pounds ground beef
3 (6-ounce) cans tomato paste

2 teaspoons salt
½ teaspoon black pepper
1 teaspoon garlic powder
1 teaspoon dried oregano
1 teaspoon dried basil
2-3 bay leaves
4 cups water

Cook hot and Italian sausage in boiling water for 20 minutes. Drain. Melt butter in a Dutch oven. Add onion, bell pepper, and parsley and sauté 5 minutes. Add beef and cook until browned. Stir in sausage, tomato paste, and remaining 7 ingredients. Simmer 60 minutes. Yields 12 servings.

Steak with Sauce Bercy

Steak
4 (8-ounce, 1 inch thick) beef top
   loin or tenderloin steaks, well
   trimmed
2 tablespoons butter

1 tablespoon vegetable oil
½ teaspoon salt
½ teaspoon black pepper

Sauce Bercy
6 tablespoons unsalted butter,
   softened, divided
2 tablespoons minced green onions
½ cup dry vermouth

1 tablespoon lemon juice
2 tablespoons minced fresh parsley
¼ teaspoon salt
¼ teaspoon white pepper

Pat steaks dry with paper towels. Heat butter and oil in a large skillet. When very hot, add steaks and cook 3 minutes on each side for rare, 4 minutes per side for medium rare, or 6 minutes per side for medium. Transfer to a heated serving platter. Sprinkle with salt and pepper and keep warm. Pour off skillet juices to prepare sauce bercy. Add 1 tablespoon butter and melt over low heat. Stir in onions and sauté 1 minute. Remove from heat and add vermouth. Cook mixture over high heat, scraping brown bits from bottom and sides, for 4 to 5 minutes or until reduced to almost a syrup. Remove from heat and cool 1 minute. Whisk in remaining 5 tablespoons butter, 1 tablespoon at a time. Beat in lemon juice and remaining 3 ingredients. Spread over steaks and serve immediately. Yields 4 servings.

Marinated Flank Steak

2 pounds beef flank steak
2 tablespoons garlic salt
2 tablespoons seasoned pepper
½ cup Worcestershire sauce

¼ cup soy sauce
¼ cup olive oil
¼ cup lemon juice

Sprinkle steak with garlic salt and pepper. Place steak in a large, shallow roasting pan. In a small bowl, combine Worcestershire sauce and remaining 3 ingredients. Mix well and pour over steak. Cover and refrigerate 24 hours, turning several times. Remove from refrigerator 60 minutes before cooking. Drain, reserving marinade. Pat meat dry with paper towels. If cooking on a barbecue grill, cook 4 minutes on each side for rare or 5 minutes per side for medium rare. Baste with reserved marinade while cooking. To broil in the oven, cook 1 inch from heat for 3 minutes on each side for rare or 4 minutes per side for medium rare. Baste with marinade while cooking. Carve, beginning at the small end of steak, into thin, diagonal slices with the grain of meat. Yields 4 servings.

Steak Au Poivre Flambé

4 (8-ounce, 1 inch thick) beef
   tenderloin, top sirloin, or club
   steaks, well trimmed
2 tablespoons crushed black pepper
½ cup beef broth
1 tablespoon cornstarch
1 tablespoon Dijon mustard
5 tablespoons unsalted butter,
   divided

½ teaspoon coarse salt
¼ cup minced green onions
2 tablespoons brandy
½ cup dry red wine
1 teaspoon Worcestershire sauce
2 teaspoons lemon juice
2 teaspoons minced fresh parsley

Pat steaks dry with paper towels. Press steaks into pepper. Work pepper into steaks with the back of a spoon. Allow to stand at room temperature for 60 minutes. Combine broth, cornstarch, and mustard in a bowl. In a large skillet, melt 3 tablespoons butter over high heat. When butter starts to brown, add steaks and sear for 1 minute on each side. Reduce heat and cook 2 minutes longer on each side for rare, 3 minutes per side for medium rare, or 4 minutes per side for medium. Transfer to a heated platter. Sprinkle with salt and keep warm. Pour off skillet drippings. Add 1 tablespoon butter and melt over low heat. Add onions and sauté 1 minute. Remove from heat. In a small saucepan over low heat, warm brandy. Ignite and pour into skillet. Stir until flames stop. Add wine. Bring to a boil over high heat, stirring constantly and scraping brown bits from bottom and sides of skillet. Cook 3 minutes or until liquid reduces by half. Stir in broth mixture and bring to a boil. Reduce heat and continue to cook and stir 3 minutes or until sauce thickens. Reduce heat to low and add remaining 1 tablespoon butter, Worcestershire sauce, and lemon juice. Cook and stir 1 minute. Pour sauce over steaks and sprinkle with parsley. Yields 4 servings.

Stuffed Flank Steak

Steak and Marinade
1 (3-pound) flank steak, butterflied
¼ cup olive oil
¼ cup soy sauce
¼ cup lemon juice
2 cloves garlic, pressed

1 tablespoon powdered rosemary
1 teaspoon powdered thyme
1 tablespoon salt
2 teaspoons black pepper

Stuffing
8 slices bacon, cooked and
  crumbled, grease reserved
1 cup minced yellow onion
¾ cup unpeeled grated zucchini
¾ cup unpeeled grated yellow
  squash
¼ teaspoon dried oregano

½ cup fresh breadcrumbs
2 tablespoons minced fresh parsley
1 tablespoon lemon juice
1 egg, lightly beaten
¼ teaspoon salt
¼ teaspoon black pepper

Pound steak lightly with a meat mallet. Place in a large, shallow roasting pan. Combine oil and next 7 ingredients in a small bowl. Reserve 3 tablespoons of marinade. Mix well and pour over steak. Cover with foil and refrigerate 24 hours, turning several times. Remove from refrigerator at least 60 minutes before cooking. To prepare stuffing, heat 4 tablespoons reserved bacon grease in a Dutch oven. Add onion and sauté 5 minutes. Stir in zucchini, squash, and oregano and sauté 5 minutes. Remove from heat and add bacon, breadcrumbs, and remaining 5 ingredients. Moisten with 3 tablespoons of meat marinade. Mix well. Place steak flat and spread stuffing to within 1 inch of each edge. Roll in jelly roll fashion and secure tightly with a thick string at 1 to 2-inch intervals. Return steak to pan and baste with marinade. Roast at 450° for 20 minutes for rare, 30 minutes for medium rare, or 40 minutes for medium. Every 10 minutes, turn and baste. Carve in ½-inch slices and arrange on a heated platter. Yields 6 servings.

Baked Brisket

Brisket

4 pounds beef brisket, untrimmed
2 teaspoons garlic salt
3 tablespoons all-purpose flour
3 tablespoons vegetable oil
4½ cups water, divided

24 small red potatoes, unpeeled
6 carrots, quartered
1½ teaspoons salt
1 teaspoon black pepper
2 tablespoons minced parsley

Mustard Cream Sauce

2 tablespoons dry mustard
2 tablespoons cold water
½ cup sour cream

1 teaspoon white vinegar
¼ teaspoon salt

Pat beef dry with paper towels. Sprinkle all sides with garlic salt and lightly coat with flour. Heat oil in a Dutch oven over high heat. Add beef and brown. Cover and transfer to oven. Bake at 275° for 4 hours. After 2 hours of cooking, place 2 cups water in each of 2 saucepans. Bring to a boil. Add potatoes to 1 saucepan and cook 15 minutes. Add carrot to other saucepan and cook 5 minutes. Drain vegetables. After 2 hours, 30 minutes of cooking, turn beef and add vegetables, remaining ½ cup water, salt, and pepper. Return to oven and complete baking. When done cooking, remove brisket and trim excess fat. Carve across the grain into very thin slices. Arrange on a large heated platter and surround with vegetables. Sprinkle parsley over top and serve with Mustard Cream Sauce. To prepare sauce, place mustard in a small bowl. Very gradually add water, stirring constantly until creamy. Let stand 15 minutes. Stir in sour cream, vinegar, and salt. Yields 8 servings.

Creamy Pasta Casserole

1 (5-ounce) package noodles
2 tablespoons butter
1 large clove garlic, pressed
1 pound ground beef
4 ounces fresh mushrooms, sliced
2 cups tomato sauce
1 teaspoon salt

1 teaspoon sugar
1 (3-ounce) package cream cheese, softened
1 cup sour cream
1 cup chopped green onions
½ cup grated cheddar cheese

Cook, rinse, and drain noodles. Melt butter in a skillet. Add garlic and sauté 1 minute. Add beef and brown. Drain fat. Add mushrooms, and next 3 ingredients. Cook over low heat for 20 minutes. In a bowl, blend cream cheese, sour cream, and onions. Combine meat and cream cheese mixtures. Spread half of noodles in a 1½-quart casserole dish. Top with half of meat mixture. Repeat layers and top with cheese. Bake at 350° for 30 minutes or until hot and bubbly. Yields 6 servings.

Pot Roast

1 (4-pound) rump roast
½ cup all-purpose flour
2 tablespoons vegetable oil
1 teaspoon salt
½ teaspoon black pepper
2 yellow onions, thickly sliced
2 teaspoons minced garlic
½ cup water

⅓ cup sherry
¼ cup tomato sauce
¼ teaspoon powdered rosemary
¼ teaspoon dry mustard
¼ teaspoon dried marjoram
¼ teaspoon powdered thyme
1 bay leaf
8 ounces mushrooms, thinly sliced

Pat roast dry with paper towels. Dredge in flour. Heat oil in a Dutch oven. Add meat and brown on all sides. Remove roast and season with salt and pepper. Pour off all but 2 tablespoons pan drippings. Add onion to drippings and sauté 3 minutes. Add garlic and sauté 2 minutes. Stir in water and next 7 ingredients. Return roast to pan and cover. Reduce heat and simmer 3 hours, 30 minutes. Transfer to a carving board, cover loosely with foil, and let stand 15 minutes. Add mushrooms to pot and cook over medium heat for 10 minutes. Remove bay leaf. Reduce heat to very low and keep gravy warm. Carve roast into thin slices and arrange on a large, heated platter. Pour some of gravy over meat and serve remaining gravy in a heated sauceboat. Yields 8 servings.

Spicy Fried Liver

2 pounds calf liver, sliced ½-inch
  thick
2 cloves garlic, pressed
1 tablespoon white vinegar
1 teaspoon turmeric
1 teaspoon ground ginger

¼ teaspoon cayenne pepper
¼ teaspoon black pepper
4 tablespoons butter, divided
1 teaspoon lemon juice
1 teaspoon salt
3 yellow onions, thinly sliced

Rinse liver and pat dry with paper towels. Combine garlic and next 5 ingredients in a small bowl. Rub liver on both sides with mixture. Heat 2 tablespoons butter in a large skillet. When very hot, add liver and cook 1 minute. Turn and cook 3 minutes on other side. Transfer to a heated platter. Sprinkle with lemon juice and salt and keep warm. In same skillet, melt remaining 2 tablespoons butter. Add onion and sauté 8 minutes or until soft and golden. Top liver with onion and serve immediately. Yields 4 servings.

Blanquette De Veau

4 pounds boneless veal shoulder or
  breast, cut into 1½-inch cubes
2 teaspoons paprika
½ teaspoon powdered rosemary
6 tablespoons butter, divided
1 tablespoon vegetable oil
2 teaspoons salt
1 teaspoon white pepper
2 pounds mushrooms, thinly sliced
1 cup minced yellow onion
4 cloves garlic, pressed

2 cups veal or chicken broth
2 tablespoons all-purpose flour
1 cup dry white wine
12 pearl onions, peeled
3 egg yolks
2 cups sour cream, room
  temperature
2 tablespoons lemon juice
¼ teaspoon nutmeg
2 tablespoons minced fresh parsley

Pat meat dry with paper towels. Sprinkle with paprika and rosemary. Heat 2 table-spoons butter and oil in a Dutch oven. Cook veal in small batches, removing with a slotted spoon as pieces brown. Season browned meat with salt and pepper. Melt 2 tablespoons butter in a skillet. Add mushrooms and sauté 3 minutes. Add minced onion to Dutch oven and sauté 3 minutes. Add garlic and sauté 2 minutes. Return meat to Dutch oven. Stir in broth and mushrooms. In a cup, blend flour into wine. Stir flour mixture into Dutch oven. Cover and simmer 1 hour, 30 minutes or until meat is tender. Remove from heat. In a saucepan, melt remaining 2 tablespoons butter. Add pearl onions, cover, and cook 8 minutes. Add onions to Dutch oven. In a bowl, whisk together egg yolks, sour cream, and lemon juice. Slowly stir into meat mixture. Add nutmeg. Cook over very low heat for 10 minutes, stirring occasionally. Do not allow sauce to simmer. Serve in a heated deep dish or a platter surrounded with rice or noodles. Sprinkle with parsley. Yields 8 to 10 servings.

Veal Birds

1½ pounds veal cutlets, cut into 5X3
   inch pieces, ⅜-inch thick
1 cup milk
5 strips bacon, cooked and
   crumbled
1 cup dry breadcrumbs
1 egg yolk, lightly beaten
¼ teaspoon Worcestershire sauce
¼ teaspoon dried thyme
7 tablespoons butter, divided
1 cup finely chopped yellow onion
½ cup finely chopped celery
¼ pound pork sausage

1 teaspoon black pepper, divided
1 teaspoon salt
¼ teaspoon nutmeg
¼ cup all-purpose flour
1 tablespoon olive oil
1 cup dry white wine
1 cup chicken broth
8 ounces mushrooms, thinly sliced
¼ cup finely chopped bell pepper
¼ cup finely chopped green onions
2 tablespoons brandy
1 cup heavy cream
1 teaspoon minced parsley

Soak cutlets in milk in a large, deep dish for 60 minutes. Pat dry with paper towels. Place cutlets between 2 sheets of wax paper and pound lightly with a smooth meat mallet to ¼-inch thick. Combine bacon and next 4 ingredients in a bowl. Mix well. In a large skillet, melt 2 tablespoons butter. Add yellow onion, celery, and sausage and sauté 10 minutes. Mix into breadcrumb mixture. Place equal amounts of stuffing in the center of each cutlet. Roll up and tie with string. Combine ½ teaspoon black pepper and next 3 ingredients. Roll veal birds in flour mixture and shake off excess. Heat 3 tablespoons butter and oil in a skillet. Add birds and brown quickly on all sides. Transfer to a deep ovenproof dish. Remove skillet from heat. Add wine and cook over high heat for 3 minutes or until liquid reduces by half. Scrape brown bits from bottom and sides of pan. Reduce heat and stir in broth. Cook 3 minutes. In a skillet, melt remaining 2 tablespoons butter. Add mushrooms, bell pepper, and green onions and sauté 3 minutes. Spoon over birds. Sprinkle with remaining ½ teaspoon black pepper. Pour sauce over top and cover with foil. Bake at 350° for 45 minutes. Transfer birds to a large, heated platter and remove string. Keep warm. Return sauce to skillet. In a small saucepan, warm brandy. Ignite and pour flaming liquid into skillet. Shake skillet until flames stop. Over high heat, stir in cream and cook 4 to 5 minutes or to desired consistency. Pour sauce over birds, sprinkle with parsley, and serve immediately. Yields 8 servings.

Veal with Artichokes and Mushrooms

1 pound veal cutlets, 8 slices,
   ³/₈-inch thick
1 teaspoon salt
1 teaspoon white pepper
3 tablespoons all-purpose flour
1 egg
2 tablespoons water

5 tablespoons butter, divided
1 tablespoon olive oil
2 cups sliced artichoke bottoms
8 ounces mushrooms, thinly sliced
2 tablespoons minced green onions
1 tablespoon lemon juice
1 tablespoon minced fresh parsley

Using a smooth meat mallet, pound cutlets lightly between 2 sheets of wax paper to ¹/₄-inch thick. Pat dry with paper towels. Combine salt, pepper, and flour. Dredge cutlets on both sides in flour mixture and shake off excess. Lightly beat egg and water together and brush over both sides of cutlets. In a large skillet, heat 2 tablespoons butter and oil. When very hot, add cutlets and sauté 2 minutes on each side. Transfer to a heated platter and keep warm. In a Dutch oven, melt remaining 3 tablespoons butter. Add artichoke, mushrooms, and green onions and sauté 5 minutes. Add lemon juice and parsley and cook and stir 2 minutes. Spoon over cutlets and serve immediately. Yields 4 servings.

Veal Vermouth

1 pound veal cutlets, 8 slices,
   ³/₈-inch thick
2 cloves garlic, sliced lengthwise
1 teaspoon salt
1 teaspoon white pepper
3 tablespoons all-purpose flour

2 tablespoons butter
1 tablespoon olive oil
8 ounces mushrooms, thinly sliced
¹/₂ cup dry vermouth
2 teaspoons lemon juice
2 tablespoons minced fresh parsley

Using a smooth meat mallet, pound cutlets lightly between 2 sheets of wax paper to ¹/₄-inch thick. Pat dry with paper towels. Rub veal with cut side of garlic. Combine salt, pepper, and flour. Dredge veal on both sides in flour mixture and shake off excess. Heat butter and oil in a Dutch oven. When very hot, add veal and sauté 2 minutes on each side. As they brown, remove cutlets from pan. After all meat is browned, return veal to pan. Place mushrooms over veal and add vermouth. Reduce heat, cover, and simmer 25 minutes. Transfer veal and mushrooms to a heated platter. Sprinkle with lemon juice and parsley. Serve immediately. Yields 4 servings.

Veal Taormina

1 large eggplant, peeled and cut into
   1/4-inch slices
2 eggs, beaten
1 1/2 cups seasoned breadcrumbs
3/4 cup olive oil
1 1/2 pounds veal, ground once
3 (8-ounce) cans tomato sauce

2 teaspoons sugar
1 teaspoon dried oregano
1/2 teaspoon dried basil
1/2 teaspoon salt
1/2 cup Parmesan cheese
8 ounces mozzarella cheese, sliced

Dip eggplant slices in egg and then in breadcrumbs. Fry in oil and drain on paper towels. Shape veal into a large patty and brown 5 minutes on each side. Break patty into chunks and stir in tomato sauce and next 4 ingredients. Simmer 10 minutes. Arrange a third of eggplant in a greased 9X13 inch baking dish. Cover with a third of meat sauce. Sprinkle a third of Parmesan cheese over the top and add a third of mozzarella cheese. Repeat layers until all ingredients are used. Bake at 350° for 40 minutes or until cheese is bubbly. Yields 8 to 10 servings.

Breaded Veal Cutlets

1 1/2 pounds veal cutlets, 12 slices,
   3/8-inch thick
1 teaspoon salt
1 teaspoon white pepper
1/4 cup all-purpose flour
1 1/2 cups dry breadcrumbs
1/2 cup Parmesan cheese

1 egg
2 tablespoons water
4 tablespoons butter
2 tablespoons olive oil
1/2 cup dry white wine
2 tablespoons minced fresh parsley
4 lemon wedges

Using a smooth meat mallet, pound cutlets lightly between 2 sheets of wax paper to 1/4-inch thick. Pat dry with paper towels. Combine salt, pepper, and flour. Dredge cutlets in flour mixture and shake off excess. Combine breadcrumbs and cheese. Lightly beat together egg and water. Dip cutlets in egg, then coat with breadcrumb mixture. Allow coating to dry 10 minutes. In a large skillet, heat butter and oil. When very hot, add cutlets and sauté 2 minutes on each side. Remove and drain on paper towels. Transfer to a heated serving platter and keep warm. Remove pan from heat and deglaze with wine, scraping brown bits from bottom and sides of pan. Cook 3 minutes or until liquid reduces by half. Pour sauce over cutlets. Sprinkle with parsley and garnish with lemon wedges. Yields 4 servings.

Veal with Mushrooms, Prosciutto, and Cheese

1½ pounds veal cutlets, 12 slices,
⅜-inch thick
1 teaspoon salt
1 teaspoon freshly ground white
pepper
3 tablespoons all-purpose flour
7 tablespoons butter, divided
1 tablespoon olive oil

¼ cup minced green onions, divided
½ cup dry white wine
2 cups heavy cream, divided
3 cups finely chopped mushrooms
¼ cup finely grated Swiss cheese
⅓ cup Parmesan cheese
12 thin slices prosciutto or ham

Using a smooth meat mallet, pound cutlets lightly between 2 sheets of wax paper to ¼-inch thick. Pat dry with paper towels. Combine salt, pepper, and flour. Dredge veal in flour mixture and shake off excess. In a large skillet, heat 3 tablespoons butter and oil. When very hot, add veal and brown 2 minutes on each side. Transfer to a heated baking sheet and keep warm. Reduce heat and add 2 tablespoons onions to skillet. Sauté 1 minute. Remove skillet from heat and add wine. Cook over high heat for 2 minutes or until liquid reduces by half. Scrape brown bits from bottom and sides of skillet. Reduce heat and slowly stir in 1½ cups cream. Cook and stir over high heat until sauce reduces by half. Keep warm. In a separate skillet, melt remaining 4 tablespoons butter. Add remaining 2 tablespoons onions and sauté 1 minute. Add mushrooms and sauté 3 to 4 minutes or until all moisture evaporates. Add remaining ½ cup cream. Cook and stir over high heat for 4 minutes or until cream reduces by half. Combine cheeses. Divide mushroom mixture evenly among cutlets. Top each with a slice of prosciutto and sprinkle with cheese mixture. Broil 2 to 3 minutes or until cheese browns. Transfer cutlets to warmed plates. Top with cream sauce and serve immediately. Yields 6 servings.

Stuffed Veal Pocket

Stuffing

1 stick butter
3 cups finely chopped bell pepper
2½ cups finely chopped celery
2 cups finely chopped green onions
1½ cups finely chopped yellow
    onion
2 cloves garlic, minced

2 tablespoons minced fresh parsley
1½ cups dry breadcrumbs
1 egg, lightly beaten
1 pound ham
1 teaspoon salt
1 teaspoon black pepper

Veal

1 (5-pound) veal shoulder roast,
    boned, well trimmed
½ teaspoon salt
¼ teaspoon black pepper
1 yellow onion, quartered

1 tomato, quartered
2 stalks celery, halved
2 carrots, sliced lengthwise
2 slices rye bread, cubed

Gravy

½ cup red wine
1 teaspoon salt
½ teaspoon black pepper

4 tablespoons butter
8 ounces mushrooms, thinly sliced

Heat butter in a Dutch oven. Add bell pepper and next 5 ingredients and sauté 7 minutes. Add breadcrumbs and next 4 ingredients. Reduce heat, cover, and cook 20 minutes. Transfer to a bowl and cool. Cover with foil and refrigerate overnight. To prepare veal, cut a slit in roast to form a pocket. Pat meat dry with paper towels. Sprinkle inside pocket with salt and pepper. Place half of stuffing inside pocket and secure shut with toothpicks, allowing some stuffing to spill out. Place remaining stuffing in a greased casserole dish. Place meat in a shallow roasting pan and surround with onion and next 4 ingredients. Add water to a 1-inch depth. Roast at 350° for 3 hours, basing occasionally with pan juices. Transfer meat to a carving board, cover loosely with foil, and let stand 20 minutes. Place stuffing casserole in oven and bake 20 to 30 minutes. To make gravy, strain pan juices into a large, deep skillet. Add wine and bring to a boil. Cook and stir 2 minutes. Add salt and pepper. Keep warm. In a separate skillet, melt butter. Add mushrooms and sauté 3 minutes. Add to gravy and serve in a heated sauceboat. Carve meat in thin slices and arrange on a heated platter. Yields 10 to 12 servings.

Braised Veal Roast with Tarragon

1 (5-pound) bone-in veal rump roast
1 teaspoon dried tarragon, divided
4 tablespoons butter
2 tablespoon vegetable oil
1½ teaspoons salt, divided
1 teaspoon black pepper, divided
2½ cups coarsely chopped green
    onions

2 carrots, sliced in ¼-inch rounds
1 bay leaf
¾ cup white wine
1 egg yolk
1 cup heavy cream
8 ounces mushrooms, thinly sliced

Pat roast dry with paper towels. Sprinkle with ½ teaspoon tarragon. Heat butter and oil in a Dutch oven. When very hot, add roast and brown on all sides. Season with 1 teaspoon salt and ½ teaspoon pepper. Reduce heat and cover. Cook 30 minutes, turning once. Stir in remaining ½ teaspoon tarragon, ½ teaspoon salt, ½ teaspoon pepper, and next 4 ingredients. Cover and simmer 1 hour, 30 minutes. Transfer roast to a heated serving platter, cover loosely with foil, and let stand 15 minutes. Place Dutch oven over high heat and bring pan juices to a boil. Remove from heat. In a bowl, whisk egg yolk and cream. Slowly mix into pan juices. Add mushrooms and cook, stirring occasionally, over low heat for 10 minutes. Do not simmer. Carve roast into thin slices. Serve sauce in a heated sauceboat. Yields 6 servings.

Veal Marsala

1½ pounds veal cutlets, 12 slices,
    ⅜-inch thick
1 teaspoon salt
1 teaspoon white pepper
½ teaspoon paprika
¼ cup all-purpose flour

6 tablespoons butter, divided
1 tablespoon olive oil
2 teaspoons lemon juice
½ cup dry Marsala
2 tablespoons minced fresh parsley
2 tablespoons Parmesan cheese

Using a smooth meat mallet, pound cutlets lightly between 2 sheets of wax paper to ¼-inch thick. Pat dry with paper towels. Combine salt and next 3 ingredients. Dredge cutlets in flour mixture and shake off excess. In a large skillet, heat 3 tablespoons butter and oil. When very hot, add cutlets and sauté 1 minutes on each side. Transfer to a heated platter and sprinkle with lemon juice. Pour off fat from skillet. Add Marsala and scrape brown bits from bottom and sides of skillet. Bring to a boil and cook 1 minute. Stir in remaining 3 tablespoons butter until melted. Return veal to skillet and add parsley. Cook 2 minutes, turning cutlet several times. Transfer cutlets to a heated serving platter and top with sauce. Sprinkle with cheese. Yields 4 to 6 servings.

Veal with Mushrooms in Cream Sauce

1 pound veal cutlets, 8 slices,
   3/8-inch thick
1 teaspoon salt
1 teaspoon white pepper
3 tablespoons all-purpose flour
2 tablespoons butter

1 tablespoon olive oil
1/2 cup Calvados or dry white wine
1 cup heavy cream
8 ounces mushrooms, thinly sliced
2 tablespoons lemon juice
2 tablespoons minced fresh parsley

Using a smooth meat mallet, pound cutlets lightly between 2 sheets of wax paper to 1/4-inch thick. Pat dry with paper towels. Combine salt, pepper, and flour. Dredge cutlets in flour mixture and shake off excess. In a large skillet, heat butter and oil. When very hot, add cutlets and sauté 2 minutes on each side. Transfer to a heated serving platter and keep warm. Remove skillet from heat and deglaze with Calvados, scraping brown bits from bottom and sides of pan. Cook about 1 1/2 minutes over high heat to reduce liquid slightly. Reduce heat and add cream and mushrooms. Cook and stir 5 to 6 minutes or until sauce reduces by half and is lightly browned. Add lemon juice and parsley. Cook and stir 2 minutes. Pour over veal and serve. Yields 4 servings.

Veal Piccata

1/2 cup white wine, divided
1 egg yolk, lightly beaten
1/3 cup beef broth
1 pound veal cutlets, 8 slices,
   3/8-inch thick
1 teaspoon salt
1 teaspoon white pepper
1/8 teaspoon dried oregano

3 tablespoons Parmesan cheese
3 tablespoons all-purpose flour
2 tablespoons butter
1 tablespoon olive oil
2 tablespoons lemon juice
2 tablespoons minced fresh parsley
1 lemon, sliced and seeded
1 tablespoon capers

Combine 1/4 cup wine, egg yolk, and broth in a cup. Blend well and set aside. Using a smooth meat mallet, pound cutlets lightly between 2 sheets of wax paper to 1/4-inch thick. Pat dry with paper towels. Combine salt and next 4 ingredients. Dredge cutlets in flour mixture and shake off excess. In a large skillet, heat butter and oil. When very hot, add cutlets and sauté 2 minutes on each side. Sprinkle with lemon juice while cooking. Transfer to a heated serving platter and keep warm. Remove skillet from heat and deglaze with remaining 1/4 cup wine, scraping brown bits from bottom and sides of skillet. Cook over high heat for 2 minutes or until liquid reduces by half. Reduce heat and stir in broth mixture. Add parsley and cook and stir 1 minute. Pour sauce over cutlets and garnish with lemon and capers. Yields 4 servings.

Veal with Shrimp and Crabmeat

1½ pounds veal cutlets, 12 slices,
⅜-inch thick
1 teaspoon salt
1 teaspoon white pepper
3 tablespoons all-purpose flour
6 tablespoons butter, divided
1 tablespoon olive oil
2 tablespoons minced green onions
½ cup dry white wine

1 cup heavy cream
8 ounces mushrooms, thinly sliced
1 tablespoon lemon juice
2 tablespoons minced fresh parsley,
divided
¼ pound cooked shrimp, peeled and
deveined
½ pound crabmeat

Using a smooth meat mallet, pound cutlets lightly between 2 sheets of wax paper to ¼-inch thick. Pat dry with paper towels. Combine salt, pepper, and flour. Dredge cutlets in flour mixture and shake off excess. In a large skillet, heat 3 tablespoons butter and oil. When very hot, add cutlets and sauté 2 minutes on each side. Transfer to a heated serving platter and keep warm. Reduce heat and add onions to skillet. Sauté 1 minute. Remove skillet from heat and deglaze with wine, scraping brown bits from bottom and sides of skillet. Cook over high heat for 2 minutes or until liquid reduces by half. Reduce heat and stir in cream. Simmer 4 minutes or until sauce thickens slightly. Add mushrooms and cook and stir 3 minutes. Add lemon juice and 1 tablespoon parsley and cook and stir 1 minute. Pour over veal and keep warm. In a separate skillet, melt remaining 3 tablespoons butter. Add shrimp and crabmeat and cook until heated. Spoon over veal and sprinkle with remaining 1 tablespoons parsley. Yields 6 servings.

Creole Veal Chops

6 tablespoons butter, divided
⅔ cup finely chopped yellow onion
¾ cup finely chopped bell pepper
¾ cup finely chopped celery
2 cloves garlic, minced
8 ounces mushrooms, thinly sliced
1 (14½-ounce) can whole tomatoes, undrained
¾ cup tomato paste
2 bay leaves

½ teaspoon sugar
4½ cups veal or beef broth
1 tablespoon salt, divided
2 teaspoons black pepper, divided
10 (½-inch thick) shoulder veal chops, well trimmed
1 tablespoon dried rosemary
½ cup all-purpose flour
1 tablespoon vegetable oil
2 tablespoons minced fresh parsley

Melt 4 tablespoons butter in a Dutch oven. Add onion, bell pepper, and celery and sauté 5 minutes. Add garlic and sauté 2 minutes. Stir in mushrooms and next 4 ingredients. Reduce heat and simmer 15 minutes. Slowly stir in broth and simmer 15 minutes. Season with 1 teaspoon salt and 1 teaspoon black pepper. Pat chops dry with paper towels. Combine remaining 2 teaspoons salt, remaining 1 teaspoon black pepper, rosemary, and flour. Dredge chops in flour mixture and shake off excess. In a large skillet, heat remaining 2 tablespoons butter and oil. When very hot, add chops and brown 3 minutes on each side. Transfer to a large ovenproof dish. Pour sauce over chops. Cover with foil and bake at 350° for 1 hour, 30 minutes. Remove bay leaf and sprinkle with parsley. Yields 10 servings.

Cold Veal Tongue with Horseradish Sauce

Horseradish Sauce
1/2 cup mayonnaise
1/2 cup sour cream
2 tablespoons minced fresh parsley
3 tablespoons horseradish
1/2 teaspoon prepared yellow
   mustard

1/2 teaspoon Worcestershire sauce
1/2 teaspoon lemon juice
1/4 teaspoon salt
1/4 teaspoon black pepper

Veal Tongue
1 1/2 pounds fresh veal tongue
salt
1 large yellow onion, unpeeled and
   studded with 8 cloves
3 stalks celery with leaves, halved

1 carrot, halved lengthwise
1 clove garlic, halved
2 bay leaves
8 peppercorns

Combine all sauce ingredients in a bowl and mix well. Cover and refrigerate overnight. To prepare meat, scrub tongue under warm running water. Soak in cold water for 60 minutes. Place tongue in a Dutch oven. Add enough water to cover by 6 inches. Add 1 1/2 teaspoons salt per quart of water added. Add onion and remaining 5 ingredients. Bring just to a boil. Reduce heat and cover. Simmer 2 hours or until tender. Remove tongue and plunge into cold water for less than 1 minute. Skin immediately. Remove roots and gristle. Return to pot and cool completely in liquid. Transfer to a serving platter and carve in 1/4-inch thick slices. To carve, cut nearly through to hump parallel to base. Toward the tip, slice on diagonal. Serve with horseradish sauce. Yields 4 servings.

Grillades

This dish freezes well and is best made a day ahead.

2 pounds (³⁄₈-inch thick) boneless
   veal rounds, well trimmed
2 teaspoons salt, divided
1 teaspoon white pepper
¹⁄₃ cup all-purpose flour
1 stick butter, divided
2 tablespoons vegetable oil
1 cup finely chopped green onions
¹⁄₂ cup finely chopped bell pepper
1 clove garlic, minced

8 ounces mushrooms, thinly sliced
3 cups peeled and chopped
   tomatoes
2 tablespoons tomato paste
¹⁄₂ cup red wine
1¹⁄₂ cups water
2 tablespoons minced fresh parsley
1 bay leaf
¹⁄₂ teaspoon dried thyme

Using a smooth meat mallet, pound veal lightly between 2 sheets of wax paper to ¹⁄₄-inch thick. Pat dry with paper towels. Combine 1 teaspoon salt, pepper, and flour. Dredge veal in flour mixture and shake off excess. In a large, deep skillet, heat 4 tablespoons butter and oil. Add veal and sauté 2 minutes on each side. Remove veal pieces as they brown. Reduce heat and melt 2 tablespoons butter. Add onions and bell pepper and sauté 3 minutes. Add garlic and sauté 2 minutes. Remove from heat. In a separate skillet, melt remaining 2 tablespoons butter. Add mushrooms and sauté 3 minutes. To first skillet, add mushrooms, remaining 1 teaspoon salt, tomatoes, and remaining 6 ingredients. Return veal to skillet and stir. Bring just to a boil. Reduce heat and cover. Simmer 40 minutes. Uncover, remove bay leaf, and cook 20 minutes longer. Yields 8 servings.

Porcupine Pork Roast

1 (7-pound) pork loin roast, ribs
  cracked, untrimmed
¼ cup olive oil
1½ teaspoons salt
1 teaspoon black pepper
1½ teaspoons dried oregano
½ teaspoon dried thyme
⅓ cup all-purpose flour
2 yellow onions, sliced

3 cups water, divided
3 beef bouillon cubes
2 chicken bouillon cubes
1¼ cups white wine
2 cloves garlic, pressed
¾ cup sour cream, room
  temperature
2 tablespoons cornstarch

Using a knife, score fat of roast in a diamond pattern. Rub roast with oil and season with salt and next 3 ingredients. Coat with flour. Arrange onions on scored surface and secure with toothpicks. Place in a shallow roasting pan. Cover tightly and refrigerate overnight. Remove from refrigerator at least 60 minutes prior to cooking. Bake at 375° for 30 minutes. While roast bakes, prepare a basting sauce. Bring 2¼ cups water to a boil in a saucepan. Add bouillon cubes and dissolve. Reduce to low heat and add wine and garlic. Simmer 5 minutes. Remove from heat and stir in sour cream. After baking 30 minutes, reduce oven temperature to 325° and pour sauce over roast. Bake 4 hours, basting every 30 minutes. Transfer roast to a heated serving platter, cover loosely with foil, and let stand 15 minutes. Place roasting pan on stove top. Combine remaining ¾ cup water and cornstarch and add to pan. Simmer 10 minutes, scraping brown bits from bottom of pan. Serve sauce in a heated sauceboat. Yields 6 servings.

Roast Tenderloin of Pork

Pork and Marinade

1 (4 to 5 pound) pork tenderloin
6 cloves garlic, pressed
1 (6-ounce can) frozen limeade
    concentrate, thawed

3 tablespoons soy sauce
1 tablespoon black pepper
1 teaspoon salt

Sauce

3 tablespoons butter
2 tablespoons minced green onions
½ cup dry red wine
1 tablespoon cornstarch

3 tablespoons water
1 cup heavy cream
¼ teaspoon salt
¼ teaspoon black pepper

Place tenderloin in a shallow roasting pan. In a bowl, combine garlic and next 4 ingredients. Mix well and pour over pork. Cover with foil and refrigerate 24 hours, turning several times. Remove meat from refrigerator 60 minutes before cooking. Drain and reserve marinade. Bake pork at 400° for 20 minutes. Reduce heat to 325° and bake 30 minutes longer, basting with reserved marinade every 10 minutes. Transfer pork to a carving board, cover loosely with foil, and let stand 15 minutes. To prepare sauce, discard drippings from roasting pan. Place pan on stove top and melt butter. Add onions and sauté 2 minutes. Add wine and bring to a boil, constantly stirring and scraping bottom of pan. In a cup, blend cornstarch and water. Reduce heat and stir in cornstarch mixture, cream, salt, and pepper. Simmer 5 minutes. Carve roast into thin slices. Serve sauce on the side in a heated sauceboat. Yields 8 to 10 servings.

Pork Loin Roast with Cream Sauce

Roast and Marinade

1 (4-pound) pork loin roast,
    untrimmed, boned, tied
½ cup fresh lime juice
¼ cup soy sauce
½ cup olive oil

½ cup minced green onions
2 tablespoons Worcestershire sauce
½ teaspoon salt
½ teaspoon black pepper

Cream Sauce

2 tablespoons butter
¼ cup minced yellow onion
½ cup white wine
1 cup heavy cream

¼ cup brandy
1 teaspoon salt
½ teaspoon black pepper

Place meat in a shallow roasting pan. In a bowl, combine lime juice and next 6 ingredients. Mix well and pour over roast. Cover with foil and refrigerate 24 hours, turning several times. Remove from refrigerator 60 minutes before cooking. Strain and reserve marinade. Pat meat dry with paper towels. Return roast to pan, fat-side up, and insert a meat thermometer. Bake at 350° for 1 hour, 45 minutes or until thermometer registers 160°. Baste roast with reserved marinade every 20 minutes. Transfer roast to a carving board, cover loosely with foil, and let rest 15 minutes. Carve into thin slices and arrange on a heated serving platter. To prepare cream sauce, melt butter in a skillet. Add onion and sauté 3 minutes. Reduce heat and add wine. Simmer 15 minutes. Gradually stir in cream. Add brandy, salt, and pepper. Over medium-high heat, cook and stir 3 to 4 minutes or until liquid reduces by a third. Serve in a heated sauceboat. Yields 8 to 10 servings.

Pork Chops with Mushroom Stuffing

2 tablespoons butter
⅓ cup coarsely chopped mushrooms
⅔ cup finely chopped yellow onion
½ cup dry breadcrumbs
2 tablespoons minced fresh parsley
⅛ teaspoon dried thyme

½ teaspoon salt
¼ teaspoon black pepper
1 egg, lightly beaten
4 (1¾-inch thick) double center-cut
    pork chops, well trimmed
2 tablespoons vegetable oil

Heat butter in a skillet. Add mushroom and next 6 ingredients and sauté 5 minutes. Remove from heat and stir in egg. Cut a slit in each chop to form a pocket. Fill pockets with equal amounts of stuffing. Dry chops with paper towels. Heat oil in a skillet. When very hot, add chops and brown 3 minutes on each side. Transfer to a shallow roasting pan and cover with foil. Bake at 325° for 60 minutes. Yields 4 servings.

Pork Crown Roast with Prune and Apricot Stuffing

Stuffing

1 pound ground hot sausage	½ teaspoon sage
1 pound ground mild sausage	½ teaspoon cinnamon
½ cup finely chopped yellow onion	1½ teaspoons salt
½ cup finely chopped celery	1 teaspoon black pepper
½ cup finely chopped fresh parsley	2 eggs, lightly beaten
2 tablespoons butter	1½ cups chopped prunes
1 cup dry breadcrumbs	1½ cups chopped dried apricots
2 tablespoons packed light brown sugar	

Pork Roast

1 (12-pound) crown pork roast, ribs cracked, laced in a circle, trimmed	1 teaspoon freshly ground black pepper
2 teaspoons salt	2 (9-ounce) jars kumquats, optional
	1 (16-ounce) can apricot halves, optional

Sauce

1 tablespoon cornstarch	1 clove garlic, pressed
½ cup water	¼ cup minced fresh parsley
1 cup Madeira	½ teaspoon lime juice

Cook sausages in a Dutch oven for 10 minutes or until browned. Remove and drain on paper towels. In pan drippings, sauté onion, celery, and parsley for 5 minutes. In a separate skillet, melt butter. Add breadcrumbs and cook, tossing frequently, for 8 minutes or until lightly browned. In a large bowl, combine sausage, onion mixture, breadcrumbs, sugar, and next 7 ingredients. Cover and refrigerate overnight. To prepare meat, season roast with salt and pepper. Place a piece of heavy foil around bottom of roast to allow stuffing to be easily transferred from roasting pan to serving platter. Cover rib tips with foil. Place roast in a large, shallow roasting pan and insert a meat thermometer. Cook, uncovered, for 60 minutes. Fill center cavity of roast with stuffing and cook 60 minutes longer or until thermometer registers 165°. Transfer roast to a heated serving platter and let stand 15 to 20 minutes. Remove foil from rib tips. Slit kumquats on 1 end and place on rib tips to garnish. Place apricot halves, hollow-side down, in center of stuffing. To make sauce, blend cornstarch and water in a cup. Skim fat from pan drippings and discard all but 3 tablespoons of remaining drippings. Place roasting pan with drippings on stove top and add Madeira. Cook over high heat for 3 minutes or until reduced by half, stirring to dissolve brown bits from bottom of pan. Remove from heat and stir in cornstarch mixture. Return to heat and add garlic, parsley, and lime juice. Simmer 10 minutes. Serve in a heated sauceboat. Yields 10 to 12 servings.

Pork Tenderloin Medallions

2 pounds pork tenderloin, well
   trimmed
1 teaspoon salt
½ teaspoon black pepper
½ cup all-purpose flour
2 eggs
¼ cup water

1 cup dry breadcrumbs
6 tablespoons butter
2 tablespoons olive oil
½ cup dry white wine
8 ounces mushrooms, thinly sliced
1 tablespoon lemon juice
2 tablespoons minced fresh parsley

Cut pork crosswise into 1-inch thick medallions. Pat meat dry with paper towels.
Combine salt, pepper, and flour. Dredge medallions in flour mixture and shake off
excess. Beat eggs and water together. Dip medallions in egg mixture and coat with
breadcrumbs. Allow coating to dry 10 minutes. In a Dutch oven, heat butter and
oil. Add medallions and sauté 8 minutes on each side. Drain on paper towels.
Transfer to a heated platter and keep warm. Remove pan from heat and add wine.
Cook over high heat, scraping brown bits from bottom and sides of pan, for 3
minutes or until reduced by half. Add mushrooms and cook and stir 2 minutes.
Add lemon juice and cook and stir 1 minute. Pour sauce over meat. Sprinkle with
parsley and serve immediately. Yields 6 servings.

Creole Pork Chops

8 (¾-inch thick) loin pork chops,
   well trimmed
3 tablespoons vegetable oil
1 cup finely chopped yellow onion
1 cup finely chopped bell pepper
1 cup finely chopped celery
2 cloves garlic, minced
1 (28-ounce) can whole tomatoes,
   undrained

3 tablespoons tomato paste
3 cups beef broth
1 teaspoon sugar
1 bay leaf
1 teaspoon dried oregano
1½ teaspoons salt
1 teaspoon black pepper
2 tablespoons minced fresh parsley

Pat chops dry with paper towels. Heat oil in a Dutch oven. When very hot, add
chops and brown 3 minutes on each side. Remove chops as they brown and keep
warm. Discard all but 3 tablespoons pan drippings. Add onion and next 3 ingredients and sauté 5 minutes. Stir in tomatoes and next 7 ingredients. Reduce heat and
cover. Simmer 30 minutes, stirring occasionally. Return chops to Dutch oven and
cook 30 minutes, turning once. Transfer chops to a large, deep, heated platter.
Remove bay leaf and pour sauce over top. Sprinkle with parsley. Yields 6 servings.

Roast Suckling Pig

If grapes are not available, string uncooked green peas onto heavy thread for a double-stand necklace. Use ribbon, fresh mint leaves, parsley, celery leaves, flowers, or any combination of these to garnish pig and platter.

Roast Pig
1 (10 to 12-pound) suckling pig, cleaned of hair, eyes removed
1 tablespoon salt
1 teaspoon black pepper
6 cloves
½ teaspoon sage
½ teaspoon dried oregano
4 tablespoons butter

2½ cups finely chopped yellow onion
2 cups finely chopped celery
1 clove garlic, minced
½ cup oil, divided
1 lime
2 cherries or cranberries

Frosted Grapes
2 pounds red or green grapes
2 egg whites

2 tablespoons water
1 cup sugar

Wash pig, inside and out, under cold running water. Dry thoroughly with paper towels. Season inside cavity with salt and next 4 ingredients. Melt butter in a large skillet. Add onion and celery and sauté 3 minutes. Add garlic and sauté 2 minutes. Cool. Spread mixture in cavity. Run 4 skewers through both sides of cavity. Skewer front and back legs in place; back legs folded under rump, front legs extended with head resting in between. Place a 2-inch diameter ball of foil in pig's mouth. Cover ears and tail with foil and place a small ball of foil in each eye socket. Cover and refrigerate until ready to cook. Remove from refrigerator 3 hours prior to cooking. Place a rack diagonally in a shallow roasting pan. Cross 2 sheets of heavy foil, 1½ times the length of pig, on rack. Place pig on rack and fold foil up loosely around pig to allow for drippings. Rub surface of pig with 3 tablespoons oil. Insert a meat thermometer in the thickest part of the thigh. Roast pig at 450° for 15 minutes. Brush with some of remaining oil. Roast 15 minutes more and brush with oil. Reduce heat to 350° and bake 3 hours or until thermometer registers 165°. Continue to baste every 20 minutes, using oil until gone, then using pan drippings. When done, turn off heat and let stand in oven 30 minutes. Remove pig from rack, drain, and place on a heated platter. Remove skewers and foil. Place lime in mouth and cherries in eye sockets. At intervals around pig's neck, place toothpicks. Attach clusters of frosted grapes to toothpicks and garnish platter with clusters of frosted grapes. To make grapes, divide into small clusters. Beat egg whites and water in a bowl until frothy. Place sugar in a large, shallow dish. Dip grapes into egg white, shake off excess. Roll grapes in sugar, shake off excess. Refrigerate until dry and ready to use. Yields 10 to 12 servings.

Pork Chops Provençale

¼ cup chopped garlic cloves
¼ cup basil
1 tablespoon coarse salt
1 tablespoon crushed black pepper
12 (½-inch thick) pork chops, well
   trimmed

3 tablespoons vegetable oil
1 cup white wine
2 tablespoons butter
8 ounces mushrooms, thinly sliced
1 tablespoon minced fresh parsley

Mash garlic in a bowl with a fork. Mix in basil, salt, and pepper. Coat both sides of chops with garlic mixture and let stand at room temperature at least 60 minutes. Heat oil in a large skillet. Add chops and brown 2 minutes on each side. Transfer to a shallow roasting pan, overlapping slightly. Pour off excess fat from skillet and add wine. Cook over high heat for 3 minutes or until reduced by half, scraping brown bits from bottom and sides of skillet. Remove from heat. In a separate skillet, melt butter. Add mushrooms and sauté 3 minutes. Combine mushrooms and wine sauce and set aside. Bake chops at 350° for 35 minutes. Remove from oven and drain off pan drippings. Pour wine sauce into roasting pan. Return to oven and bake 15 minutes longer. Arrange chops on a heated platter. Pour sauce over top and sprinkle with parsley. Yields 8 servings.

Pork Chops with Apple Stuffing

¾ cup dry breadcrumbs
1 cup finely chopped tart apple
1 tablespoon finely chopped yellow
   onion
½ teaspoon salt
¼ teaspoon freshly ground black
   pepper
1 teaspoon poultry seasoning
2 tablespoons butter, melted

4 (1¾-inch thick) double center-cut
   pork chops, well trimmed
¼ cup all-purpose flour
3 tablespoons vegetable oil
¾ cup white wine
¾ cup chicken broth
1 tablespoon cornstarch, optional
3 tablespoons water, optional
4 ounces mushrooms, thinly sliced

Combine breadcrumbs and next 6 ingredients in a large bowl. Mix well. Cut a slit in each chop to form a pocket. Fill pockets with equal amounts of stuffing and secure each with a toothpick. Reserve extra stuffing. Dredge chops on both sides in flour and shake off excess. Heat oil in a Dutch oven. When very hot, add chops and brown on each side for 3 minutes. Pour wine and broth over chops. Reduce heat, cover, and simmer 1 hour, 30 minutes. After 1 hour, add reserved stuffing. If sauce needs thickening, blend cornstarch and water and gradually stir into Dutch oven. Add mushrooms and cook and stir 3 minutes. Arrange chops on a deep, heated platter. Place extra stuffing on chops and top with sauce. Yields 4 servings.

Pork Chops With Wild Rice

6 (¾ to 1-inch thick) rib pork chops, well trimmed
3 tablespoons bacon fat or vegetable oil
1 teaspoon salt
½ teaspoon black pepper
¾ cup finely chopped celery

½ cup finely chopped yellow onion
¼ cup finely chopped bell pepper
8 ounces mushrooms, thinly sliced
2 beef bouillon cubes
2 cups cooked wild rice
⅓ cup heavy cream
1 tablespoon minced fresh parsley

Pat chops dry with paper towels. Heat fat in a large skillet. When very hot, add chops and brown on each side for 3 minutes. Remove chops and season with salt and pepper. Discard all but 2 tablespoons pan drippings. Reduce heat and add celery and next 3 ingredients to skillet. Sauté 3 minutes. Add bouillon cubes, crush, and stir to dissolve. Spread rice in an 8X12 inch baking dish. Place chops, overlapping slightly, on rice. Cover with sautéed vegetables. Pour cream around edge. Cover with foil and bake at 350° for 30 minutes. Uncover and bake 30 minutes longer. Sprinkle with parsley and serve. Yields 4 to 6 servings.

Spiced Ham Loaf with Creamy Horseradish Sauce

Ham Loaf
1 tablespoon unflavored gelatin
1¼ cups water, divided
½ cup lemon juice
2 tablespoons Worcestershire sauce
2 cups ground ham
2 tablespoons mayonnaise
1 tablespoon horseradish

1 tablespoon chopped pimiento
¼ teaspoon Dijon mustard
⅛ teaspoon ground cloves
⅛ teaspoon nutmeg
1 teaspoon seasoned salt
⅛ teaspoon cayenne pepper

Creamy Horseradish Sauce
1½ tablespoons horseradish
1 tablespoon lemon juice

¼ teaspoon salt
½ cup heavy cream, whipped

Sprinkle gelatin over ¼ cup water in a bowl. Do not stir. Let soak 5 minutes or until water is absorbed. In a saucepan, combine remaining 1 cup water and lemon juice. Heat just to a boil. Stir into gelatin until thoroughly mixed. Add Worcestershire sauce. Chill until slightly thickened. Stir in ham and next 8 ingredients. Mix well. Pour into a small, greased loaf pan and chill until firm. Unmold and cut into thin slices. Serve with horseradish sauce. To make sauce, fold horseradish, lemon juice, and salt into cream. Yields 8 to 10 servings.

Glazed Party Ham

1 (10 to 14-pound) whole cooked
   ham, bone-in
1½ cups peach preserves
whole cloves

2 cups Burgundy
1 bay leaf
½ cup packed light brown sugar

Place ham, fat-side up, in a deep roasting pan. Using a knife, score fat ¼-inch deep in a diamond pattern. Spoon preserves over surface and stud with cloves. Pour wine into pan and add bay leaf. Cover and bake at 350° for 30 minutes. Uncover and sprinkle with brown sugar. Continue to bake, uncovered, for 30 minutes, basting with pan juices once or twice. Transfer ham to a large platter. Cool and refrigerate 24 hours. Yields 20 to 30 servings.

Baked Ham with Guava Jelly Glaze

1 (5 to 7-pound) cooked ham, boned
2 cups guava jelly

½ cup Dijon mustard

Cut ham into ¼-inch thick slices and tie loosely. Place, fat-side up, in a shallow roasting pan. Heat jelly and mustard in a saucepan over low heat until a liquid consistency. Pour half over ham, allowing mixture to run between slices. Bake at 350° for 60 minutes, basting every 20 minutes with remaining mixture. Transfer ham to a heated platter and let stand 15 minutes. Discard string. Pour pan juices and any remaining jelly mixture into a heated sauceboat and serve with ham. Yields 12 to 14 servings.

Sag Gosht

2 pounds boneless lamb shoulder or
   leg, well trimmed
¼ cup all-purpose flour
3 tablespoons vegetable oil
1 cup finely chopped yellow onion
3 large cloves garlic, minced

2 (10-ounce) packages frozen
   chopped spinach, cooked and
   drained
2 cups sliced artichoke bottoms
1 teaspoon ground ginger
½ teaspoon turmeric
1½ teaspoons salt
1 teaspoon black pepper

Cut lamb into 1-inch cubes. Pat dry with paper towels. Dredge meat in flour and shake off excess. Heat oil in a Dutch oven. In batches, add lamb and brown on all sides. Remove lamb with a slotted spoon. Add onion to Dutch oven and sauté 3 minutes. Add garlic and sauté 2 minutes. Return lamb to Dutch oven. Mix in spinach and remaining 5 ingredients. Reduce heat, cover, and cook 30 minutes. Yields 6 servings.

Roast Leg of Lamb with Chutney Sauce

Lamb
1 (4-pound) leg of lamb, boned, rolled, and tied
1 teaspoon salt

½ teaspoon black pepper
½ teaspoon powdered rosemary

Chutney Sauce
1 stick butter
1½ cups Indian chutney, puréed
¼ cup soy sauce

½ teaspoon powdered rosemary
2 cloves garlic, pressed

Season lamb with salt, pepper, and rosemary. Place in a shallow roasting pan, fat-side up. To prepare sauce, melt butter in a saucepan. Add chutney and remaining 3 ingredients. Simmer and stir 3 minutes. Brush meat with a small amount of sauce. Bake at 325° for 1 hour, 45 minutes. Remove from oven and pour remaining sauce over lamb. Increase temperature to 400° and bake 10 minutes. Transfer lamb to a carving board, cover with foil, and let stand 10 minutes. Carve into thin slices and arrange on a heated serving platter. Pour sauce over lamb or serve in a heated sauceboat. Yields 6 servings.

Rack of Lamb

2 (8-rib) racks of lamb, ribs cracked, bones shortened and cleaned, well trimmed
2 tablespoons olive oil
3 tablespoons Dijon mustard
2 cloves garlic, pressed

½ teaspoon powdered rosemary
½ teaspoon powdered thyme
½ teaspoon salt
½ teaspoon black pepper
2 watercress or parsley bouquets

Place lamb in a large, shallow roasting pan, meat-side up. Cover rib tips with foil to prevent burning. Using a knife, score thin layer of fat ¼-inch deep in a diamond pattern. Combine oil and next 6 ingredients in a bowl. Brush over lamb. Insert a meat thermometer. Roast at 450° for 35 minutes or until thermometer registers 150° for rare, 40 to 45 minutes or 160° for medium rare, or 45 to 50 minutes or 170° for medium. Transfer to a heated serving platter and remove foil. Arrange racks facing each other with ribs interlaced. Let stand 8 to 10 minutes. Garnish between racks with watercress bouquets. Yields 8 servings.

Butterflied Leg of Lamb

1 (6-pound) leg of lamb, boned
   and butterflied
1 cup olive oil
½ cup red wine vinegar
2 tablespoons lemon juice
⅔ cup coarsely chopped yellow
   onion
2 cloves garlic, pressed

1 bay leaf, crumbled
1 tablespoon Dijon mustard
1 tablespoon dried rosemary
1 tablespoon dried marjoram
½ teaspoon dried basil
½ teaspoon dried thyme
1 teaspoon salt
1 teaspoon black pepper

Make a series of small incisions in lamb so meat will lie as flat as possible. Place in a large, shallow pan. In a bowl, combine oil and remaining 12 ingredients to make a marinade. Mix well and pour over lamb. Cover tightly with foil and refrigerate at least 12 hours, turning several times. Remove lamb from refrigerator at least 60 minutes prior to cooking. Remove lamb from marinade and dry with paper towels. Place marinade in a saucepan and bring to a boil. Reduce heat to low and keep warm. Place lamb in a pan, fat-side down. Broil 4 to 5 inches from heat for 15 minutes. Turn, baste with marinade, and broil 20 minutes. Transfer to a carving board, cover loosely with foil, and let stand 15 minutes. Carve diagonally across the grain into thin slices. Yields 8 to 10 servings.

Lamb Chops With Herbs

1 egg, lightly beaten
1 teaspoon salt
½ teaspoon black pepper
2 teaspoons minced fresh parsley
½ teaspoon powdered rosemary
½ teaspoon powdered thyme

8 (1 to 1½-inch thick) loin lamb
   chops, well trimmed
4 tablespoons butter
½ cup heavy cream
⅛ teaspoon sage
1 tablespoon mint sauce

Combine egg and next 5 ingredients in a bowl. Mix well and brush over both sides of chops. Cover chops and let stand 60 minutes at room temperature. Melt butter in a large skillet. Add chops and cook 8 minutes on each side. Transfer to a heated platter and keep warm. Add cream, sage, and mint sauce to skillet. Cook and stir 3 to 4 minutes or until sauce thickens. Pour over chops and serve immediately. Yields 4 servings.

Lamb Curry

Entrée

4 pounds boneless lamb shoulder or
   leg, well trimmed
1 cup golden raisins
1 cup grated coconut
2 cups water, divided
5 tablespoons vegetable oil, divided
1 teaspoon salt
1 cup coarsely chopped yellow
   onion
5 cloves garlic, coarsely chopped
1¼ cups chicken broth

⅔ cup Indian chutney
¼ cup curry powder
2 tablespoons coriander seed
¼ teaspoon mace
¼ teaspoon cayenne pepper
¼ teaspoon ground cloves
¼ teaspoon cinnamon
4 chicken bouillon cubes
4 cups steamed rice
poppadums (plain Indian curry
   biscuits), optional

Condiments

1 cup Indian chutney
1 cup finely chopped peanuts
1 cup finely chopped red onion
1 cup finely chopped green onion
   tops
1 cup finely chopped cucumber
1 cup finely chopped tomato
1 cup finely chopped bell pepper
1 cup finely chopped canned beets

1 cup mashed banana
1 cup chopped apple, sprinkled with
   lemon juice
1 cup unsweetened pineapple
   chunks
1 cup mandarin oranges
1 hard-cooked egg, finely grated
1 cup cooked and crumbled bacon

Cut lamb into 1-inch cubes. Pat dry with paper towels. In separate bowls, soak raisins and coconut in 1 cup water each for 60 minutes. Drain, reserving liquid. Blot coconut with paper towels. Heat 1 tablespoon oil in a skillet. Add coconut and cook, tossing frequently until golden brown. In a Dutch oven, heat 3 tablespoons oil. Add lamb and brown in small batches. Remove with a slotted spoon and season with salt. Reduce heat and add remaining 1 tablespoon oil to Dutch oven. Add onion and sauté 5 minutes. Add garlic and sauté 3 minutes. Remove from heat. Stir in broth. Add chutney and next 6 ingredients. Pour reserved raisin and coconut liquid into a saucepan and bring just to a boil. Remove from heat. Add bouillon cubes and stir to dissolve. Stir into curry mixture. Return lamb to Dutch oven and cover. Simmer 60 minutes or until lamb is tender. Serve with rice and condiments of choice. If serving poppadums, heat at 350° for 7 minutes and crumble over curry. Serve the raisins and coconut as condiments. Yields 8 to 10 servings.

Lamb Roll with Currant Sauce

Lamb Roll
1 (5-pound) leg of lamb, boned,
  rolled, and tied
1 teaspoon coarse salt
½ teaspoon crushed black pepper
½ teaspoon powdered rosemary
½ teaspoon powdered thyme

½ teaspoon sage
2 cloves garlic, cut into lengthwise
  slices
10 celery leaves
1 tablespoon all-purpose flour

Currant Sauce
1 stick butter
¾ cup currant jelly
¼ cup brandy

¼ cup ketchup
¼ cup fresh mint leaves
1 tablespoon orange zest

Remove strings and unroll lamb. Season with salt and next 4 ingredients. Add garlic and celery leaves. Re-roll meat, jelly roll fashion, and tie tightly at 1 to 2-inch intervals. Sprinkle with flour. Place lamb, fat-side up, in a shallow roasting pan. Bake at 325° for 2 hours, 30 minutes. Transfer to a carving board, cover with foil, and let stand 10 minutes. To make sauce, melt butter in a small saucepan. Add jelly and remaining 4 ingredients. Simmer and stir 10 minutes. Slice lamb and arrange on a heated serving platter. Pour sauce over lamb or serve in a heated sauceboat. Yields 10 servings.

Moussaka

Make recipe several days in advance, if desired, preparing sauce and baking just prior to serving.

Entrée

1 (2 to 2½-pound) eggplant, unpeeled
4 teaspoons salt, divided
5 tablespoons olive oil, plus extra as needed, divided
2 cups finely chopped yellow onion
3 cloves garlic, minced
1 pound ground lamb

½ teaspoon dried oregano
½ teaspoon powdered thyme
½ cup red wine
1 tomato, peeled, seeded, and chopped
⅔ cup tomato sauce
2 egg whites, room temperature
½ cup dry breadcrumbs, divided

Béchamel Sauce

2 tablespoons butter
2 tablespoons all-purpose flour
½ teaspoon salt

1½ cups milk, heated
2 egg yolks, beaten
½ teaspoon nutmeg

Cut eggplant lengthwise into ¼-inch thick slices. Sprinkle with 3 teaspoons salt and drain on paper towels for 30 minutes. Pat dry with paper towels. Heat 3 tablespoons oil in a large skillet. Add eggplant and brown on both sides, adding extra oil as needed. Drain on paper towels. In a separate skillet, heat 2 tablespoons oil. Add onion and sauté 4 minutes. Add garlic and sauté 2 minutes. Stir in lamb, remaining 1 teaspoon salt, oregano, and next 4 ingredients. Cover and simmer 30 minutes. Remove from heat and cool slightly. Whisk in egg whites. Add ¼ cup breadcrumbs and mix well. Place remaining ¼ cup breadcrumbs in a 2-quart rectangular casserole dish. Alternate layers of eggplant and lamb mixture, ending with eggplant. To make sauce, melt butter in a saucepan. Stir in flour until smooth. Add salt and gradually stir in milk. Cook and stir until sauce is thick and smooth. Reduce to very low heat. Mix some sauce into egg yolk in a thin stream. Return mixture to saucepan and add nutmeg. Blend well and pour over eggplant. Bake at 350° for 60 minutes or until top is puffed and golden. Cool 20 minutes before cutting into squares. Yields 6 servings.

Chicken and Sausage Jambalaya

1 small frying chicken
1 stalk celery with leaves
1 onion, halved
3 cloves garlic, divided
2 cups dry converted long-grain rice
1 pound smoked sausage, cut into
  ½-inch slices
1 pound ham, cubed
4 tablespoons butter

1 cup chopped yellow onion
¾ cup chopped bell pepper
¼ cup chopped fresh parsley
1 (6-ounce) can tomato paste
1 large bay leaf
¼ teaspoon dried thyme
2 teaspoons salt
½ teaspoon black pepper
¼ teaspoon Tabasco sauce

Place chicken in a large pot and cover with water. Add celery, onion, and 1 clove garlic and boil 60 minutes or until tender. Strain broth and reserve. Remove chicken meat from bone and cut into bite-size pieces. Cook rice in 5 cups of reserved broth for 25 minutes or until all liquid is absorbed. Fry sausage and ham in a Dutch oven for 3 to 5 minutes or until lightly browned. Remove meat and set aside. Add butter and next 3 ingredients and sauté 3 minutes or until tender. Add chicken, sausage, and ham. Mince remaining 2 cloves garlic. Add minced garlic, tomato paste, and remaining 5 ingredients to Dutch oven. Mix in rice. Cook over low heat for 15 minutes, stirring frequently. Remove bay leaf and serve. Yields 8 to 10 servings.

Chicken Trièste

6 chicken breasts
½ teaspoon salt, divided
½ teaspoon black pepper, divided
⅛ teaspoon dried thyme
4 tablespoons butter

½ cup sliced green onions
8 ounces fresh mushrooms, sliced
1 cup dry white wine
½ teaspoon dried tarragon
1 cup sour cream

Pat chicken dry. Season with ¼ teaspoon salt, ¼ teaspoon pepper, and thyme. Melt butter in a large skillet. Add chicken and brown. Remove chicken and set aside. Add onions and mushrooms to skillet and sauté. Mix in remaining ¼ teaspoon salt, remaining ¼ teaspoon pepper, wine, and tarragon. Return chicken to skillet and simmer 45 minutes. Transfer chicken and vegetables using a slotted spoon to a warm platter. Boil pan juices 3 minutes. Remove from heat and cool a few minutes. Add sour cream and mix well. Cook, stirring frequently, until hot, but do not boil. Pour sauce over chicken and serve immediately. Yields 6 servings.

Chicken Diablo

8 chicken breasts, skinned and boned	3 tablespoons Dijon mustard
½ teaspoon salt	1 teaspoon Worcestershire sauce
¼ teaspoon black pepper	1½ cups breadcrumbs
3 tablespoons dry white wine	4 tablespoons butter
	1 cup vegetable oil

Place chicken breasts between sheets of wax paper and pound lightly to flatten. Sprinkle with salt and pepper. In a small bowl, combine wine, mustard, and Worcestershire sauce. Brush chicken on all sides with mustard mixture, then roll in breadcrumbs. Heat butter and oil in a large skillet over medium heat. Add chicken and brown on both sides until fully cooked. Yields 8 servings.

Chicken À L'Orange

1½ teaspoons salt, divided	1 medium onion, thinly sliced into rings
¼ teaspoon black pepper	4 thin slices bell pepper, cut into rings
¼ teaspoon paprika	2 cups orange juice
¼ cup all-purpose flour	¼ cup dry sherry
1 (3-pound) frying chicken, cut into pieces	2 tablespoons packed brown sugar
2 tablespoons plus 1 teaspoon butter, divided	2 teaspoons orange zest
1 tablespoon vegetable oil	¼ cup water
1 cup sliced mushrooms	2 tablespoons cornstarch
½ teaspoon Worcestershire sauce	

Combine ½ teaspoon salt and next 3 ingredients in a shallow dish. Roll chicken in flour mixture. Heat 2 tablespoons butter and oil in a skillet. Add chicken and cook until lightly browned. Arrange in a single layer in a shallow baking dish. Sauté mushrooms in remaining 1 teaspoon butter and Worcestershire sauce. Place mushrooms, onion, and bell pepper over chicken. In a saucepan, combine remaining 1 teaspoon salt, juice, and next 3 ingredients. Bring to a boil and remove from heat. Blend water and cornstarch and stir into juice mixture. Simmer 5 minutes or until mixture thickens, stirring frequently. Pour over chicken and bake at 350° for 60 minutes, basting with pan juices every 20 minutes. Yields 4 servings.

Creole Chicken Pie

Chicken and Broth
1 (3-pound) frying chicken
4 cups water
½ teaspoon poultry seasoning
½ teaspoon salt
¼ teaspoon black pepper
1 onion, quartered
2 stalks celery, sliced

Pastry
2 cups all-purpose flour
1 teaspoon salt
⅔ cup vegetable shortening
5 tablespoons ice water
1 egg yolk, beaten

Sauce
⅓ cup vegetable oil
½ cup all-purpose flour
¾ cup chopped celery
¼ cup chopped bell pepper
¾ cup chopped onion
½ cup chopped green onions
1 clove garlic, minced
1½ cups chicken broth, heated
1 bay leaf
¼ teaspoon Tabasco sauce
1½ teaspoons salt
¼ teaspoon black pepper
¼ teaspoon dried thyme
1 teaspoon Worcestershire sauce
1 pound mushrooms, sliced
2 tablespoons butter
¼ cup finely chopped fresh parsley
2 teaspoons chopped pimiento

Combine chicken and next 6 ingredients in a large saucepan. Simmer 45 to 60 minutes or until tender. Remove chicken meat from bone, dice, and reserve. Strain broth, skim fat, and reserve. To make pastry, combine flour and salt in a bowl. Cut in shortening with a pastry blender or with 2 knives until mixture resembles corn-meal. Sprinkle with ice water and toss lightly with a fork. Add extra ice water if needed for dough to bind together. Chill. To prepare sauce, heat oil in a skillet. Gradually add flour and cook and stir until dark brown. Add celery and next 4 ingredients. Cook 5 minutes, stirring frequently. Slowly stir in broth until smooth. Add bay leaf and next 5 ingredients. Simmer 20 minutes, stirring occasionally. In a small skillet, sauté mushrooms in butter. Add mushrooms, parsley, pimiento, and reserved chicken to sauce. Simmer 20 minutes. Remove bay leaf. To assemble pie, divide chilled dough in half. Roll each half between 2 sheets of wax paper until dough is ½-inch larger than a 9-inch pie pan. Line pan with 1 sheet of dough and trim excess. Fill with sauce mixture. Top with second sheet of dough. Trim excess dough and pinch edges to seal. Brush top with egg yolk and place on a baking sheet. Bake at 425° for 30 minutes. If necessary, brown under the broiler. Yields 6 servings.

Chicken with Oyster Dressing

Oyster Dressing
2 tablespoons butter
1 clove garlic, minced
¼ cup finely chopped onion
2 tablespoons finely chopped green onions
1 tablespoon finely chopped bell pepper
¼ cup finely chopped celery
3 tablespoons minced fresh parsley

1 cup oysters, drained and chopped, ½ cup liquid reserved
1 cup plain breadcrumbs
¾ teaspoon salt
¼ teaspoon black pepper
⅛ teaspoon cayenne pepper
⅛ teaspoon dried thyme
1 tablespoon lemon juice
1 teaspoon Worcestershire sauce

Chicken
2 (1½ pound) frying chickens or Cornish game hens, halved
2⅔ tablespoons butter, divided

½ cup water
½ teaspoon salt
¼ teaspoon black pepper

Oyster Dressing
2 tablespoons breadcrumbs

To make dressing, melt butter in a large skillet. Add garlic and next 5 ingredients and sauté 5 minutes. Add oysters and sauté 3 minutes. Remove from heat. Mix in reserved oyster liquid, breadcrumbs and next 6 ingredients. Arrange chicken, skin-side up, in a single layer in a large baking dish. Place 1 teaspoon butter on each half. Add water and bake at 375° for 20 minutes. Broil until skin is lightly browned. Sprinkle with salt and pepper. Place skin-side down in baking dish. Fill each cavity with oyster dressing. Sprinkle with breadcrumbs and dot each half with 1 teaspoon butter. Bake 25 minutes. Broil until brown. Yields 4 servings.

Chicken Carondelet

¾ cup finely chopped onion
1 clove garlic, minced
5 tablespoons butter, divided
¼ cup all-purpose flour
1½ cups chicken broth, heated
¼ cup dry white wine
1 teaspoon salt
¼ teaspoon black pepper

⅛ teaspoon Tabasco sauce
8 ounces mushrooms, sliced
3 cups diced cooked chicken
6 slices bacon, cooked and
    crumbled
½ cup sour cream
6 patty shells, warmed

Sauté onion and garlic in 4 tablespoons butter until softened. Add flour and cook 3 minutes, stirring constantly. Slowly add broth and whisk until smooth. Add wine and next 3 ingredients. Simmer 5 minutes, stirring occasionally. In a small skillet, sauté mushrooms in remaining 1 tablespoon butter. Add mushrooms, chicken, bacon, and sour cream to sauce. Simmer 20 minutes, stirring occasionally. Do not allow sauce to boil. Serve in patty shells. Yields 6 servings.

Chicken Curry

1 cup chopped onion, divided
¾ teaspoon salt, divided
½ teaspoon black pepper, divided
4 chicken breasts
3 cups water
½ cup chopped celery
½ teaspoon poultry seasoning
4 tablespoons butter

2 tablespoons all-purpose flour
1½ teaspoons curry powder
2 tablespoons mango chutney
2 tablespoons black currant jelly
1 cup chopped apple
¼ cup raisins
2 cups steamed rice

Combine ½ cup onion, ½ teaspoon salt, ¼ teaspoon pepper, and next 4 ingredients in a saucepan. Simmer 30 minutes or until tender. Skin, debone, and chop chicken. Reserve broth. Melt butter in a skillet. Add remaining ½ cup onion and sauté until soft. Blend in flour and curry powder and cook 3 minutes, stirring constantly. Heat broth and add slowly to skillet, stirring until well blended. Bring to a boil. Reduce heat and simmer 5 minutes or until thickened. Blend in chutney and jelly. Season with remaining ¼ teaspoon salt and remaining ¼ teaspoon pepper. Add chicken to sauce. Cover and simmer 10 minutes. Stir in apple and raisins. Cover and simmer 10 minutes longer. Serve over rice. Yields 4 servings.

Chicken and Garlic Stew

6 chicken thighs
¾ teaspoon salt, divided
¾ teaspoon white pepper, divided
3 cups water
20 cloves garlic, separated and
  unpeeled
2 tablespoons olive oil

½ cup chopped celery, including
  leaves
½ cup chopped fresh parsley
⅛ teaspoon dried thyme
1 cup dry white wine
French bread, heated

Season chicken with ¼ teaspoon salt and ¼ teaspoon pepper. Bring water to a boil. Add garlic and cook 1 minute. Drain and rinse under cold water and peel. Coat the bottom of a shallow 2-quart casserole dish with oil. Add garlic, remaining ½ teaspoon salt, remaining ½ teaspoon pepper, celery, parsley, and thyme. Stir in wine. Add chicken, skin-side down, and baste. Cover tightly and bake at 375° for 35 minutes. Turn chicken, baste, and bake 40 minutes longer. Serve with French bread. Yields 4 servings.

Chicken Fillets in Wine Sauce

6 chicken breasts, skinned and
  boned
½ teaspoon salt
¼ teaspoon black pepper

½ cup all-purpose flour
5 tablespoons butter, divided
1 tablespoon vegetable oil
⅔ cup dry white wine

To prepare chicken fillets, separate tenderloins from breasts and remove tendons. Place large portion of breasts on a cutting board, skinned-side up. Press down on chicken with palm of hand and halve with a knife blade running parallel to cutting board. Each large portion should be divided in 2 equal portions; each breast will yield 3 fillets. Sprinkle with salt and pepper. Dredge in flour. In a large skillet, heat 3 tablespoons butter and oil. Add chicken in a single layer and sauté until lightly browned. Remove chicken and keep warm. Add wine to skillet. Cook over high heat for 2 minutes or until sauce thickens slightly. Stir to loosen pan drippings. Remove from heat and add 1 tablespoon butter. When melted, add remaining 1 tablespoon butter and stir until melted. Pour sauce over chicken and serve immediately. Yields 4 servings.

Chicken Bonne Femme

1 frying chicken, cut into pieces
1½ teaspoons salt, divided
½ teaspoon black pepper, divided
½ cup vegetable oil
2 large baking potatoes, thinly sliced

2 tablespoons butter
1 large white onion, thinly sliced
8 ounces mushrooms, sliced
1 tablespoon Parmesan cheese
1 teaspoon chopped fresh parsley

Dry chicken thoroughly and season with ½ teaspoon salt and ¼ teaspoon pepper. Heat oil in a large skillet. Add chicken and cook until done. Drain on paper towels and keep warm. Add potatoes to oil in skillet and cook until browned. Drain potatoes and keep warm. Discard oil in skillet. Add butter, onion, and mushrooms and sauté until onion is softened. Drain. Place chicken on a heated platter. Arrange potatoes around chicken. Spread mushrooms and onion over chicken. Season with remaining 1 teaspoon salt and remaining ¼ teaspoon pepper. Sprinkle with cheese and parsley. Yields 4 servings.

Chicken Provençal

½ cup all-purpose flour
2½ teaspoons salt, divided
½ teaspoon black pepper, divided
1 frying chicken, cut into pieces
½ cup olive oil
½ cup chopped bell pepper
12 pearl onions, peeled
¼ cup chopped green onions
4 cloves garlic, minced
2 chicken bouillon cubes

1 cup boiling water
3 tablespoons chopped fresh
  parsley, divided
½ cup dry white wine
1 bay leaf
6 medium tomatoes, peeled, seeded,
  and cut into strips
½ cup black olives, halved
¼ teaspoon dried thyme
¼ teaspoon Tabasco sauce

Combine flour, ½ teaspoon salt, and ¼ teaspoon pepper in a shallow dish. Dry chicken thoroughly and roll in flour mixture. Heat oil in a large skillet. Add chicken and brown slowly. Transfer chicken to a shallow 2-quart casserole dish. Discard all but 1 tablespoon of oil in skillet. Add bell pepper and next 3 ingredients and sauté 5 minutes. Dissolve bouillon cubes in boiling water. Add bouillon, remaining 2 teaspoons salt, remaining ¼ teaspoon pepper, 2 tablespoons parsley, and remaining 6 ingredients. Simmer 5 minutes. Pour over chicken and cover. Bake at 350° for 45 minutes. Remove bay leaf and garnish with remaining 1 tablespoon parsley. Yields 4 servings.

Tarragon Chicken

6 chicken breasts, skinned and
  boned
4 tablespoons butter, divided
¼ cup brandy
¼ cup minced onion
2 tablespoons all-purpose flour
1 tablespoon tomato paste

½ cup chicken broth
¾ cup dry white wine
¾ teaspoon dried tarragon, crushed,
  or 1 tablespoon chopped fresh
½ teaspoon salt
¼ teaspoon black pepper
dash of Tabasco sauce

Brown chicken in 3 tablespoons butter in a large skillet. Warm brandy, ignite, and pour over chicken. When flames stop, transfer chicken to a shallow 2-quart casserole dish. Reduce brandy until it barely coats skillet. Add remaining 1 tablespoon butter and onion and sauté 3 minutes. Add flour and cook 3 minutes, stirring constantly. Slowly stir in tomato paste, broth, and wine. Simmer until sauce is smooth, stirring constantly. Add tarragon and remaining 3 ingredients. Cover and bake at 350° for 30 minutes or until tender. Yields 6 servings.

Chicken Crêpes

2 whole chickens
2½ teaspoons salt, divided
2 onions, quartered
½ cup coarsely chopped celery tops
2 carrots, chopped
1 stick plus 3 tablespoons butter
1 cup all-purpose flour
3½ cups chicken broth, heated

½ cup chopped green onions
4 ounces mushrooms, chopped
¼ cup dry sherry
¼ cup finely chopped fresh parsley
¼ teaspoon white pepper
¼ teaspoon Tabasco sauce
24 crêpes (page 218)
1½ cups hollandaise sauce (page 66)

Place chickens in a large pot and cover with water. Add 1½ teaspoons salt and next 3 ingredients. Simmer 45 minutes or until tender. Skin and debone chicken and dice meat. Strain broth, skim fat, and reserve. Melt 9 tablespoons butter in a large skillet. Blend in flour and cook and stir 3 minutes without browning. Remove from heat and slowly blend in broth. Return to low heat and simmer 5 minutes or until smooth, stirring frequently. Sauté onions and mushrooms in remaining 2 tablespoons butter in a small skillet. Add to sauce along with diced chicken, remaining 1 teaspoon salt, sherry, and next 3 ingredients. Mix gently. Fill each crêpe with ⅓ cup chicken mixture. Roll and place seam-side down in a shallow 3-quart baking dish. Cover and bake at 350° for 30 minutes. Serve with hollandaise sauce. Yields 12 servings.

Chicken Cleveland

10 chicken breasts, skinned and
    boned
1 stick butter, divided
6 tablespoons dry sherry
½ teaspoon salt
⅛ teaspoon black pepper

8 ounces fresh mushrooms, sliced
    and sautéed
1 clove garlic, pressed
¼ cup all-purpose flour
2 cups chicken broth, heated
½ cup dry white wine
1 cup slivered almonds, toasted

In a skillet, brown chicken breasts in batches in 6 tablespoons butter. Transfer breasts as they get done to a heated platter. When all are browned, return breasts to skillet. Warm sherry in a small pan. Ignite and pour over chicken. When flames stop, transfer chicken to a plate and sprinkle with salt and pepper. Melt remaining 2 tablespoons butter in skillet. Add mushrooms and garlic and sauté 3 minutes or until lightly browned. Add flour and cook 3 minutes, stirring constantly. Remove from heat and pour in broth. Return to heat and stir constantly until sauce is smooth. Slowly stir in wine until sauce begins to bubble. Turn chicken and simmer 20 to 25 minutes or until tender. Sprinkle almonds over chicken when ready to serve.

Rolled Chicken Breasts

8 ounces mushrooms, sliced
1 stick butter, divided
6 chicken breasts, skinned and
    boned
6 thin slices ham
6 slices Swiss cheese
6 tablespoons all-purpose flour

½ teaspoon salt, divided
½ teaspoon black pepper, divided
1 tablespoon vegetable oil
1 cup chicken broth, heated
¼ cup dry white wine
Tabasco sauce to taste
¼ cup slivered almonds, toasted

Sauté mushrooms in 2 tablespoons butter. Pound chicken breasts until flattened to ¼-inch thick. Place a slice of ham and a slice of cheese on each breast. Starting at narrow end, roll toward wider end. Secure with toothpicks. Combine flour, ¼ teaspoon salt, and ¼ teaspoon pepper in a shallow dish. Coat chicken in flour mixture. Reserve flour mixture. In a large skillet, heat 4 tablespoons butter and oil. Add chicken and brown. Transfer chicken to a greased, shallow 2-quart casserole dish in a single layer. Discard fat in skillet and add remaining 2 tablespoons butter. Gradually add 2 tablespoons of reserved flour mixture, stirring constantly until light brown. Slowly add broth, stirring constantly until smooth. Add remaining ¼ teaspoon salt, remaining ¼ teaspoon pepper, sautéed mushrooms, wine, and Tabasco sauce. Simmer 5 minutes. Pour over chicken and cover. Bake at 350° for 30 minutes. Sprinkle with almonds. Yields 6 servings.

Coq Au Vin

¼ pound thick-sliced bacon, cut into
   1-inch pieces
6 cups water
1 stick butter, divided
1 (3-pound) frying chicken, cut into
   pieces
1½ teaspoons salt, divided
½ teaspoon black pepper, divided
⅛ teaspoon dried thyme
24 pearl onions, peeled

2 cloves garlic, pressed
8 ounces fresh mushrooms, halved
⅓ cup brandy
2 cups red wine, preferably
   Burgundy
1 cup chicken broth
1 bay leaf
¼ cup all-purpose flour
2 teaspoons finely chopped fresh
   parsley

Simmer bacon in water for 10 minutes. Drain, rinse under cold water, and dry on paper towels. In a Dutch oven, sauté bacon in 4 tablespoons butter for 10 minutes. Dry chicken thoroughly and season with ½ teaspoon salt, ¼ teaspoon pepper, and thyme. Remove bacon with a slotted spoon. Add chicken, brown, and remove. Add onions and garlic, sauté 5 minutes, and remove. Add mushrooms and sauté 3 minutes. Remove mushrooms and discard butter. Warm brandy in a small saucepan. Remove from heat, ignite, and pour into Dutch oven. When flames stop, add remaining 1 teaspoon salt, remaining ¼ teaspoon pepper, wine, broth, and bay leaf. Return bacon, chicken, and sautéed vegetables to pot. Cook until sauce starts to bubble. Reduce heat and cover. Simmer 45 minutes. Remove chicken and onions from Dutch oven. In a saucepan, melt remaining 4 tablespoons butter. Slowly add flour and cook and stir until roux is dark brown. Mix roux into sauce and remove bay leaf. Return chicken and onions to Dutch oven and simmer 15 minutes. Transfer to a deep serving dish and sprinkle with parsley. Yields 4 servings.

Lemon Chicken

4 chicken breasts, skinned and
   boned
2 tablespoons butter
1 tablespoon vegetable oil
2 tablespoons dry sherry
2 tablespoons lemon juice

¼ teaspoon salt
⅛ teaspoon black pepper
1 cup half-and-half
4 slices lemon, seeded for garnish
1 tablespoon minced fresh parsley
   for garnish

In a skillet, brown chicken in butter and oil. Remove chicken and discard fat from skillet. Add sherry and next 3 ingredients. Simmer 2 minutes, stirring constantly. Remove from heat and slowly add half-and-half. Heat until sauce starts to bubble. Add chicken and simmer 20 minutes or until tender. Transfer chicken to a serving dish and pour sauce over top. Garnish with lemon slices and parsley. Yields 4 servings.

Cold Chicken and Spaghetti

2 teaspoons salt, divided
4 chicken breasts
¼ teaspoon poultry seasoning
1 onion, quartered
1 stalk celery, chopped
8 ounces mushrooms, sliced
1 tablespoon lemon juice
6 ounces thin spaghetti, cooked
   al dente

¼ cup olive oil
2 tablespoons white wine vinegar
½ teaspoon Dijon mustard
½ cup chopped green onion tops
½ cup chopped celery
½ cup mayonnaise
⅛ teaspoon cayenne pepper
¼ teaspoon black pepper
¼ teaspoon paprika

Combine 1 teaspoon salt and next 4 ingredients in a large pot. Cover with water and simmer 45 minutes or until tender. Skin and debone chicken and dice meat. Refrigerate 60 minutes. Sprinkle mushrooms with lemon juice. Place spaghetti in a colander and rinse under cold water. Transfer to a 3-quart bowl. In a small bowl, beat together oil and vinegar. Pour over spaghetti and toss lightly until well coated. Return to colander to drain. Combine chicken, mushrooms, mustard, and next 3 ingredients in 3-quart bowl. Add spaghetti, remaining 1 teaspoon salt, cayenne pepper, and black pepper. Toss well. Sprinkle with paprika. Refrigerate 4 to 6 hours. Yields 4 servings.

Chicken and Wild Rice

2 (3-pound) frying chickens
1 cup water
1 cup dry sherry
2 stalks celery
1½ teaspoons salt
1 yellow onion, quartered
½ teaspoon curry powder
¼ teaspoon black pepper

¼ teaspoon poultry seasoning
2 (6-ounce) packages long-grain and
   wild rice mix
1 stick butter
1 pound mushrooms, sliced
1 cup sour cream
1 (10¾-ounce) can condensed
   cream of mushroom soup

Combine chickens and next 8 ingredients in a large pot. Cover and simmer until chicken is tender, turning chickens every 15 minutes. Skin and debone chickens and cube meat. Strain broth and use to cook rice mix according to package directions. Add water to make required amount of liquid. In a small skillet, melt butter. Add mushrooms and sauté. In a 4-quart casserole dish, combine chicken, rice, mushrooms, sour cream, and soup. Cover and bake at 350° for 20 to 25 minutes. Yields 12 servings.

Mistletoe Chicken

Chicken
4 chicken breasts
4 cups water
1 onion, quartered
1 stalk celery, chopped

½ teaspoon salt
¼ teaspoon black pepper
¼ teaspoon poultry seasoning

Sauce
1 cup chopped green onions
1 clove garlic, minced
2 tablespoons minced fresh parsley
1 stick plus 1 tablespoon butter,
  divided
7 tablespoons all-purpose flour
¼ cup dry sherry
½ teaspoon salt

¼ teaspoon black pepper
⅛ teaspoon Tabasco sauce
½ teaspoon Worcestershire sauce
8 ounces mushrooms, sliced
1 pound shrimp, cooked, peeled,
  and deveined
6 patty shells, warmed

Combine chicken and next 6 ingredients in a saucepan. Simmer 45 minutes or until tender. Skin and debone chicken and dice meat. Strain broth, skim fat, and reserve 3¼ cups. To prepare sauce, in a Dutch oven, sauté onions, garlic, and parsley in 7 tablespoons butter until softened. Gradually add flour and cook and stir about 3 minutes. Whisk in reserved broth until smooth. Add sherry and next 4 ingredients. Simmer 5 minutes, stirring occasionally. In a separate pan, sauté mushrooms in remaining 2 tablespoons butter. Add mushrooms, chicken, and shrimp to sauce. Simmer 10 minutes. Serve in patty shells. Yields 6 servings.

Chicken and Artichoke Casserole

2 teaspoons salt, divided
1 (3-pound) frying chicken
4 cups water
2 cups chopped celery, including
  leaves
1 large onion, quartered
3 large artichokes
8 ounces mushrooms, sliced
7 tablespoons butter, divided
½ cup chopped green onions
1 clove garlic, pressed

¼ cup all-purpose flour
1 cup half-and-half, heated
1 cup milk, heated
¼ teaspoon white pepper
1 teaspoon Worcestershire sauce
¼ teaspoon Tabasco sauce
2 tablespoons freshly grated
  Parmesan cheese
¼ cup grated Swiss cheese
2 tablespoons breadcrumbs

Combine 1 teaspoon salt and next 4 ingredients in a large pot. Simmer 60 minutes. Skin and debone chicken and cube meat. Boil artichokes for 60 minutes in salted water. Drain. Scrape artichoke leaves and chop hearts. In a small skillet, sauté mushrooms in 2 tablespoons butter. Melt remaining 5 tablespoons butter in a large skillet. Add green onions, garlic, and artichoke scrapings and sauté 3 minutes. Add flour and cook and stir 3 minutes. Remove from heat and slowly add half-and-half and milk, stirring constantly until smooth. Heat sauce until it starts to bubble. Remove from heat and add remaining 1 teaspoon salt, pepper, and next 4 ingredients. Stir until cheese melts. Gently stir in chicken, artichoke heart, and mushrooms. Transfer to a greased 2-quart casserole dish and sprinkle with breadcrumbs. Bake at 350° for 30 minutes. Yields 4 servings.

Chicken and Rice Casserole

1 stick butter
½ cup finely chopped yellow onion
½ cup minced bell pepper
8 ounces mushrooms, sliced
¼ cup chopped fresh parsley
½ cup chopped celery
1 clove garlic, pressed
1 teaspoon dried thyme
1 teaspoon beau monde seasoning

1 teaspoon Worcestershire sauce
½ teaspoon Tabasco sauce
1 teaspoon salt
¼ teaspoon black pepper
1 cup sour cream
1½ cups chicken broth
3 cups diced cooked chicken
3 cups steamed rice
½ cup slivered almonds, toasted

Melt butter in a large skillet. Add onion, bell pepper, and mushrooms and sauté 10 minutes. Add parsley, celery, and garlic and cook 5 minutes. Mix in thyme and next 5 ingredients. Stir in sour cream. Slowly add broth. Fold in chicken and rice. Place mixture in a 2½-quart casserole dish and sprinkle with almonds. Bake at 375° for 30 minutes. Yields 10 servings.

Persian Chicken with Peaches

⅓ cup all-purpose flour
1¼ teaspoons salt
1 teaspoon black pepper
1¼ teaspoons dried marjoram
2 tablespoons finely chopped fresh
  parsley
4 chicken breasts
½ cup milk

2 tablespoons butter
¼ cup vegetable oil
¾ cup finely chopped onion
¼ cup lemon juice
1 tablespoon honey (optional)
1 cup peach syrup
8 canned peach halves

Combine flour and next 4 ingredients in a shallow dish. Dip chicken in milk, then roll in flour mixture. Reserve unused flour mixture. Heat butter and oil in a large skillet. Add chicken and brown until crisp. Transfer chicken, in a single layer, to a 2-quart baking dish. Add onion to skillet and sauté until softened. Remove onion using a slotted spoon and sprinkle over chicken. Add reserved flour mixture to skillet and brown. Add lemon juice, honey, and peach syrup. Cook 5 minutes or until slightly thickened, stirring frequently. Arrange peach halves on top of onion and chicken and cover with sauce. Bake at 350° for 45 minutes. Yields 4 servings.

Turkey Noodle Casserole

Casserole
8 ounces fine noodles, cooked and
  drained
4 tablespoons butter, melted
1 (4-ounce) can mushrooms, drained

2 cups diced cooked turkey
¾ teaspoon salt
¼ teaspoon black pepper

Sauce
4 tablespoons butter
¼ cup all-purpose flour
½ teaspoon salt
¼ teaspoon black pepper

2 cups chicken broth
½ cup freshly grated Parmesan
  cheese
1 cup grated Swiss cheese

Combine noodles and butter and transfer to a shallow 2-quart casserole dish. In a bowl, combine mushrooms and next 3 ingredients. Place mixture over noodles. To prepare sauce, melt butter in a saucepan. Blend in flour, salt, and pepper. Add broth and cook and stir 5 minutes or until thick and smooth. Add Parmesan cheese and mix well. Pour sauce over chicken and noodles. Sprinkle with Swiss cheese. Bake at 350° for 30 minutes. Yields 6 servings.

Duck Jambalaya

Duck Meat
2 large ducks
1 tablespoon salt
1 teaspoon black pepper

1 onion, quartered
2 stalks celery
1 bay leaf

Jambalaya
3 tablespoons bacon fat
3 tablespoons all-purpose flour
1 cup chopped bell pepper
2 medium onions, chopped
1 cup chopped green onions
2 tablespoons chopped fresh parsley
2 cloves garlic, minced

1 cup chopped celery
2 cups chicken broth
1 cup dry rice
2 teaspoons salt
½ teaspoon cayenne pepper
4 cups Duck Meat

Combine ducks and next 5 ingredients in a large pot. Cover with water and cook 1 hour, 30 minutes or until tender. Remove ducks and cool. Remove meat from bone and cut into bite-size pieces. This should equal about 4 cups. To prepare jambalaya, heat bacon fat in a large pot. Gradually add flour. Cook and stir until dark brown. Add bell pepper and next 5 ingredients and cook until soft. Add broth and remaining 4 ingredients. Bring to a boil. Reduce heat as low as possible and cover tightly. Cook 60 minutes, stirring occasionally. When rice is tender, un-cover and cook a few minutes to allow rice to steam dry. Yields 4 to 6 servings.

Doves Oporto

2 tablespoons butter
1 cup chopped onion
1½ cups all-purpose flour
4 teaspoons salt

2 teaspoons black pepper
16 doves, cleaned and washed
1 cup port or dry sherry

Melt butter in a large skillet. Add onion and sauté until lightly browned. Combine flour, salt, and pepper. Dust doves with flour mixture. Add to skillet and brown on all sides over high heat. Reduce heat and pour in port. Cover and simmer 20 minutes or until done, turning once. Add more port if needed. Transfer doves to a heated serving platter. Scrape brown bits from bottom and sides of skillet and stir. Pour over doves and serve. Yields 8 servings.

Quail Supreme

8 quail, cleaned and washed
salt and pepper to taste
6 tablespoons butter
8 green onions, chopped

½ cup dry sherry
2 cups chicken broth
1 cup heavy cream

Season quail inside and out with salt and pepper. Melt butter in a Dutch oven. Add quail and onions and brown. Pour sherry over quail and ignite. Stir over low heat until flame stops. Pour broth over quail. Bake at 350° for 10 minutes. Add cream and bake 20 minutes longer or until tender. Yields 4 servings.

Quail in Wine Sauce

8 quail, cleaned and washed
1 stick butter, melted
¾ cup dry red wine

¼ teaspoon salt
¼ teaspoon black pepper
¼ cup soy sauce

Lay 8 squares of foil on a counter top. Place 1 quail in the center of each square. Fold foil around quail, leaving an opening at the top. Combine butter and remaining 4 ingredients. Divide among quail and close foil tightly. Bake at 325° for 60 minutes. Yields 8 servings.

Marinated Doves Supreme

Marinade is also good with quail, duck breasts, and back strap of venison.

1 stick butter, melted
½ cup vegetable oil
⅓ cup lemon juice
¼ cup soy sauce
1 teaspoon dried oregano
1 tablespoon chopped fresh parsley

½ teaspoon salt
¼ teaspoon black pepper
1 clove garlic, minced
8 doves, cleaned and washed
1 cup water

Combine butter and next 8 ingredients. Pour over doves in a shallow baking dish. Cover and refrigerate overnight. Drain and reserve marinade. Add water to doves and bake at 375° for 30 minutes or until browned. Baste generously with reserved marinade. Cover and bake 15 minutes longer or until tender. Yields 4 servings.

Quail with Mushrooms

12 quail, cleaned, washed, and dried
5 tablespoons vegetable oil, divided
1½ teaspoons salt, divided
1½ teaspoons black pepper, divided
1½ sticks butter
½ cup all-purpose flour
½ cup finely chopped onion
½ cup finely chopped green onions
2 cloves garlic, minced

½ cup finely chopped fresh parsley
1 bay leaf
½ teaspoon dried thyme
1 cup chopped carrot
2 cups water
1 pound mushrooms, sliced
2 cups chicken broth
1 cup dry white wine

An hour before cooking, rub quail with 2 tablespoons oil. Season inside and out with ½ teaspoon salt and ½ teaspoon pepper. In a non-iron Dutch oven, brown quail in remaining 3 tablespoons oil. Transfer quail, breast-side down, to a deep baking pan. Cover and keep warm. Melt butter in Dutch oven. Slowly add flour and cook and stir until golden brown. Add remaining 1 teaspoon salt, remaining 1 teaspoon pepper, onion, and next 5 ingredients. Cook 15 minutes or until tender. Cook carrot in water for 10 minutes. Drain. Add carrot, mushrooms, broth, and wine to Dutch oven. Cook and stir 5 minutes. Remove bay leaf. Pour over quail and cover. Bake at 325° for 45 minutes. Yields 6 servings.

Doves with Curry

1 cup olive oil, divided
1 tablespoon soy sauce
¼ teaspoon salt
½ teaspoon black pepper
1 tablespoon wine vinegar
8 doves, cleaned and washed
2 cups water
1 tablespoon butter

¼ cup chopped white onion
2 cloves garlic, minced
⅓ cup chopped celery
⅓ cup chopped bell pepper
⅓ cup chopped green onions
1 small piece fresh ginger, chopped
1½ tablespoons Madras curry
  powder

Combine ½ cup oil and next 4 ingredients. Pour over doves in a shallow baking dish. Cover and refrigerate 3 hours or overnight. In a skillet, brown doves in remaining ½ cup oil. Transfer doves to a Dutch oven. Pour water in skillet and stir well. Pour over doves and stir with a wooden spoon. Melt butter in skillet. Add white onion and next 5 ingredients and sauté until browned. Blend in curry powder. Add to doves and cover. Simmer 1 hour, 30 minutes or until tender. Yields 4 servings.

Skillet-Simmered Doves

1 stick butter	½ teaspoon salt
2 cloves garlic	½ teaspoon black pepper
12 doves, cleaned and washed	toast points
cayenne pepper	

Melt butter in a large skillet. Add garlic. Sprinkle doves with cayenne pepper and brown in skillet. Season with salt and black pepper. Cover tightly and cook over low heat for 60 minutes. Serve on toast points. Yields 6 servings.

Louisiana Honey-Glazed Canard

4 small ducks, preferably teal or gray, cleaned and washed	1 teaspoon dried thyme
salt and pepper to taste	¾ cup honey
1½ quarts chicken broth	1 tablespoon cider vinegar
1 large onion, coarsely chopped	1 teaspoon dry mustard
2 bay leaves	4 slices bacon

Generously season ducks inside and out with salt and pepper. Combine broth and next 3 ingredients in a large Dutch oven. Bring to a boil and add ducks. Add extra broth if needed to cover ducks. Cover and simmer until tender. Transfer ducks, breast-side up, to a roasting pan. Combine honey, vinegar, and mustard. Baste ducks with honey mixture. Place a slice of bacon on each duck. Bake at 375° for 30 minutes or until bacon is crisp. Baste several times during final 15 minutes of baking. Transfer to a heated platter and brush with remaining sauce. Yields 4 servings.

Cold Duck Salad

5 ducks, cleaned and washed	2 bay leaves
2 tablespoons salt	½ cup chopped green onions
1 teaspoon black pepper	1 cup chopped celery
3 onions, quartered	2 cups mayonnaise
3 stalks celery	½ cup finely chopped chutney

Place ducks in a large pot and cover with water. Add salt and next 4 ingredients. Bring to a boil and simmer 60 minutes or until tender. Skin and debone ducks and cube meat. Chill. When cold, combine meat, green onions, and remaining 3 ingredients. Serve as an entrée or with crackers as an hors d'oeuvre. Yields 4 servings.

Wild Duck with Mushroom Stuffing

3 tablespoons butter
1 cup chopped mushrooms
1 cup chopped yellow onion
¼ cup chopped green onions
½ pound chicken livers, chopped
2 tablespoons chopped fresh parsley
4 slices bacon, cooked and
  crumbled
½ teaspoon salt, plus to taste

1 teaspoon black pepper, plus to
  taste
2 tablespoons dry sherry
6 teal, or 3 large ducks, cleaned and
  washed
1¾ cups water
¼ cup chopped celery
¼ cup chopped bell pepper
2 cloves garlic, minced

Melt butter in a skillet. Add mushrooms and yellow and green onions and sauté. Add livers and simmer 5 to 10 minutes. Mix in parsley and next 4 ingredients. Simmer until liquid evaporates. Lightly season ducks with salt and pepper. Fill each cavity with mushroom stuffing. Place ducks, breast-side down, in a Dutch oven. Pour water around ducks, but do not cover. Combine celery, bell pepper, and garlic and sprinkle over ducks. Cover and bake at 400° for 45 minutes. Baste with pan juices. Bake, uncovered, 45 minutes longer, basting every 15 minutes. If using large ducks, split in half when done baking. Yields 6 servings.

Duck with Orange Sauce

Duck can be simmered in advance and refrigerated. When ready to serve, place on platter and bake as directed.

1 cup orange marmalade
½ cup orange juice
2 tablespoons orange zest
2 tablespoons orange-flavored
  liqueur
1 (4-pound) duck, or 2 teal, cleaned
  and washed

salt and pepper to taste
1 orange, sliced
1 small onion, sliced
2 cloves garlic
2 cups water

Combine marmalade and next 3 ingredients in a saucepan. Cook over low heat until smooth. Keep warm. Prick skin of duck with a fork several times. Generously sprinkle duck cavity with salt and pepper. Place orange, onion, and garlic in a Dutch oven. Place duck on top and add water. Cover and simmer 2 hour, 30 minutes to 3 hours or until tender. Transfer to an oven-proof platter. Wipe and prick skin again. Pour off all fat and liquid. Brush with orange sauce. Bake at 425°, basting occasionally with orange sauce, for 20 to 30 minutes or until skin is browned and crisp. Yields 2 servings.

Vegetables, Rice, Pasta & Grits

Lagniappe

Only in New Orleans will you find the word 'lagniappe' used in casual conversation on a regular basis. Lagniappe -- pronounced lan-yap -- is one of those French words that crept into the Crescent City's parlance back in the days when explorers such as Iberville and Bienville were settling the Vieux Carre, and it's become a kind of motto for the way of life down here.

According to the dictionary, a lagniappe is "something given or obtained gratuitously or by way of good measure", in other words, 'a little somethin' extra'. It may be a nod and a smile from a streetcar driver or friendly help given by a local to a lost tourist. Traditionally however, lagniappe has meant a little extra food -- the proverbial baker's dozen. It's a tradition that's alive and well in this city. Sometimes it's an extra bunch of grapes to sweeten the deal with the fruitstand vendor, or perhaps a couple of free crabs to go along with your redfish filets, or maybe a thirteenth petit four to round out your dozen. In whatever form, lagniappe is the basic ingredient of all New Orleans cooking.

That's why we've decided to call the dessert section our cookbook "Lagniappe." These are the extras, the recipes that sweeten the meal -- literally and figuratively. In "Lagniappe" you'll find dozens of local favorites like Bread Pudding (p. 208), Creole Pecan Pie (p. 214), and Praline Pumpkin Pie (p. 217). We also highly recommend the Crêpes Suzette (p. 220), Créme Brulee (p. 222), and Praline Sauce (p. 227). These are the kind of classic Crescent City desserts served in the finest restaurants here, and they're the 'little something extra' that turn a good meal into a great one. That's what makes them lagniappe.

Jambalaya Grits

2 tablespoons bacon fat
2 tablespoons all-purpose flour
½ cup chopped onion
1 bell pepper, chopped
½ cup chopped celery

1 cup quick grits
3 fresh tomatoes, peeled and
   chopped (about 1 cup)
1 cup ground ham
bacon, cooked and crumbled

Heat fat in a skillet. Gradually add flour and cook and stir until lightly browned. Add onion, bell pepper, and celery and cook 5 minutes. Cook grits according to package directions. Add grits, tomato, and ham to skillet. Sprinkle with bacon and serve immediately. Yields 6 servings.

Onion and Bacon Grits

8 slices bacon
⅔ cup minced onion
4 cups milk
1 stick butter, divided

1 cup quick grits, uncooked
1 teaspoon salt
½ teaspoon black pepper
1 cup Parmesan cheese

Cook bacon in a skillet. Drain on paper towels and crumble. Discard all but 1 tablespoon fat from skillet. Add onion and sauté. In a saucepan, bring milk and 6 tablespoons butter to a boil. Stir in grits, cover, and reduce heat. Simmer 5 minutes. Remove from heat and add onion, salt, and pepper. Beat 5 minutes or until creamy. Mix in half of bacon. Pour into a greased 9X13 inch casserole dish and chill until firm. Cut into 6 rectangular bars and place on a baking sheet, 2 inches apart. Sprinkle with remaining bacon and cheese. Melt remaining 2 tablespoons butter and drizzle over each bar. Bake at 400° for 25 minutes. Yields 6 servings.

Artichoke Mushroom Casserole

Cream Sauce
4 tablespoons butter
¼ cup all-purpose flour
1¼ teaspoons salt

¼ teaspoon white pepper
2 cups milk

Casserole
6 artichokes, boiled
1 stick butter, divided
¼ cup minced green onions
1 pound mushrooms, halved

2 teaspoons Worcestershire sauce
½ teaspoon Tabasco sauce
¾ cup seasoned breadcrumbs

Melt butter over low heat in a saucepan. Stir in flour, salt, and pepper. Remove from heat and slowly stir in milk. Return to low heat and cook and stir 5 minutes or until thickened. To prepare casserole, scrape artichoke leaves and quarter bottoms. Melt 6 tablespoons butter in a large skillet. Add onions and sauté until softened, but not browned. Add mushrooms and sauté 2 to 3 minutes. Reduce heat and stir in cream sauce, Worcestershire sauce, and Tabasco sauce. Add artichoke scrapings and bottoms. Pour into a 1½-quart casserole dish. Sprinkle with breadcrumbs and dot with remaining 2 tablespoons butter. Bake at 350° for 25 minutes. Yields 6 servings.

Anchovied Artichokes

½ cup sour cream
1½ teaspoons anchovy paste
½ teaspoon salt
½ teaspoon white pepper
⅛ teaspoon garlic salt

⅛ teaspoon Tabasco sauce
½ teaspoon paprika
1 teaspoon lemon juice
1 (8-ounce) can artichoke hearts,
    drained and chopped

Combine sour cream and next 7 ingredients in a saucepan. Cook over low heat for 5 minutes, stirring occasionally until well blended. Gently fold in artichoke. Heat 5 to 10 minutes. Yields 4 servings.

Broccoli Amandine Casserole

1 bunch broccoli, trimmed, or 2
   (10-ounce) packages frozen
   florets
1 beef bouillon cube
¾ cup hot water
4 tablespoons butter
¼ cup all-purpose flour
1 cup light cream

2 tablespoons dry sherry
2 tablespoons lemon juice
½ teaspoon salt
¼ teaspoon white pepper
½ cup Parmesan cheese
¼ cup grated Gouda cheese
¼ cup sliced almonds, toasted

Cook broccoli in rapidly boiling water for 6 minutes or until just tender. Drain and place in a greased 2-quart casserole dish. Dissolve bouillon cube in hot water. Melt butter in a 1-quart saucepan. Add flour and cook and stir 1 to 2 minutes. Vigorously beat in cream and bouillon with a wire whisk. Bring to a boil. Cook and stir 3 to 5 minutes or until thick and smooth. Remove from heat and add sherry and next 3 ingredients. Pour over broccoli. Sprinkle with cheeses and almonds. Bake at 350° for 20 minutes. Yields 6 to 8 servings.

Spicy Broccoli Ring

1 pound carrots, sliced
1 cup oil and vinegar salad dressing
1 (¼-ounce) package unflavored
   gelatin
1 (10¾-ounce) can consommé
   mixed with 1 can water, divided
2 teaspoons lemon juice
5 teaspoons Worcestershire sauce

½ teaspoon Tabasco sauce
1½ teaspoons salt
1 teaspoon white pepper
1 bunch broccoli, cooked, drained,
   and chopped
5 hard-cooked eggs, chopped
¾ cup mayonnaise

Cook carrots until crisp-tender. Drain. Cover with dressing and refrigerate. Dissolve gelatin in ¼ cup consommé mixture. Heat remaining consommé mixture and add to gelatin. Stir until dissolved. Stir in lemon juice and next 5 ingredients. Cool. Mix in egg and mayonnaise. Pour into a greased 8-cup ring mold. Chill at least 6 hours. Unmold and place marinated carrots in center of ring. Yields 12 servings.

Broccoli Onion Au Gratin

3 pounds pearl onions, peeled
2 bunches broccoli, trimmed
6 tablespoons butter
¾ cup all-purpose flour
4 cups milk

2 cups light cream
1 tablespoon salt
¼ teaspoon white pepper
½ cup Parmesan cheese

Boil onions in salted water until tender. Drain. Cut broccoli into bite-size pieces. Boil until crisp-tender. Drain and place in a shallow, 2-quart baking dish. Melt butter over low heat in a large saucepan. Slowly blend in flour. Add milk and cream. Cook and stir until sauce thickens. Season with salt and pepper. Mix in onions. Pour sauce over broccoli and sprinkle with cheese. Bake at 350° for 30 to 45 minutes or until bubbly and browned. Yields 12 servings.

Garden Casserole

2 cups cooked brown rice
2 cups broccoli, cut into ½-inch
   strips from flower through stalk
2 cups julienned carrots
1 cup diagonally sliced zucchini

1 cup green beans
1 teaspoon soy sauce
1 (16-ounce) jar marinara sauce
1 cup grated longhorn cheese
1 cup grated Monterey Jack cheese

Place rice in a greased 6X10X2 inch baking dish. Cook broccoli and next 3 ingredients in boiling salted water for 5 to 7 minutes or until tender. Drain. Reserve 4 zucchini slices for garnish. Spoon vegetables over rice. Combine soy sauce and marinara sauce and pour over vegetables. Cover dish with foil and bake at 375° for 30 minutes. Combine cheeses. Uncover casserole and sprinkle with cheeses. Continue to bake, uncovered, for 5 minutes or until cheeses melt. Garnish with zucchini slices. Yields 6 servings.

St. Patrick's Day Special

6 cups diced carrot
6 cups diced white turnip
2 cups water
4 tablespoons butter

1 teaspoon salt
1 teaspoon white pepper
½ cup packed light brown sugar

Combine all ingredients in a Dutch oven. Cover and bring to a boil. Reduce heat and simmer 30 minutes. Remove from heat and mash. Mixture should be moist, but not watery. Remove excess liquid, if necessary. Reheat and serve. Yields 12 servings.

Summer Veggie Mold

Fill center with green peas, mushrooms, broccoli florets, or spinach.

2 tablespoons butter
2 tablespoons all-purpose flour
¾ cup milk
¼ cup dry white wine
2½ cups cooked, mashed carrot
1½ tablespoons minced yellow
   onion

2 tablespoons chopped fresh parsley
½ teaspoon sugar
⅛ teaspoon nutmeg
2 teaspoons salt
1 teaspoon white pepper
3 eggs, beaten

Melt butter in a large skillet. Stir in flour and add milk. Cook and stir until mixture is thick and smooth. Blend in wine and next 7 ingredients. Remove from heat and cool 10 minutes. Stir in egg. Pour into a greased 1-quart ring mold and set in a shallow pan of hot water. Bake at 350° for 40 to 50 minutes or until firm. Remove from oven and water and let stand 5 minutes. Unmold onto a heated serving platter. Yields 8 to 10 servings.

Vegetable Lasagna

8 ounces lasagna noodles, cooked al
   dente
2 tablespoons olive oil
4 cloves garlic, minced
2 cups peeled and chopped tomato
2 medium eggplants, peeled and
   sliced ¹⁄₁₆-inch thick
vegetable oil for deep-frying

salt to taste
2 (10-ounce) packages frozen
   chopped spinach, cooked and
   drained
8 ounces ricotta cheese
black pepper to taste
1½ cups Parmesan cheese

Drain noodles and place in ice water until ready to use. Heat olive oil in a saucepan. Add garlic and sauté 3 minutes. Add tomato and simmer 15 minutes. Deep-fry eggplant in vegetable oil until golden brown. Drain on paper towels and season with salt. Combine spinach and ricotta cheese. Season with salt and pepper. Alternate layers of drained noodles, eggplant, spinach mixture and tomato mixture in a greased, 2-quart rectangular baking dish. Top with Parmesan cheese. Bake at 350° for 30 minutes. Yields 10 servings.

Zucchini Lasagna

6 cups sliced zucchini
½ pound ground beef
1 clove garlic, minced
1 (8-ounce) can tomato sauce
1 teaspoon salt
¼ teaspoon dried oregano

¼ teaspoon dried basil
1 cup small-curd cottage cheese
1 egg, beaten
1 tablespoon chopped fresh parsley
¼ cup dry breadcrumbs
1 cup grated mozzarella cheese

Cook zucchini in boiling water for 5 minutes. Drain. Cook beef and garlic in a skillet for 5 minutes. Stir in tomato sauce and next 3 ingredients. In a small bowl, combine cottage cheese, egg, and parsley. In a greased, 8-inch square baking dish, layer half of each of the following in order listed: zucchini, breadcrumbs, cottage cheese mixture, beef mixture, and mozzarella cheese. Repeat layers, except mozzarella cheese. Bake at 350° for 25 minutes. Sprinkle with remaining mozzarella cheese. Bake 3 minutes longer or until cheese melts. Yields 6 servings.

Creole Squash

4 pounds white squash, peeled and
   diced
2 eggs
1 cup milk
1½ teaspoons salt
¼ teaspoon white pepper
1 cup peeled and chopped tomato

2 slices white bread, cubed
4 tablespoons butter, cut into small
   pieces
2 teaspoons chopped fresh parsley
1 teaspoon paprika
¼ cup grated Romano cheese

Cook squash in boiling water for 6 minutes or until tender. Drain and mash. In a large bowl, combine eggs and next 3 ingredients. Gently mix in squash and tomato. Fold in bread and butter. Blend well. Pour into a 2-quart casserole dish. Bake at 350° for 45 minutes. Sprinkle with parsley, paprika and cheese. Yields 8 servings.

Yellow Squash and Tomatoes

2 tablespoons butter
1/2 cup chopped yellow onion
2 large tomatoes, peeled, chopped,
   and drained (about 2 cups)
1 teaspoon sugar
2 1/4 pounds yellow squash, sliced

1 teaspoon salt
1/2 teaspoon black pepper
1/8 teaspoon Tabasco sauce
1/2 cup Parmesan cheese
4 slices uncooked bacon, cut into
   small pieces

Melt butter in a large skillet. Add onion and sauté 5 minutes or until softened. Add tomato and sugar and cook 10 minutes. Reduce heat and add squash and salt. Cover and cook until tender. Season with pepper and Tabasco sauce. Pour into a shallow, 1 1/2-quart baking dish. Top with cheese and bacon. Broil 10 minutes or until browned. Yields 6 to 8 servings.

Deviled Corn

5 tablespoons butter, divided
2 tablespoons all-purpose flour
1 teaspoon Dijon mustard
1/2 teaspoon Worcestershire sauce
1 tablespoon lemon juice
1/2 teaspoon salt
1/2 teaspoon black pepper
1/2 cup milk
3 slices bacon, cooked and
   crumbled

1 (16-ounce) can yellow corn,
   drained
1 (16-ounce) can cream-style yellow
   corn
1/2 cup Parmesan cheese
1/2 cup seasoned breadcrumbs
3 hard-cooked eggs, cut into wedges
8 green olives, sliced

Melt 4 tablespoons butter in a large saucepan. Stir in flour and next 6 ingredients. Cook 8 minutes or until mixture thickens. Remove from heat and stir in bacon, corn, and cream-style corn. Pour into a 1 1/2-quart casserole dish. Sprinkle with cheese. In a small saucepan, melt remaining 1 tablespoon butter. Mix in breadcrumbs. Sprinkle over corn mixture. Bake at 350° for 45 minutes. Garnish with egg and olive slices. Yields 8 to 10 servings.

Fried Eggplant

1 (1-pound) eggplant, peeled
1 tablespoon salt
vegetable oil for deep-frying
2 eggs, beaten

¾ cup Italian-style breadcrumbs
3 tablespoons powdered sugar,
   optional

Cut eggplant into round, ¼-inch thick slices, or into large strips. Place in a bowl and sprinkle with salt. Let stand 30 minutes. Rinse with cool water, drain, and pat dry with paper towels. Heat oil in a large frying pan. Dip eggplant in egg, then in breadcrumbs. Fry in hot oil for 5 minutes or until golden brown. Drain and sprinkle with sugar. Yields 6 servings.

Stuffed Eggplant

3 eggplants, halved lengthwise
6 slices bacon, cut into small pieces
2½ cups chopped yellow onion
¾ cup chopped celery
¾ cup chopped bell pepper
1 cup chopped green onions
1 pound ham, chopped

3 cloves garlic, crushed
½ cup chopped fresh parsley
1 teaspoon Worcestershire sauce
½ teaspoon salt
½ teaspoon black pepper
¼ cup seasoned breadcrumbs
4 tablespoons butter

Place eggplant in a large pot and cover with cold water. Cook 30 minutes or until tender. Do not let eggplant break. Drain and cool. Scoop out pulp of eggplant, drain, and reserve. Place eggplant shells on a baking sheet. Cook bacon in a skillet. Add yellow onion and cook until lightly browned. Add celery and bell pepper and sauté until tender. Add green onions and ham and cook 5 minutes. Add reserved eggplant pulp, garlic, and next 4 ingredients. Cook over low heat for 10 minutes. Fold in breadcrumbs. Remove from heat. Mix in butter. Divide among eggplant shells. Bake at 350° for 30 minutes. Yields 6 servings.

Ratatouille Niçoise

4 tablespoons butter
2 cloves garlic, minced
1¾ cups thinly sliced yellow onion
2 tablespoons all-purpose flour
1 pound zucchini, cubed
1 pound eggplant, peeled and cubed

2 bell peppers, cut into strips, divided
8 ounces cherry tomatoes
1 tablespoon salt
¼ teaspoon black pepper
1 teaspoon sugar

Melt butter in a Dutch oven. Add garlic and onion and sauté 5 minutes. Sprinkle flour over zucchini and eggplant. Place half of zucchini, eggplant, and bell pepper in Dutch oven. Cover and cook, stirring occasionally, for 10 minutes or until vegetables start to soften. Add tomatoes and remaining zucchini, eggplant, and bell pepper. Season with salt, pepper, and sugar. Cook 10 minutes. Yields 8 to 10 servings.

Eggplant and Tomatoes

2 (1-pound) eggplants, peeled
4 tablespoons butter, divided
1½ teaspoons salt, divided
¾ teaspoon white pepper, divided
¾ cup chopped yellow onion
2 cups peeled and chopped tomato

¼ teaspoon dried thyme
⅛ teaspoon garlic powder
¼ cup chopped fresh parsley
2 slices white bread, cubed
1 cup grated Swiss cheese

Cut eggplant into 1-inch thick circles. Boil 10 minutes and drain. Cube enough eggplant to measure ¾-cup. Place remaining eggplant circles in a greased 9X13 inch baking dish. Melt 2 tablespoons butter and brush over circles. Season with ½ teaspoon salt and ½ teaspoon pepper. In a large skillet, melt remaining 2 tablespoons butter. Add onion and sauté. Add cubed eggplant and tomato. Cook over low heat for 15 to 20 minutes or until thickened. Stir in remaining 1 teaspoon salt, ¼ teaspoon pepper, thyme and next 3 ingredients. Cook and stir 2 minutes. Place about 2 tablespoons of eggplant mixture on each eggplant circle. Sprinkle with cheese. Bake at 350° for 20 minutes. Yields 6 to 8 servings.

Pisto

2 tablespoons butter
¼ cup diced lean ham
2 cups thinly sliced red onion
1 red bell pepper, diced
2 cloves garlic, minced

1 (1-pound) eggplant, unpeeled and
  cut into bite-size pieces
1 (10-ounce) package frozen
  artichokes, thawed
2 teaspoons salt
1 cup peeled and chopped tomato

Melt butter in a Dutch oven. Add ham and sauté 10 minutes. Add onion, bell
pepper, and garlic and cook 10 minutes. Add eggplant and remaining 3 ingredients. Reduce heat and cover. Cook 20 minutes or until artichokes are tender and
tomato is soft. Serve hot or cold. Yields 8 servings.

Baked Tomatoes

6 small tomatoes
1 cup seasoned breadcrumbs
1 stick melted butter
1½ teaspoons salt

1 teaspoon black pepper
¾ cup very thinly sliced yellow
  onion
6 teaspoons butter

Slice off tomato tops and scoop out 1 tablespoon pulp. Invert and drain tomatoes
for 10 minutes. Combine breadcrumbs and melted butter in a small mixing bowl.
Season inside of each tomato with salt and pepper. Fill with breadcrumb mixture.
Top each tomato with onion and 1 teaspoon butter. Place in a shallow, 1½-quart
baking dish. Bake at 325° for 35 minutes. Yields 6 servings.

Tomatoes Provençal

6 large tomatoes
1 tablespoon salt
¾ teaspoon black pepper
¾ cup seasoned breadcrumbs
3 cloves garlic, minced

3 tablespoons minced fresh parsley
½ cup grated Romano or Swiss
  cheese
¼ teaspoon dried oregano
4 tablespoons butter, melted

Slice off tomato tops and scoop out 2 tablespoons pulp. Season with salt and
pepper. Combine breadcrumbs and next 4 ingredients in a medium bowl. Mix
thoroughly. Divide among tomatoes. Transfer tomatoes to a 2-quart baking dish.
Drizzle with butter. Bake at 325° for 60 minutes, basting twice while cooking.
Yields 6 servings.

Spinach Timbales

2 tablespoons butter
½ cup chopped yellow onion
1 (3-ounce) package cream cheese, softened
½ cup sour cream
2 (10-ounce) packages frozen chopped spinach, cooked and drained

2 eggs, beaten
1 teaspoon salt
½ teaspoon black pepper
½ teaspoon nutmeg
1½ cups hollandaise sauce (page 66)

Melt butter in a large skillet. Add onion and sauté 5 minutes. Remove from heat. Stir in cream cheese and next 6 ingredients. Divide among 6 greased custard cups. Bake at 325° for 30 minutes. Invert onto a serving platter and top with hollandaise sauce. Yields 6 servings.

Greek Spinach Pie

White Sauce
2 tablespoons butter
2 tablespoons all-purpose flour
½ teaspoon salt

⅛ teaspoon white pepper
1 cup milk

Pie
1½ sticks butter, divided
1 cup chopped yellow onion
2 pounds fresh spinach
½ teaspoon salt
¼ teaspoon black pepper

6 eggs, beaten
1½ cups crumbled feta cheese
1 cup white sauce
6 sheets phyllo pastry dough

Melt butter in a small saucepan. Blend in flour, salt, and pepper. Remove from heat and slowly stir in milk. Return to heat and cook and stir until thick and smooth. To make pie, melt 6 tablespoons butter in a Dutch oven. Add onion and spinach and sauté 20 minutes. Season with salt and pepper. Cool. Combine egg, cheese, and white sauce in a bowl. Pour into spinach mixture and stir until blended. Melt remaining 6 tablespoons butter. Place a sheet of phyllo dough in a 9X13 inch baking dish. Brush with butter and top with some of spinach mixture. Repeat layers, ending with phyllo dough. Bake at 350° for 30 minutes. Yields 12 servings.

Spinach and Artichoke Hollandaise

8 cooked artichoke bottoms
2 (10-ounce) packages frozen
   chopped spinach, cooked and
   DRAINED

1 cup sour cream
2 teaspoons salt
1 teaspoon white pepper
1½ cups hollandaise sauce (page 66)

Place artichoke bottoms in a 1½-quart baking dish. Combine spinach and next 4 ingredients. Place a mound of spinach mixture on each artichoke bottom. Cover with foil. Bake at 350° for 15 minutes. Top with hollandaise sauce just prior to serving. Yields 8 servings.

Mirliton Casserole

4 mirlitons
1 stick plus 4 teaspoons butter,
   divided
2 pounds raw small shrimp, peeled
1 cup minced yellow onion
2 cloves garlic, pressed
2 bay leaves

1 tablespoon chopped fresh parsley
¾ cup Italian breadcrumbs, divided
1 teaspoon salt
¼ teaspoon black pepper
1 tablespoon Worcestershire sauce
¼ teaspoon Tabasco sauce

Boil whole mirlitons for 45 minutes or until tender. Peel, remove seed and center strings, and mash pulp. Melt 1 stick butter in a large skillet. Stir in pulp, shrimp, and next 4 ingredients. Simmer 20 minutes, stirring occasionally. Gradually stir in ½ cup breadcrumbs. Add salt and remaining 3 ingredients. Simmer 5 minutes, stirring constantly. Remove bay leaves and pour into a 2-quart casserole dish. Sprinkle with remaining ¼ cup breadcrumbs. Dot with remaining 4 teaspoons butter. Bake at 350° for 20 to 25 minutes. Yields 6 to 8 servings.

Baked Bananas

8 ripe bananas
¼ cup lemon juice
1 stick butter

½ cup sugar
3 tablespoons cinnamon
8 lemon wedges

Peel bananas and slice lengthwise. Place in a shallow baking dish. Sprinkle with lemon juice and dot with butter. Sprinkle sugar and cinnamon over top. Bake at 350° for 25 minutes. Garnish with lemon wedges. Yields 8 servings.

Hot Curried Fruit

1 (8¾-ounce) can apricot halves,
   drained
1 (8½-ounce) can sliced pears,
   drained
1 (8½-ounce) can sliced peaches,
   drained
1 (8-ounce) can sliced grapefruit,
   drained
1½ cups sliced banana

1 (17-ounce) jar dark pitted
   cherries, drained
2 tablespoons cornstarch
1 tablespoon curry powder
1 tablespoon cinnamon
1 cup packed brown sugar
1 stick butter, melted
¼ cup brandy or sherry

Place apricot halves and next 5 ingredients in a greased 2-quart baking dish. Combine cornstarch and next 3 ingredients. Sprinkle over fruit. Mix butter and brandy together and pour over fruit. Toss gently. Bake at 350° for 30 minutes. Yields 10 to 12 servings.

Stuffed Baked Apples

12 Rome apples
1 cup packed brown sugar
1 stick butter, melted

½ cup chopped pecans
½ cup currants or raisins
6 cinnamon sticks, halved

Cut a thin slice from the bottom of each apple. Core each apple from the top, being careful not to pierce the bottom. Scoop out 2 or 3 tablespoons pulp from each. Combine sugar and next 3 ingredients in a bowl. Blend well and spoon into apples. Place in a greased, shallow 2½-quart baking dish. Place a cinnamon stick half in center of each apple. Bake at 300° for 30 to 35 minutes. Yields 12 servings.

Fried Mushrooms

1 cup all-purpose flour
¾ cup beer
½ teaspoon garlic salt
1½ teaspoons salt
1 teaspoon baking powder

1 teaspoon white pepper
1 pound fresh mushrooms, washed,
   dried, and stems trimmed
vegetable oil for frying

Combine flour and next 5 ingredients in a bowl. Dip mushrooms in beer batter. Fry in hot oil until golden brown. Drain well and serve immediately. Yields 4 servings.

Mushroom Pie

3 tablespoons butter
¼ cup chopped yellow onion
1 pound mushrooms, sliced
1 tablespoon all-purpose flour
½ cup light cream

1 tablespoon brandy or sherry
1 teaspoon salt
¼ teaspoon white pepper
basic pie crust (page 214)
1 egg white, beaten

Melt butter in a large skillet. Add onion and sauté 10 minutes. Add mushrooms and cook 4 to 5 minutes. Blend in flour and cream. Bring to a boil, stirring constantly. Stir in brandy, salt, and pepper. Cool. Brush pie crust with egg white. Pour in mushroom mixture. Bake at 350° for 20 minutes. Serve hot or cold. Yields 8 to 10 servings.

Almond Fried Rice

4 tablespoons butter
½ cup chopped onion
¼ cup chopped bell pepper
¼ pound ham, finely chopped
¼ teaspoon salt

⅛ teaspoon black pepper
¼ cup soy sauce
¼ cup slivered almonds, toasted
3 cups steamed rice, cooled

Melt butter in a large skillet. Add onion and bell pepper and sauté until tender. Add ham and remaining 5 ingredients. Cook and stir 5 minutes. Yields 4 servings.

Okra Jambalaya

3 tablespoons butter
½ cup minced yellow onion
2 cloves garlic, minced
½ cup minced bell pepper
3 cups chopped tomato

1 teaspoon minced fresh parsley
1½ teaspoons salt
¼ teaspoon black pepper
⅛ teaspoon cayenne pepper
48 okra, trimmed

Melt butter in a Dutch oven. Add onion, garlic, and bell pepper and sauté 6 to 8 minutes. Add tomato and remaining 5 ingredients. Cook 20 minutes or until tender. Yields 6 to 8 servings.

Mushrooms Stuffed with Eggplant

2 (1-pound) eggplants, peeled and
   diced
1½ sticks butter
½ cup chopped yellow onion
¼ cup chopped bell pepper
2 cloves garlic, minced
2 teaspoons salt
¼ teaspoon black pepper

½ teaspoon chili powder
¼ teaspoon Tabasco sauce
½ cup Italian breadcrumbs
24 large fresh mushrooms, washed,
   dried, and stems removed
½ cup dry sherry
1 cup grated Muenster cheese

Soak eggplant in salted water for 30 minutes. Drain. Melt butter in a large skillet. Add onion, bell pepper, and garlic and sauté 10 minutes. Add eggplant and cook over low heat for 25 minutes. Mix in salt and next 4 ingredients. Cook 5 minutes. Spoon mixture into mushrooms. Place, stuffed-side up, in a greased 2-quart baking dish. Drizzle sherry over tops. Bake at 350° for 15 minutes. Sprinkle with cheese and bake 15 minutes longer. Yields 8 servings.

Potato Soufflé

3 cups mashed potato
4 tablespoons butter, softened
1 pound small-curd cottage cheese
½ cup sour cream
2 eggs, beaten
2 teaspoons salt

⅛ teaspoon cayenne pepper
½ cup minced green onions
¼ cup Parmesan cheese
chopped fresh parsley or chives, or
   paprika for garnish

Blend potato and butter in a large bowl. Beat in cottage cheese and next 5 ingredients. Pour into a 2-quart soufflé dish. Sprinkle with Parmesan cheese. Bake at 425° for 50 minutes. Garnish. Yields 8 servings.

Sweet Potato Ring

8 sweet potatoes, peeled
1½ sticks butter, softened, divided
½ cup packed light brown sugar
1 (5⅓-ounce) can evaporated milk
1 teaspoon nutmeg

1 egg, lightly beaten
¾ cup raisins
¾ cup packed dark brown sugar
1 cup pecan halves

Cook sweet potatoes in boiling water for 25 minutes or until tender. Drain. Mash potatoes in a large bowl. Add 1 stick butter and next 4 ingredients. Mix well. Gently fold in raisins. Use remaining 4 tablespoons butter to grease a 9-cup ring mold. Sprinkle dark brown sugar inside ring mold. Place pecan halves on the bottom. Gently spoon in sweet potato mixture. Bake at 350° for 45 to 60 minutes. Cool 5 minutes and unmold onto a heated serving platter. Yields 10 to 12 servings.

Sweet Potato Soufflé

Potatoes
1 pound fresh sweet potatoes or
    yams, cooked, or 1 (29-ounce)
    can, drained
¾ cup milk

1 teaspoon vanilla
¼ cup sugar
2 eggs
6 tablespoons butter, melted

Topping
6 tablespoons butter, softened
½ cup chopped pecans

½ cup packed dark brown sugar
¾ cup crushed corn flakes

Beat together potatoes and next 5 ingredients. Place in an ungreased 1½-quart baking dish. Bake at 300° for 45 minutes or until edges leave sides of pan. Mix together all topping ingredients in a bowl until smooth. Spread over baked soufflé. Cook under the broiler for 1 minute or until topping browns. Yields 8 servings.

Penne Pierro

6 slices bacon, cut into 1-inch pieces
⅓ cup chopped onion
1 (10-ounce) can tomato purée
⅓ cup water
½ teaspoon salt
⅛ teaspoon cayenne pepper

8 ounces penne, cooked al dente
 and drained
¾ cup freshly grated Parmesan
 cheese
½ cup heavy cream

Cook bacon until browned but not crisp. Add onion and cook until softened. Add tomato purée and next 3 ingredients. Cook 20 minutes. Place mixture in a large bowl. Stir in penne and cheese. Add cream and toss well. Yields 4 to 6 servings.

Pasta Primavera

8 ounces cauliflower, cut into bite-
 size pieces
8 ounces broccoli, cut into bite-size
 pieces
8 ounces zucchini, cut into 1-inch
 pieces
4 spears asparagus, cut into thirds
8 ounces green beans, cut into
 1-inch lengths
⅔ cup green peas
5 tablespoons butter, divided
½ cup chopped green onions
8 ounces mushrooms, thinly sliced
1 teaspoon minced red or green chili
 peppers, or ½ teaspoon crushed
 red pepper flakes

¼ cup chopped fresh parsley
6 tablespoons olive oil, divided
1 teaspoon minced garlic
3 cups diced tomato
1 teaspoon salt
½ teaspoon black pepper
6 fresh basil leaves, or 1 teaspoon
 dried basil
2 ounces ham, chopped
¼ cup chicken broth
¾ cup heavy cream
⅔ cup Parmesan cheese
1 pound spaghetti, cooked al dente
 and drained
⅓ cup pine nuts, toasted

Cook cauliflower and next 4 ingredients in boiling, salted water until crisp-tender. Drain, rinse with cold water, and drain again. Add peas. Heat 1 tablespoon butter in a skillet. Add onions and mushrooms and sauté 3 minutes. Stir in chili peppers and parsley. Add to vegetable mixture and set aside. Heat 3 tablespoons oil in a saucepan. Add garlic and next 3 ingredients. Cook 4 minutes, stirring gently. Mix in basil and ham. Heat remaining 3 tablespoons oil in a large skillet. Add vegetable mixture and cook and gently stir until thoroughly heated. Melt remaining 4 tablespoons butter in a large saucepan. Stir in broth, cream, and cheese. Cook over very low heat until smooth. Add spaghetti and toss. Toss in half of vegetable mixture and liquid from tomato mixture. Mix in remaining vegetables. If sauce is too dry, add extra cream. Sauce should not be soupy. Add nuts and toss. Serve in soup or spaghetti bowls. Spoon tomato mixture over top. Yields 8 servings.

Linguine Mollusca

¼ cup olive oil
2 tablespoons all-purpose flour
½ cup chopped green onions
5 tomatoes, peeled and chopped
(about 4 cups)
2 cloves garlic, minced
½ teaspoon dried oregano
2 bay leaves

1 pint oysters
½ cup oyster liquid
1 teaspoon salt
¼ teaspoon black pepper
12 ounces linguine, cooked al dente
and drained
¾ cup freshly grated Parmesan
cheese

Heat oil in a saucepan. Stir in flour. Add onions and next 4 ingredients. Simmer 20 minutes. Add oysters and liquid. Simmer 15 minutes. Add salt and pepper and remove bay leaves. Fold in linguine. Sprinkle with cheese and serve. Yields 6 servings.

Fettuccine Caesar

8 ounces fettuccine
1 stick butter
¼ cup olive oil
2 green onions, minced

3 cloves garlic, minced
8 ounces mushrooms, chopped
¼ cup half-and-half
1 cup Parmesan cheese

Boil fettuccine in salted water. In a pan, heat butter and oil. Add onions and garlic and sauté 3 minutes. Add mushrooms and cook 3 minutes. Drain fettuccine and return to pot. Pour vegetable mixture over noodles and toss lightly. Add half-and-half and sprinkle with cheese. Serve immediately. Yields 4 to 6 servings.

Fettuccine with Julienned Veggies

1½ sticks butter, divided
8 ounces mushrooms, sliced
1½ pounds zucchini, julienned
1 cup heavy cream
12 ounces fettuccine

2 tablespoons salt
1 tablespoon vegetable oil
¾ cup Parmesan cheese
½ cup chopped fresh parsley

Melt 4 tablespoons butter in a very large skillet. Add mushrooms and sauté 2 minutes. Add zucchini, cream, and remaining 1 stick butter, cut into small pieces. Bring to a boil and simmer 3 minutes. Cook fettuccine in a large pot, adding salt and oil to water. Drain and add fettuccine to skillet. Mix well. Add cheese and parsley and toss. Yields 6 to 8 servings.

Broccoli Rice Casserole

1¼ cups rice
6 cups chicken broth, divided
2 (10-ounce) packages frozen
   broccoli
1¼ sticks butter, divided
¾ cup minced onion

¾ cup chopped mushrooms
½ cup all-purpose flour
1 cup evaporated milk
1 teaspoon salt
¼ teaspoon black pepper
½ cup dry breadcrumbs

Cook rice in 3 cups broth. Fluff with a fork and place in a greased 2½ to 3-quart casserole dish. Parboil broccoli and drain thoroughly. Spread over rice. Melt 1 stick butter in a 12-inch skillet. Add onion and mushrooms and sauté until softened. Blend in flour and cook and stir 2 to 3 minutes. Add remaining 3 cups broth and milk. Bring to a boil, stirring constantly. Add salt and pepper. Pour over broccoli. Melt remaining 2 tablespoons butter in a small saucepan. Add breadcrumbs and cook and stir until lightly browned. Sprinkle over casserole. Bake at 350° for 30 minutes or until bubbly. Yields 8 to 10 servings.

Corn and Rice Stuffed Tomatoes

8 tomatoes
½ cup chopped onion
½ cup chopped bell pepper
2 tablespoons butter
8 ounces mushrooms, sliced
½ cup corn
2 cups steamed rice

1 teaspoon salt, plus to taste
¼ teaspoon black pepper, plus to
   taste
½ cup grated sharp cheddar cheese,
   divided
dried oregano to taste

Slice tops off tomatoes. Scoop out pulp and reserve. Cook onion and bell pepper in butter until tender. Add mushrooms and sauté. Add tomato pulp, corn, and rice. Season with salt and pepper and cook until heated. Stir in ¼ cup cheese. Sprinkle inside tomato shells with salt, pepper, and oregano to taste. Spoon vegetable mixture into shells. Top with remaining ¼ cup cheese. Fill a rectangular baking dish with ½-inch water. Place tomatoes in water. Bake at 375° for 25 minutes. Yields 8 servings.

Wild Rice with Water Chestnuts

This recipe makes a good stuffing for Cornish game hens.

¾ cup wild rice
3 cups chicken or beef broth
6 tablespoons butter
¼ cup minced onion
1 cup chopped mushrooms

½ cup sliced water chestnuts
2 tablespoons minced fresh parsley
¼ teaspoon sage
1 teaspoon salt
¼ teaspoon black pepper

Wash rice in cold water 3 or 4 times. Bring broth to a boil in a saucepan. Slowly add rice. Reduce heat, cover, and simmer 50 to 60 minutes. Melt butter in a skillet. Add onion and mushrooms and sauté 5 minutes. Add rice, water chestnuts and remaining 4 ingredients. Fluff with a fork and serve immediately. Yields 4 servings.

Fruit Spiced Rice

A good side dish for ham or pork.

5 cups water
2 cups brown rice
¾ teaspoon cinnamon
¾ teaspoon nutmeg
½ teaspoon salt

½ cup raisins
½ cup dried apricots, chopped
4 tablespoons butter
½ cup blanched almonds
2 tablespoons sugar

Combine water and next 6 ingredients in a saucepan. Bring to a boil. Stir once and reduce heat. Cover and simmer 45 minutes. Melt butter in a skillet. Add almonds and sauté until golden. Sprinkle with sugar. Pour over rice and serve. Yields 8 to 10 servings.

Sausage Dressing

5-6 slices bread
2 tablespoons butter
½ cup pork sausage
½ cup chopped celery
¼ cup chopped onion
¼ cup chopped tart apple

¼ teaspoon salt
1 tablespoon poultry seasoning
¼-½ cup chicken broth
½ cup raisins, optional
⅓ cup sherry, optional

Place bread on center rack in oven to dry overnight. Spread butter on slices and crumble to equal 2 cups. Cook sausage in a skillet. Drain. Add bread crumbs, celery and next 4 ingredients. Moisten with broth. Plump raisins in sherry and add to mixture. Serve with ham. Yields 4 servings.

Evangeline Rice with Peas

If using frozen peas, thaw and add 5 minutes before stirring in cheese.

4 tablespoons butter
¼ cup chopped onion
¼ cup chopped celery
1 slice bacon, diced
2 cups fresh or frozen green peas
½ cup diced ham

1 cup rice
2¼ cups chicken broth
1 teaspoon salt
¼ teaspoon black pepper
2 tablespoons Parmesan cheese

Melt butter in a large saucepan. Add onion, celery, and bacon and sauté 5 minutes. Add peas and ham and cook 5 minutes. Add rice and cook and stir 3 minutes. Stir in broth, salt, and pepper. Bring to a boil. Cover and cook over low heat for 25 minutes. Stir in cheese. Yields 4 to 6 servings.

Spinach Dressing

1 loaf stale French bread, cubed
  (about 10 cups)
2 cups chicken broth
4 tablespoons butter
1 tablespoon vegetable oil
½ pound pork sausage
½ pound ground beef
3 green onions, minced
½ cup minced onion
2 stalks celery, minced
1 tablespoon chopped fresh parsley

2 (10-ounce) packages frozen
  chopped spinach, cooked and
  drained
2 eggs, beaten
2 tablespoons Parmesan cheese
1 tablespoon dried thyme
1 tablespoon beau monde seasoning
1 teaspoon salt
¼ teaspoon black pepper
cayenne pepper to taste

Soak bread in broth and squeeze dry. Heat butter and oil in a large skillet. Add sausage and beef and sauté. Stir in green onions and next 3 ingredients. Add bread, spinach, and remaining 7 ingredients. Mix well and place in a 2-quart casserole dish. Bake at 350° for 20 minutes, or use as a stuffing for chicken, turkey, or Cornish game hens. Yields 6 to 8 servings.

Walnut Stuffing

1 cup rice
3½ cups beef broth, divided
1 bay leaf
1 cup chopped green onions
2 cloves garlic, pressed
1 cup chopped celery
3 tablespoons bacon fat
1 pound pork sausage
¼ cup chopped ham

2 cups stale French bread crumbs
1 teaspoon salt
½ teaspoon black pepper
1½ teaspoons dried thyme
1 teaspoon sage
2 tablespoons chopped fresh parsley
½ cup water
¾ cup chopped walnuts

Cook rice in 2 cups broth with bay leaf for 20 minutes. Remove bay leaf. Sauté onions, garlic, and celery in bacon fat in a large skillet. In a separate skillet, cook sausage and drain. Add sausage and ham to onion mixture. Stir in crumbs and rice. Add salt and next 4 ingredients. Moisten with water and remaining 1½ cups broth. Add walnuts. Place in a 3-quart casserole dish. Bake at 350° for 25 to 30 minutes or stuff loosely into a bird. Yields 12 servings.

Louisiana Oyster and Pecan Stuffing

1½ cups stale French bread cubes
¼ cup chopped white onion
2 small green onions, minced
¼ teaspoon minced garlic
½ cup chopped celery
¼ cup minced bell pepper
¼ teaspoon dried thyme
1 teaspoon poultry seasoning

1 bay leaf
½ teaspoon salt
¼ teaspoon black pepper
1½ cups coarsely chopped pecans
1 stick butter, melted
1 pint large oysters, liquid reserved
1 egg, lightly beaten

Combine bread cubes and next 12 ingredients. Stir in oysters and moisten with a small amount of oyster liquid. Add egg. Stuff into a 4 to 5 pound bird. Yields 4 servings.

Breads, Cookies and Desserts

New Orleans kicks off the year with King Cake

While most of the world spends January recovering from the holidays, New Orleanians spend it gearing up for the Carnival season, which officially begins on the 12th day after Christmas: Twelfth Night. Also known as Epiphany, Twelfth Night commemorates the visit of the Three Wise Men to the infant Jesus. In the Catholic Church it is a Holy Day, and in New Orleans, long a predominantly Catholic city, it's also the kick off of Carnival, traditionally celebrated with the serving of a special confection, the King Cake.

Depending on where you buy it -- or how you make it -- King Cake can take any one of several forms. At its simplest, it is a sweet, brioche-like pastry, fashioned in a ring shape. Often king cakes are more elaborate, featuring stuffings or fruit filling, nuts, cream cheese or cinnamon swirls, and topped with icing and sprinkled sugar of purple, green and gold -- the colors of Mardi Gras.

In keeping with the spirit of the feast day it symbolizes, baked into each King Cake is a small token. Once it was a small bean, but today, hidden somewhere in the sweet ring is a small, plastic figure of a baby, meant to represent the infant Jesus. Whoever finds the baby in their slice of cake is named 'king', and, according to tradition, is obliged to bring the King Cake to the next gathering.

King Cake can only be eaten during the Carnival season, which means you can't serve them before Twelfth Night or after midnight on Mardi Gras, when Carnival officially ends. But that's what makes them so special, so enjoy them while you can!

For a great King Cake recipe that you can customize to fit your tastes see our recipe on page 196.

Muffins Jambalaya

Seal cooled muffins in a plastic bag to freeze. Thaw in bag for 15 minutes when ready to serve. Remove from bag, wrap tightly in foil, and warm at 400° for 15 minutes.

3 tablespoons butter
½ cup minced green onions
½ cup minced bell pepper
1 cup yellow cornmeal
1¼ cups all-purpose flour
2 teaspoons baking soda

1 teaspoon salt
2 eggs
2 cups buttermilk
1 cup finely chopped ham
1 cup finely chopped cooked
   sausage

Melt butter in a skillet. Add onions and bell pepper and sauté until softened, but not browned. In a large bowl, combine cornmeal and next 3 ingredients. In a small bowl, beat together eggs and buttermilk. Add egg mixture to dry ingredients all at once, stirring only until blended. Gently fold in ham, sausage, and vegetable mixture. Spoon into well-greased muffin tins, filling two-thirds full. Bake at 400° for 30 minutes or until nicely browned. Yields 24 muffins.

French Peasant Bread

To freeze, wrap cooled loaves tightly in plastic. Thaw in plastic for 30 minutes. Remove from plastic and wrap in foil. Warm at 400° for 15 minutes.

2 cups warm water
1 tablespoon sugar
2 teaspoons salt
1 package dry yeast

4 cups unsifted, unbleached flour
2 tablespoons vegetable oil
2 tablespoons cornmeal
2 tablespoons butter, melted

Combine warm water and next 3 ingredients in a warm, large bowl. Stir until dissolved. Stir in flour. Dough will be sticky. Scrape into a greased bowl, cover with a towel, and let rise 45 minutes in a warm place. Stir dough down. Grease 2 baking sheets with oil and sprinkle with cornmeal. Mound half of dough onto each sheet. Let rise, uncovered, for 45 minutes. Brush with butter. Bake at 425° for 10 minutes. Reduce heat to 375° and bake 20 minutes. Bread will be flat and crusty. Yields 2 loaves.

French Bread

To freeze, wrap cooled loaves tightly in plastic. Reheat bare loaves at 400° for 10 to 15 minutes to restore crispness.

2 cups warm water	1 tablespoon salt
2 packages dry yeast	5-6 cups all-purpose flour, divided
3 tablespoons vegetable oil, divided	2 tablespoons margarine
1 tablespoon sugar	2 tablespoons cornmeal

Combine warm water and yeast in a large bowl. In a small bowl, combine 2 tablespoons oil, sugar, and salt. Add to yeast water. Stir in 4 cups flour. When it becomes difficult to stir, spread some of remaining flour on a smooth surface. Turn dough onto surface and knead 10 to 12 minutes or until smooth and pliable. Add more flour as needed. Use remaining 1 tablespoon oil to grease a large bowl. Place dough in bowl, turning once to grease top. Cover with a damp cloth and let rise in a warm place for 60 minutes or until doubled. Turn dough onto a floured surface and divide into fourths. Roll each section into a 6X12 inch rectangle. Roll up like a jelly roll, pulling long side towards you, keeping it as tight as possible. Pinch and shape ends. Grease two 15-inch baking sheets with margarine and sprinkle with cornmeal. Place loaves of dough, seam-side down, on sheets. Stretch, if needed, to make each loaf 15 inches long. Brush tops with water. Cut a ¼-inch deep slash along the top length of each loaf. Allow to rise, uncovered, for 60 minutes or until doubled. Place a pan of hot water in the bottom of oven. Brush loaves with water. Bake at 400° for 10 minutes. Brush with water again and bake 20 minutes longer or until bread is deep golden brown on top and sounds hollow when tapped. Yields 4 loaves.

Garlic Bread

1½ sticks butter	2 (15-inch) loaves French bread
1 tablespoon minced garlic	⅔ cup freshly grated Parmesan
1/16 teaspoon dried thyme	cheese

Melt butter in a small skillet. Add garlic and sauté until softened, but not browned. Add thyme and remove from heat. Slice loaves in half lengthwise. Place, cut-side up, on a baking sheet. Sprinkle with cheese. Pour butter mixture over top and spread evenly. Bake at 400° for 10 minutes or until brown. Cut into 1½-inch slices and serve hot. Yields 8 servings.

Herbed Dill Bread

To freeze, wrap cooled loaves tightly in plastic. Thaw in plastic for 30 minutes. Remove from plastic and wrap in foil. Warm at 400° for 15 to 20 minutes.

1 cup milk
½ cup sour cream
1 tablespoon salt
2 tablespoons sugar
3 tablespoons butter
2 packages dry yeast

½ cup warm water
2 eggs
2 tablespoons dill seed
1 cup chopped green onions
½ cup chopped fresh parsley
5-6 cups all-purpose flour, divided

Heat milk and sour cream in a saucepan. Stir in salt, sugar, and butter. Cool 30 minutes. In a small bowl, dissolve yeast in warm water. In a large mixing bowl, beat eggs. Stir in milk mixture, yeast water, dill seed, onions, and parsley. Stir in 2 cups flour and beat vigorously. Stir in another 2 cups flour until it becomes difficult to stir. Spread 1 cup flour on a smooth surface. Turn dough onto surface and knead until elastic and no longer sticky. Add more flour as needed. Place in a well-greased bowl, turning once to grease top. Cover and let rise in a warm place for 1 hour to 1 hour, 30 minutes or until doubled. Turn onto a floured surface and knead 2 to 3 minutes. Return to bowl, cover, and let rise 45 minutes or until almost doubled. Turn onto a lightly floured surface and divide into 2 balls, kneading to remove air bubbles. Place each ball in a greased 1½-quart round casserole dish. Cover and let rise 30 to 45 minutes or until dough reaches top of pan. Bake at 375° for 40 minutes or until bread is evenly browned and sounds hollow when tapped. Yields 2 loaves.

Sour Cream Bread

1½ cups sour cream
1 stick butter
½ cup sugar
½ teaspoon salt

2 packages dry yeast
⅓ cup warm water
3 eggs
4½ cups all-purpose flour

Heat sour cream in a small saucepan until warm. In a large bowl, combine butter, sugar, and salt. Add sour cream and stir until butter melts. Dissolve yeast in warm water. Add to cream mixture. Beat in eggs and flour, alternately. Let rise in a warm place for 2 hours or until doubled. Stir dough and beat. Spoon into 2 greased 9X5X3 inch loaf pans. Let rise 60 minutes or until doubled. Bake at 350° for 35 minutes. Remove from pans and cool. Yields 2 loaves.

Wine and Cheese Bread

This recipe freezes well.

3 cups all-purpose flour, divided
1 package dry yeast
½ cup dry white wine
1 stick butter
2 teaspoons sugar

1 teaspoon salt
3 eggs
4 ounces Monterey Jack, Jarlsberg,
   or cheddar cheese, cubed

Combine 1½ cups flour and yeast in a large mixing bowl. In a small saucepan, heat wine and next 3 ingredients to 115° to 120°. Stir just until butter melts. Add to flour mixture. Add eggs. Beat with an electric mixer on low speed for 30 seconds, scraping constantly. Beat 3 minutes on high speed. Stir in cheese. Add enough of remaining flour to make a soft dough. Turn onto a lightly floured board. Knead 3 to 5 minutes or until dough is smooth. Place in a well-greased bowl and cover. Let rise in a warm place for 1 hour, 30 minutes or until doubled. Punch down and let rest 10 minutes. Shape into an 8-inch round loaf. Place in a greased 9-inch pie pan. Cover and let rise 40 minutes or until doubled. Bake at 375° for 20 minutes. Cover loosely with foil and bake 20 minutes longer. Yields 1 loaf.

Cream Cheese Biscuits

1 stick butter, softened
½ (8-ounce) package cream cheese,
   softened

1 cup all-purpose flour

Cream butter and cream cheese in a mixing bowl. Add flour and continue beating until well mixed. Roll dough onto floured wax paper to ¼-inch thick. Cut with a 2-inch diameter biscuit cutter. Place on an ungreased baking sheet. Bake at 375° for 15 minutes or until golden brown. Yields 2 dozen biscuits.
To prepare in a food processor, place cold cream cheese, cold butter, and flour in a food processor fitted with a steel blade. Process 1 minute or until dough forms a ball. Roll out, cut, and bake at directed.

Onion Cheese Bread

1½ cups milk	½ cup warm water
2 tablespoons sugar	3 cups chopped onion
3 tablespoons butter	6 ounces sharp cheddar cheese,
2 teaspoons salt	grated
2 packages dry yeast	6-7 cups all-purpose flour, divided

Scald milk in a saucepan. Add sugar, butter, and salt and stir until dissolved. Let cool 30 to 40 minutes. Dissolve yeast in warm water. In a large bowl, combine milk mixture, yeast water, onion, and cheese. Stir in 4 cups flour. Spread 1 cup flour over a smooth surface. When it becomes difficult to stir dough, turn onto floured surface. Knead 10 minutes or until pliable and no longer sticky. Add remaining flour as needed. Place in a well-greased bowl, turning once to grease top. Cover and let rise in a warm place for 60 minutes or until doubled. Turn out onto a floured surface and knead 2 to 3 minutes. Return to bowl and let rise 45 minutes or until almost doubled. Transfer to a lightly floured surface and form into 2 loaves. Tuck ends under and place in 2 greased 9X5X3 inch pans. Cover and let rise 45 minutes or until dough reaches top of pan. Bake at 400° for 15 minutes. Reduce heat to 375° and bake 15 to 20 minutes or until loaf sounds hollow when tapped. Remove from pan to cool. Yields 2 loaves.

Onion Cheese Buns: When dough is divided in half after second rising, roll to less than ½-inch thick. Cut out dough with a 4-inch diameter biscuit cutter and place on greased baking sheets, leaving room for dough to rise. Let rise 1 hour to 1 hour, 30 minutes or until about doubled. Bake at 375° for 20 minutes or until tops are golden brown. To freeze, seal cooled buns in plastic bags. Thaw in bags before serving. Yields 3 dozen buns.

Onion Cheese Rolls: After first rising, roll dough to about ¼-inch thick. Cut with a 3-inch diameter biscuit cutter. Place on greased baking sheets and let rise 60 minutes. Bake at 400° for 12 to 15 minutes or until brown. To freeze, bake until rolls just start to brown. Cool and freeze in plastic bags. Thaw in bags for 30 minutes and place on baking sheets. Bake at 400° for 10 to 12 minutes or until brown. Yields 6 dozen rolls.

Sourdough French Bread

To freeze, wrap cooled loaves tightly in plastic. Thaw and reheat bare loaves at 400° for 10 to 15 minutes.

1 package dry yeast
1½ cups warm water
2 tablespoons vegetable oil, divided
6-8 cups unbleached flour, divided
1½ cups sourdough starter
    (page 189)

2 teaspoons salt
4 teaspoons sugar
1 teaspoon cornstarch
1 cup water, divided
¼ cup cornmeal

Sprinkle yeast over warm water in a large bowl. Add 1 tablespoon oil, 3 cups flour, and next 3 ingredients. Mix well. Add flour, 1 cup at a time to about 6 cups. Spread 1 cup flour on a smooth surface. Turn out dough onto surface and knead until smooth. Add remaining flour as needed. Use remaining 1 tablespoon oil to grease a large bowl. Place dough in bowl and turn to grease top. Cover with a towel and let rise in a warm place for 60 minutes or until doubled. Turn out onto a floured surface and knead 8 to 10 minutes or until smooth. Add flour as needed. Dissolve cornstarch in 1 teaspoon water. Stir in remaining water. Grease 2 baking sheets and sprinkle with cornmeal. Shape dough into 2 oblong loaves and place on baking sheets. Brush top of loaves with cornstarch mixture. Cut a ¼-inch deep slash along the top length of each loaf. Let dough rise 45 minutes or until doubled. Brush with cornstarch mixture. Place a large pan of boiling water in the bottom of oven. Bake at 375° for 20 minutes on the center rack. Brush with cornstarch mixture and bake 20 minutes longer. Yields 2 loaves.

Sourdough Orange Muffins

¼ cup granulated sugar
½ cup packed dark brown sugar
1½ cups sifted flour
½ cup sifted whole wheat flour
1 teaspoon salt
1 teaspoon baking soda
4½ teaspoons dried orange zest

1 egg, beaten
½ cup vegetable oil
¾ cup sourdough starter (page 189)
½ cup buttermilk
2 teaspoons orange extract
1 cup coarsely chopped nuts

Combine granulated sugar and next 6 ingredients in a large bowl. Make a well in the center. In a separate bowl, mix egg and next 4 ingredients. Pour into center of dry ingredients. Mix until dry ingredients are just moistened. Batter will be lumpy. Fold in nuts. Spoon into greased or paper-lined muffin tins, filling two-thirds full. Bake at 375° for 20 minutes or until browned. Yields 18 to 22 muffins.

Sourdough Starter

Inital Mixture
1½ cups unbleached flour
2 tablespoons sugar
1 tablespoon salt

1 package dry yeast
2 cups warm milk, water, or potato
  water

Starter Mixture
initial mixture
2 cups unbleached flour
1 cup warm milk, water, or potato
  water

1 tablespoon salt
2 tablespoons sugar

Combine flour, sugar, and salt in a large crock or glass bowl. Sprinkle yeast over milk. Add yeast mixture to dry ingredients and stir with a wooden spoon. Mixture will be very thick and sticky, but not stiff. Keep in a warm place. Allow to sour for 3 to 4 days. To complete starter mixture, combine initial mixture and remaining 4 ingredients. Let stand overnight. Mixture will rise and bubble. Yields 3½ cups.

Onion Rye Bread

Recipe doubles easily and freezes well.

1 cup milk
1 tablespoon sugar
1½ teaspoons salt
2 tablespoons butter
2 tablespoons molasses
1 packet dry yeast
¼ cup warm water

½ cup minced onion
1 tablespoon caraway seed
2 cups all-purpose flour
2 cups rye flour
cornmeal
cream
salt

Scald milk in a saucepan. Stir in sugar and next 3 ingredients. Cool 20 to 30 minutes. Dissolve yeast in warm water. In a large bowl, combine milk mixture, yeast mixture, onion, and caraway seed. Stir in flours. Flour a smooth surface with rye flour. When dough becomes difficult to stir, turn out onto surface. Knead 5 to 10 minutes or until flour is incorporated. Place in a greased bowl. Cover and let rise in a warm place for 1 hour, 30 minutes or until doubled. Turn out onto a rye-floured surface and knead 3 to 5 minutes. Return to greased bowl and cover. Let rise 60 minutes or until doubled. Dust a greased 9X5X3 inch loaf pan with cornmeal. Remove dough from bowl and shape into a loaf. Place in loaf pan, brush with cream, and sprinkle with salt. Let rise 45 minutes or until dough almost reaches top of pan. Bake at 400° for 40 minutes. Cool on a wire rack. Yields 1 large loaf.

Biscuits

2 cups all-purpose flour
1 tablespoon baking powder
1 teaspoon salt

½ cup vegetable shortening
1 cup milk

Sift together flour, baking powder, and salt in a large bowl. Cut in shortening until mixture resembles coarse crumbs. Add just enough milk to moisten all ingredients. Place on a floured surface. Knead, if necessary, to get dough to hold together. Roll out to ¼-inch thick. Cut with a 2-inch diameter biscuit cutter and place on an ungreased baking sheet. Bake at 450° for 20 minutes or until browned. Yields 1½ dozen biscuits.
To freeze, bake only 15 minutes, not allowing biscuits to brown. Wrap cooled biscuits tightly in plastic. To serve, thaw completely and bake at 450° for 10 to 15 minutes or until browned.

No Knead Bread

For a softer crust, brush tops with melted butter and cover with a cloth while cooling.

2 cups milk
2 sticks butter
¾ cup sugar
3 packages dry yeast
½ cup warm water
3 eggs

4 teaspoons vanilla
2 teaspoons salt
8-9 cups all-purpose flour
1½ tablespoons vegetable oil,
    divided

Scald milk in a saucepan. Add butter and sugar. Cool. Dissolve yeast in water in a small bowl. In a very large bowl, beat eggs. Add vanilla and salt. Add milk mixture and yeast mixture. Mix in flour, 1 cup at a time, until dough is soft but still sticky. Cover and let rise in a warm place for 60 minutes or until doubled. Punch down and transfer to another large bowl greased with 1 tablespoon oil. Brush top of dough with remaining ½ tablespoon oil. Cover and let rise 45 minutes or until doubled. Punch down and scrape dough into 3 greased 9X5X3 inch loaf pans. Cover and let rise 60 minutes or until dough reaches top of pans. Bake at 400° for 10 minutes on the center rack. Reduce heat to 350° and bake 25 minutes or until bread sounds hollow when tapped. Remove from pans to cool. Yields 3 loaves.

White Bread

1 cup milk
1½ teaspoons salt
¼ cup warm water
1 package dry yeast

1½ teaspoons sugar
3 cups all-purpose flour, divided
1 tablespoon vegetable oil

Heat milk in a small saucepan. Add salt and cool to lukewarm. In a large bowl, combine water, yeast, and sugar. Let stand until frothy. Add milk mixture. Stir in 2½ cups flour. Spread remaining ½ cup flour on a smooth surface. Turn dough onto surface and knead 5 minutes or until smooth. Grease a bowl with oil. Place dough in bowl, turning to grease top. Let rise 45 minutes or until doubled. Turn dough onto a lightly floured surface and knead to remove air bubbles. Transfer to a greased 9X5X3 inch loaf pan and let rise 45 minutes or until doubled. Bake at 350° for 35 minutes or until bread sounds hollow when tapped. Yields 1 loaf.
Pizza Crust: Combine all ingredients as directed and knead until smooth. Divide in half and roll out to fit two 14 to 16-inch pizza pans. Do not bake before adding sauce and pizza toppings.

Butterflake Rolls

2 packages dry yeast
¼ cup warm water
½ cup sugar
2½ sticks butter, softened, divided

3 eggs, beaten
1 cup warm water
4½ cups all-purpose flour
2 teaspoons salt

Dissolve yeast in warm water. Cream sugar and 1 stick butter. Add eggs, 1 cup water, and yeast mixture. Stir in flour and salt. Dough will be very moist and sticky. Refrigerate 6 hours or overnight. Place dough onto a well-floured cloth or surface. Roll out into a 10X22 inch rectangle. Dough will be sticky. Spread 1 stick butter over dough. Roll up along the long side. Stretch to an equal thickness. Cut dough in ¾ to 1-inch slices with a floured knife. Melt remaining 4 tablespoons butter. Dip one side of slices in butter. Place in greased muffin tins, buttered-side up. Let rise 3 hours or until doubled. Bake at 400° for 10 minutes or until lightly browned. Yields 2½ dozen rolls.

Whole Wheat Bran Rolls

To freeze, bake rolls 13 to 15 minutes or until just starting to brown. Wrap cooled rolls in plastic bags. Thaw in plastic for 30 minutes. Remove from plastic and bake at 350° for 10 to 15 minutes or until browned.

1 cup milk
1 cup bran cereal
2 packages dry yeast
½ cup warm water
¾ cup plus 1 tablespoon vegetable oil, divided
3 eggs, beaten

2 tablespoons packed dark brown sugar
2 tablespoons molasses
1½ teaspoons salt
3 cups whole wheat flour, divided
2 cups white flour

Scald milk in a saucepan. Add cereal and cool to lukewarm. Dissolve yeast in warm water in a small bowl. In a large bowl, mix together ¾ cup oil and next 4 ingredients. Beat thoroughly. Add milk and yeast mixture. Add 2 cups whole wheat flour and stir vigorously. Stir in white flour. Spread remaining 1 cup whole wheat flour on a smooth surface. Turn dough onto surface and knead 5 to 10 minutes or until smooth. Grease a large bowl with remaining 1 tablespoon oil. Place dough in bowl, turning to grease top. Cover and let rise in a warm place for 1 hour, 30 minutes or until doubled. Roll out onto a lightly floured surface to ½-inch thick. Cut with a 3-inch diameter biscuit cutter. Fold and place on a greased baking sheet. Let rise 60 minutes or until puffy. Bake at 350° for 15 to 20 minutes or until browned. Yields 2½ to 3 dozen.

Bran Muffins

3 cups bran flakes
1 cup boiling water
2 cups raisins
2 eggs
2 cups buttermilk
½ cup vegetable oil

1¼ cups sugar
2½ cups all-purpose flour
1 teaspoon salt
2½ teaspoons baking soda
½ teaspoon cinnamon

Place bran flakes in a bowl. Pour boiling water over top and stir in raisins. In a large mixing bowl, beat eggs. Add buttermilk. Beat in oil and remaining 5 ingredients. Stir in bran mixture. Spoon into paper-lined muffin tins, filling two-thirds full. Bake at 425° for 20 to 25 minutes or until browned. Yields 3 dozen muffins.

Potato Rolls

To freeze, bake 10 to 12 minutes or only until very lightly browned. Wrap cooled rolls in plastic bags. Thaw in plastic 30 minutes. Place on a baking sheet and bake at 350° for 10 to 12 minutes or until browned.

1 medium potato, peeled
1 package dry yeast
2 tablespoons vegetable shortening
1 cup milk or evaporated milk
1/4 cup sugar

1 1/2 teaspoons salt
4-5 cups all-purpose flour, divided
2 eggs, lightly beaten
melted butter

Place potato in a small saucepan and cover with water. Cook until tender. Reserve 1/4 cup potato water. Mash potato to equal 2/3 cup. Cool reserved potato water 20 to 30 minutes or until lukewarm. Add yeast. In a large bowl, mix shortening and potato until smooth. In a small saucepan, warm milk and stir in sugar and salt. Add to potato mixture and stir until smooth. Add 2 cups flour, 1 cup at a time, mixing well after each addition. Mix in egg. Add yeast water and 1/2 to 1 cup more flour as needed to make dough stiff. Let rise 2 hours. Punch down dough. Add about 2 more cups flour to make a workable dough. Turn out onto a floured surface and knead 8 to 10 minutes, using remaining flour as needed. Dough will be sticky, but using less flour makes a lighter final product. Roll out on a floured surface to 1/2-inch thick. Cut with a 3-inch diameter biscuit cutter. Brush with melted butter and fold in half, pressing edges together. Place rolls, touching each other, on a greased baking sheet. Let rise about 60 minutes. Bake at 350° for 12 to 15 minutes or until browned. Yields 3 dozen rolls.

Carrot Bread

Bread freezes well.

1 cup vegetable oil
1 1/2 cups sugar
3 eggs
1 teaspoon vanilla
1 1/2 cups sifted flour
1 1/2 teaspoons baking soda

1 teaspoon cinnamon
1/2 teaspoon salt
1/2 teaspoon nutmeg
2 cups grated carrot
1 cup chopped pecans

Beat oil and next 3 ingredients in a large mixing bowl. Sift together flour and next 4 ingredients. Add to oil mixture. Blend well. Fold in carrot and pecans. Pour into 2 greased and floured 9X5X3 inch loaf pans. Bake at 350° for 40 minutes or until a toothpick inserted in the center comes out clean. Yields 2 loaves.

Braided Bread with Fruit

To freeze, wrap cooled loaves in plastic. Thaw 30 minutes in plastic. Heat at 350°
for 15 to 20 minutes.

Bread
2 packages dry yeast
1¼ cups warm water
3 tablespoons sugar
1 tablespoon salt

5 tablespoons butter, softened,
  divided
4-6 cups all-purpose flour, divided
1 tablespoon vegetable oil

Dissolve yeast in warm water in a large bowl. Add sugar, salt, and 2 tablespoons butter. Stir until sugar and salt dissolve. Stir in 3 cups flour. Spread 1 cup flour on a smooth surface. Turn dough onto surface and need until smooth. Add remaining flour as needed. Grease a large bowl with oil. Place dough in bowl and cover with a towel. Let rise in a warm place for 60 minutes or until doubled. Punch down dough and divide into thirds. Roll each section into a 6X12 inch rectangle. Prepare fillings; amounts for each filling are for 1 loaf. Make diagonal cuts, about 1-inch apart, along outer edges of dough from filling to edge. Fold strips, alternating sides in a lattice-like fashion, over filling. Stretch strips while folding to form a compact loaf and to enclose filling. Carefully lift loaves onto greased baking sheets. Melt remaining 3 tablespoons butter and brush over loaves. Let rise in a warm place for 20 to 30 minutes. Bake at 350° for 40 minutes or until browned. Yields 3 loaves.

Filling #1
½ cup raisins
¼ cup orange juice
1 large apple, unpeeled

½ cup packed brown sugar
2 teaspoons cinnamon
½ teaspoon nutmeg

Soak raisins in orange juice for 20 to 30 minutes. Drain. Slice apple into thin wedges. Place in center along the length of prepared dough. Sprinkle with raisins. Combine sugar, cinnamon, and nutmeg. Sprinkle over fruit.

Filling #2
1 large banana, sliced   ⅓ cup orange marmalade

Place banana slices in center along the length of prepared dough. Heat marmalade and pour over banana.

Filling #3
1 large pear, or 2 peaches, under
    ripe
½ cup packed brown sugar

2 teaspoons cinnamon
½ teaspoon nutmeg

Peel and slice pear. Place in center along the length of prepared dough. Combine sugar, cinnamon, and nutmeg. Sprinkle over fruit.

Rolls

To freeze, bake 10 minutes or until rolls just start to brown. Wrap cooled rolls in plastic bags. Thaw in bags about 30 minutes. Place on a baking sheet and bake at 400° for 10 minutes or until browned.

1 cup milk
2 packages dry yeast
½ cup warm water
3 eggs, well-beaten
½ cup vegetable oil

½ cup sugar
1½ teaspoons salt
6 cups all-purpose flour, divided
1 stick butter, melted

Scald milk in a small saucepan. Allow to cool to lukewarm. Dissolve yeast in warm water. Combine egg and next 3 ingredients in a bowl. Add milk and yeast mixture. Add 3 cups flour and stir vigorously 2 to 3 minutes. Stir in 2 more cups flour. Spread remaining 1 cup flour on a smooth surface. Turn dough onto surface and knead well, incorporating flour as needed. Place in a greased bowl and cover with a towel. Let rise 2 hours in a warm place. Turn out onto a lightly floured surface. Proceed to make Crescent or Parker House rolls.

Crescent Rolls: Divide dough in half. Refrigerate half not being worked with. Roll other half into a ⅛-inch thick circle. Brush with melted butter. Cut into 16 wedges. Roll each wedge, starting at wide end. Place on a baking sheet, point down. Let rise for 30 minutes or until doubled. Bake at 400° for 10 to 15 minutes or until browned. Yields 32 rolls.

Parker House Rolls: Roll dough to ¼-inch thick. Cut with a 3-inch diameter biscuit cutter. Brush with melted butter. Fold in half and place on a baking sheet. Let rise 30 minutes or until doubled. Bake at 400° for 10 to 15 minutes or until browned. Yields 36 rolls.

King Cake

To freeze, wrap cooled cake tightly in plastic. Before serving, remove from plastic and thaw.

Cake

1 stick plus 1 tablespoon butter,
    divided
2/3 cup evaporated skim milk
1/2 cup sugar, divided
2 teaspoons salt
2 packages dry yeast

1/3 cup warm water
4 eggs
1 tablespoon lemon zest
2 tablespoons orange zest
6 cups all-purpose flour

Filling

1 stick butter, melted
1/2 cup packed dark brown sugar

3/4 cup granulated sugar
1 tablespoon cinnamon

Topping

1 egg, beaten
1 cup sugar, colored, 1/3 cup of each
    yellow, purple, and green

2 (3/4-inch) plastic babies, or 2 beans

Melt 1 stick butter in a saucepan. Stir in milk, 1/3 cup sugar, and salt. Cool to lukewarm. In a large mixing bowl, combine remaining 2½ tablespoons sugar, yeast, and warm water. Let stand 5 to 10 minutes or until frothy. Beat eggs into yeast mixture. Beat in milk mixture and zests. Stir in flour, 1/2 cup at a time, reserving 1 cup. Spread reserved 1 cup flour over a smooth surface. Turn dough onto surface and knead 5 to 10 minutes or until smooth. Grease a large mixing bowl with remaining 1 tablespoon butter. Place dough in bowl, turning to grease top. Cover and let rise in a warm place for 1 hour, 30 minutes to 2 hours or until doubled. Punch down dough and divide in half. On a floured surface, roll a dough half into a 15X30 inch rectangle. Brush with half of filling's melted butter. Cut into 3 lengthwise strips. Combine sugars and cinnamon. Sprinkle half of mixture on strips, leaving a 1-inch lengthwise edge free for sealing. Fold each strip toward the center, sealing the seam. You will now have three (30-inch) strips with a sugar filling enclosed in each. Braid the strips together and make a circle by joining the ends. Repeat with other half of dough. Place each ring on a 10X15 inch baking sheet. Cover with a damp cloth and let rise 60 minutes or until doubled. Top by brushing with egg. Sprinkle with colored sugar, alternating colors. Bake at 350°

for 20 minutes. Remove from pan immediately so sugar does not harden. While still warm, place a plastic baby in each from underneath. Yields 2 cakes.

Color sugar for topping by tinting with food coloring. For purple, use equal amounts of blue and red coloring. A food processor aids in mixing and keeps the sugar from getting too moist.

In New Orleans, this cake is served during Carnival season from the Feast of Epiphany (January 6) until Mardi Gras (the day before Ash Wednesday). The person receiving the plastic baby is considered lucky. By custom, that person must also supply the next King Cake.

Raisin Cinnamon Bread

If using honey, dough will absorb more flour than if using sugar.

2 packages dry yeast
2¼ cups warm water, divided
1 cup sugar, or ¼ cup honey
1 tablespoon salt
5 tablespoons butter, softened, divided

7-9 cups unbleached flour, divided
1½ cups raisins
½ cup packed brown sugar
4 teaspoons cinnamon
2 tablespoons water

Dissolve yeast in ½ cup warm water. Stir in remaining 1¾ cups warm water, sugar, salt, and 2 tablespoons butter. Add 3½ cups flour and stir vigorously. Add raisins and enough of remaining flour to make dough easy to handle, about 3 cups. Turn dough onto a lightly floured surface and knead until smooth and elastic. Add remaining flour as needed. Place in a greased bowl, turning to grease top. Cover and let rise in a warm place for 60 minutes or until doubled. Punch down dough and divide in half. Roll each half into a 9X18 inch rectangle. Combine sugar and cinnamon in a small bowl. Sprinkle 2 tablespoons water and sugar mixture evenly over rectangles. Roll up each rectangle, starting on the short side. Pinch seams and ends to seal. Place, seam-side down, in greased 9X5X3 inch loaf pans. Melt remaining 3 tablespoons butter and brush over loaves. Let rise 45 minutes or until dough reaches top of pan. Bake at 425° for 30 to 40 minutes or until loaves are lightly browned and sound hollow when tapped. Remove from pans and cool on racks. Serve hot with butter, or wrap tightly in plastic and freeze. Yields 2 loaves.

Buttery Bread

Bread freezes well.

1 cup milk	1 cup warm water
½ cup sugar	2 packages dry yeast
1 tablespoon salt	2 eggs, beaten
1 stick butter	6-7 cups all-purpose flour, divided

Scald milk in a saucepan. Add sugar, salt, and butter. Stir until butter melts. Cool to lukewarm. In a large bowl, dissolve yeast in water. Add milk mixture. Stir in egg. Add 3 cups flour and beat vigorously. Mix in 3 more cups flour. Turn onto a smooth surface floured with some of remaining flour. Knead until smooth, adding remaining flour as needed. Dough will be soft. Place in a greased bowl, turning to grease top. Cover with a towel and let rise in a warm place for 1 hour, 30 minutes or until doubled. Turn onto a floured surface and knead 2 to 3 minutes. Return to bowl and let rise 60 minutes or until doubled. Turn onto a lightly floured surface and form into 2 loaves, kneading to remove air bubbles. Place into greased 9X5X3 inch loaf pans. Let rise 45 minutes or until dough almost reaches top of pan. Bake at 400° for 30 minutes or until bread sounds hollow when tapped. Remove from pan and cool on wire racks. Yields 2 loaves.
Use half all-purpose and half whole wheat flour.

Substitute whole wheat flour for all-purpose flour. Loaf will be heavier and more compact.

Cranberry Bread

4 cups all-purpose flour	4 tablespoons butter, melted
2 cups sugar	¾ cup water
1 tablespoon baking powder	2 cups raw cranberries, coarsely
1 teaspoon salt	chopped
1 teaspoon baking soda	2 tablespoons orange zest
2 eggs	1 cup chopped pecans
1 cup orange juice	

Combine flour and next 4 ingredients in a bowl. In a large mixing bowl, beat eggs. Add juice and remaining 5 ingredients. Add dry ingredients and mix well. Pour into 2 greased and floured 9X5X3 inch loaf pans. Bake at 325° for 60 minutes or until a toothpick inserted in the center comes out clean. Remove from pans and cool on wire racks. Yields 2 loaves.

Strawberry Bread

2 cups all-purpose flour
1 teaspoon baking soda
1 teaspoon salt
1 tablespoon cinnamon
4 eggs

1¼ cups vegetable oil
2 cups sugar
2 (10-ounce) packages frozen
   strawberries, undrained, thawed
1¼ cups chopped pecans

Sift together flour and next 3 ingredients in a bowl. In a large mixing bowl, beat eggs. Add oil and sugar. Gradually stir in dry ingredients, strawberries, and pecans. Pour into 2 greased and floured 9X5X3 inch loaf pans. Bake at 350° for 60 minutes or until a toothpick inserted in the center comes out clean. Yields 2 loaves.

Zucchini Pineapple Bread

3 eggs
2 cups sugar
1 cup vegetable oil
2 teaspoons vanilla
3 cups all-purpose flour
2 teaspoons baking soda
1 teaspoon salt
½ teaspoon baking powder
1½ teaspoons cinnamon

1 teaspoon nutmeg
1½ cups grated, unpeeled zucchini
1 (8-ounce) can crushed pineapple,
   drained
½ cup raisins
1 cup chopped pecans
1 (4-ounce) package instant vanilla
   pudding

Beat eggs and next 3 ingredients in a large bowl until foamy. In a separate bowl, sift together flour and next 5 ingredients. Stir into egg mixture. Add zucchini and remaining 4 ingredients. Pour into 2 greased and floured 9X5X3 inch loaf pans. Bake at 350° for 60 minutes or until a toothpick inserted in the center comes out clean. Yields 2 loaves.

Whole Wheat Orange Muffins

Recipe freezes well.

2 eggs
½ cup sugar
⅓ cup vegetable oil
1 cup orange juice
2 tablespoons orange zest
1 cup all-purpose flour

1½ cups whole wheat flour
1 teaspoon baking powder
1 teaspoon baking soda
½ teaspoon salt
½ cup chopped pecans

Beat eggs in a large bowl. Beat in sugar and oil. Stir in juice and zest. In a separate bowl, sift together all-purpose flour and next 4 ingredients. With swift strokes, stir dry ingredients into egg mixture. Do not overmix. Stir in pecans. Spoon into greased or paper-lined muffin tins, filling two-thirds full. Bake at 400° for 15 to 20 minutes or until lightly browned. Yields 12 muffins.

Carrot Muffins

To freeze, wrap cooled muffins tightly in plastic. Thaw in plastic 15 minutes. Transfer to foil and wrap tightly. Warm at 400° for 15 minutes.

2 eggs
1 cup sugar
1 cup vegetable oil
½ teaspoon vanilla
2 cups grated carrot

2 cups all-purpose flour
1 teaspoon cinnamon
1 teaspoon salt
2 teaspoons baking powder

Beat eggs in a bowl. Continue to beat while adding sugar, oil, and vanilla. Stir in carrot. Sift flour and remaining 3 ingredients into a large mixing bowl. Add egg mixture and stir until just moistened. Spoon into paper-lined muffin tins, filling two-thirds full. Bake at 350° for 30 minutes or until lightly browned. Serve hot. Yields 18 to 20 muffins.

Apple Coffee Cake

4 cups peeled and diced apple
2 cups sugar
2 eggs, separated
1 cup vegetable oil
2½ cups all-purpose flour

2 teaspoons baking soda
1 teaspoon salt
1 teaspoon cinnamon
1 cup chopped pecans

Combine apple and sugar in a large bowl. In a separate bowl, beat egg whites until stiff. In a third bowl, beat egg yolks until light colored. Gradually beat oil into yolk. Mix yolk mixture into white. Add egg mixture to apple mixture and mix well. In another bowl, sift together flour and next 3 ingredients. Blend dry ingredients and pecans into apple mixture. Pour into a greased and floured Bundt pan. Bake at 350° for 60 minutes or until a toothpick inserted in the center comes out clean. Yields 10 to 12 servings.

Brown Sugar Coffee Cake

2 cups all-purpose flour
1 cup granulated sugar
½ teaspoon nutmeg
1 teaspoon cinnamon
1 teaspoon salt
4 teaspoons baking powder

1 stick butter
3 eggs
1 cup milk
1 cup peeled and grated apple
½ cup packed brown sugar
1 cup broken pecans

Sift together flour and next 5 ingredients in a large bowl. Cut in butter until mixture resembles coarse crumbs. In a separate bowl, beat eggs. Add milk. Stir in dry ingredients until smooth. Pour into a greased 8X10 inch baking pan. Sprinkle apple into batter. Top with brown sugar and pecans. Bake at 350° for 30 to 40 minutes or until a toothpick inserted in the center comes out clean. Yields 12 to 15 servings.

Cajun Cowboy Cookies

1 cup granulated sugar
1 cup packed brown sugar
2 sticks butter
1½ teaspoons vanilla
2 eggs
2 cups all-purpose flour
1 teaspoon baking soda
½ teaspoon salt

1 teaspoon baking powder
2 cups rolled oats
1 (6-ounce) package semi-sweet
   chocolate chips
½ (6-ounce) package butterscotch
   chips
2 cups finely chopped nuts

Combine granulated sugar and next 4 ingredients in a large bowl and mix until fluffy. In a separate bowl, sift together flour and next 3 ingredients. Add to sugar mixture and blend well. Stir in oats, chocolate chips, and butterscotch chips. Place nuts in a small bowl. Shape rounded teaspoonfuls of dough into balls. Roll in nuts and place on an ungreased baking sheet. Bake at 350° for 18 to 20 minutes or until lightly browned. Yields 6 dozen cookies.

Fudge Brownies

Brownies
2 (1-ounce) squares semi-sweet
   chocolate
1 stick butter
½ cup all-purpose flour

1 cup sugar
½ cup finely chopped nuts
2 eggs, beaten

Frosting
1 (1-ounce) square unsweetened
   chocolate
1 tablespoon butter

2 cups powdered sugar
2 teaspoons vanilla
2-3 tablespoons boiling water

In a small saucepan, melt chocolate and butter. In a large bowl, sift flour and sugar together. Stir in chocolate mixture, nuts, and egg. Mix well. Pour into an 8-inch square pan. Bake at 350° for 20 to 25 minutes. Brownies will be very moist. Cool, frost, and cut into squares. To prepare frosting, melt chocolate and butter in a saucepan. Stir in sugar and vanilla. Add water and beat vigorously for 3 to 5 minutes. Yields 16 servings.

Crunchy Nut Cookies

1 cup granulated sugar
1 cup packed brown sugar
1 stick butter, softened
2 eggs
1 teaspoon vanilla

3 cups all-purpose flour
1 teaspoon baking soda
½ teaspoon salt
1½ cups chopped pecans
powdered sugar

Combine granulated sugar and next 4 ingredients. Mix well. Sift together flour, baking soda, and salt. Stir into sugar mixture. Add pecans. Shape level tablespoonfuls of dough into balls. Place on an ungreased baking sheet. Flatten with the bottom of a greased glass dipped in powdered sugar. Bake at 375° for 10 to 12 minutes or until browned. Yields 5 dozen cookies.

Orange Meringue Kisses

4 egg whites
½ teaspoon cream of tartar
1 cup sugar

½ teaspoon orange zest
1 teaspoon orange juice
1 cup finely chopped pecans

Beat egg whites and cream of tartar until foamy. Slowly add sugar and beat until stiff. Fold in zest, juice, and pecans. Drop by heaping teaspoonfuls onto baking sheets lined with heavy brown paper. Bake at 250° for 45 minutes. Yields 3 dozen cookies.

Praline Meringue Kisses

½ cup granulated sugar
½ cup packed dark brown sugar
3 egg whites
½ teaspoon cream of tartar

¼ teaspoon lemon juice
¼ teaspoon vanilla
1 cup finely chopped pecans

Combine sugars in a small bowl. In a large bowl, beat egg whites and cream of tartar until stiff. Beat in sugar mixture, 1 tablespoon at a time, alternating with drops of juice and vanilla. Beat until stiff and glossy. Fold in pecans. Drop by well-rounded teaspoonfuls onto baking sheets lined with heavy brown paper. Bake at 250° for 45 minutes. Yields 4 dozen cookies.

Chocolate Chip Kisses

4 egg whites
½ teaspoon cream of tartar
1 cup sugar
1 teaspoon vanilla

1 (6-ounce) package semi-sweet
  chocolate chips
1 cup finely chopped pecans

Beat egg whites and cream of tartar in a large bowl until stiff. Gradually add sugar and vanilla. Fold in chocolate chips and pecans. Drop by heaping teaspoonfuls onto a baking sheet lined with heavy brown paper. Bake at 250° for 45 minutes. Yields 4 dozen kisses.

Chocolate Mint Kisses: Add 1 teaspoon peppermint extract with vanilla. Omit pecans and add 2 to 3 drops green food coloring.

Pecan Cookies

1 stick butter, softened
1 cup packed dark brown sugar
1 teaspoon vanilla
1 egg

1 cup all-purpose flour
½ teaspoon baking powder
1 cup coarsely chopped pecans

Cream butter and sugar in a large bowl. Mix in vanilla and egg. In a medium bowl, sift together flour and baking powder. Slowly add dry ingredients to butter mixture. Stir in pecans. Drop by well-rounded teaspoonfuls onto an ungreased baking sheet. Bake at 350° for 12 to 15 minutes. Remove from sheet immediately and cool on a wire rack. Yields 3 dozen cookies.

Ginger Cookies

⅔ cup vegetable oil
1 cup sugar
1 egg
1 tablespoon molasses
2 cups all-purpose flour

2 teaspoons baking soda
1 teaspoon ground ginger
1 teaspoon cinnamon
dash of salt

Combine oil and next 3 ingredients in a large bowl. In a separate bowl, sift together flour and remaining 4 ingredients. Add dry ingredients to oil mixture and mix well. Roll into quarter-size balls and place on an ungreased baking sheet. Bake at 350° for 10 to 12 minutes or until lightly browned. Yields 4 dozen cookies.

Sugar Cookies

3 cups all-purpose flour
1¾ cups sugar
1 teaspoon baking powder
2 sticks butter, softened

1 egg
1 tablespoon vanilla
2 tablespoons milk
½ cup colored sugar crystals

Sift together flour, sugar, and baking powder. In a large bowl, cream butter. Slowly add half of dry ingredients. In a small bowl, beat egg. Stir in vanilla and milk. Add to dough. Mix in remaining dry ingredients. Refrigerate at least 60 minutes. Roll out dough to ⅛-inch thick on lightly floured wax paper. Cut with a 2½-inch diameter, round cookie cutter. Place 2 inches apart on an ungreased baking sheet. Sprinkle with sugar crystals. Bake at 350° for 12 to 15 minutes or until lightly browned. Yields 5 to 6 dozen cookies.

Orange Cookies

1 stick butter, softened
1 cup sugar, plus extra for topping
1 egg
1 teaspoon orange extract

1½ cups all-purpose flour
1 teaspoon baking powder
½ teaspoon salt
2 teaspoons orange zest

Cream butter and sugar in a large bowl. Mix in egg and extract. In a separate bowl, sift together flour, baking powder, and salt. Stir into butter mixture. Add zest. Drop by teaspoonfuls onto a greased baking sheet, leaving room for spread. Bake at 350° for 10 to 12 minutes or until edges are golden brown. Transfer to a wire rack. While still warm, sprinkle sugar over top. Yields 3 dozen cookies.
Lemon Cookies: Substitute 1 teaspoon lemon extract for orange extract, and 2 teaspoons lemon zest for orange zest.

Almond Squares

2 sticks butter, softened
1 cup sugar
1 egg, separated

2 cups all-purpose flour
½ teaspoon almond extract
2 cups sliced, unblanched almonds

Cream butter and sugar in a mixing bowl. Blend in egg yolk. Mix in flour and extract. Batter will be stiff. Spread batter into a 10X15 inch jelly-roll pan. Sprinkle almonds over top. Press almonds gently into batter. In a small bowl, beat egg white with a fork until foamy. Brush over batter and almonds. Bake at 300° for 50 minutes or until golden. Cut into squares while warm. Yields 4 dozen squares.

Gingerbread Men

Use this recipe when making a gingerbread house.

4 cups all-purpose flour	1 stick butter, softened
1 tablespoon cinnamon	½ cup packed brown sugar
1 teaspoon salt	1 cup molasses
1 teaspoon baking soda	2 teaspoons cider vinegar
1 teaspoon ground ginger	raisins
½ teaspoon ground cloves	candies

Sift together flour and next 5 ingredients in a bowl. In a large bowl, cream butter and next 3 ingredients. Mix in dry ingredients. Dough will be very stiff; knead if necessary. Roll out on floured wax paper with a floured rolling pin. Cut out gingerbread men with a 3½-inch cutter. Lift carefully onto a greased baking sheet. Use raisins and candies for eyes, nose, and buttons. Bake at 350° for 15 minutes or until lightly browned. Cool on a wire rack. Yields 3 dozen cookies.

Jelly Roll

Cake can also be filled with whipped cream and fresh fruit.

4 eggs, separated	½ teaspoon salt
¾ cup granulated sugar, divided	¼ cup powdered sugar
½ teaspoon vanilla	1 (12 to 15-ounce) jar blackberry
¾ cup sifted cake flour	jelly or any tart preserves
1 teaspoon baking powder	

Beat egg yolks in a bowl 3 to 5 minutes or until lemon colored. Slowly beat in ¼ cup sugar and vanilla. In a large bowl, beat egg whites until soft peaks form. Gradually add remaining ½ cup sugar and beat until stiff peaks form. Fold in yolk mixture. In another bowl, sift together flour, baking powder, and salt. Fold into egg mixture. Pour batter into a greased and lightly floured 12X15 inch jelly-roll pan. Bake at 375° for 12 minutes or until cake is lightly browned and springs back when touched. Sprinkle a towel with powdered sugar. Loosen cake and turn out onto towel. Roll up lengthwise, making a 15-inch roll. Cool and unroll. Spread jelly over cake. Roll up again and slice into 1-inch pieces. Yields one 15-inch roll.

Cheesecake Cookies

Crust
1 cup all-purpose flour
¼ cup packed light brown sugar

1 cup finely chopped pecans
1 stick butter, melted

Filling
2 (8-ounce) packages cream cheese
1 cup sugar

1 teaspoon vanilla
3 eggs

Glaze
2 cups sour cream
6 tablespoons sugar

1 teaspoon vanilla

In a small bowl, mix together all crust ingredients. Press into a 9X13 inch baking dish. Bake at 350° for 10 to 15 minutes or until browned. To prepare filling, beat cream cheese, sugar, and vanilla in a bowl. Add eggs and beat well. Pour over baked crust. Bake at 350° for 20 minutes. While baking, combine all glaze ingredients in a small bowl. Pour over baked filling. Bake 3 to 5 minutes longer. Cool and refrigerate before cutting into squares. Yields 4 dozen cookies.

Christmas Fruit Cookies

1½ cups raisins
1½ cups currants
1½ cups candied pineapple
1½ cups candied cherries
½ cup thinly sliced citron
1½ cups broken nuts
2 cups all-purpose flour, divided
2 sticks butter, softened
1½ cups packed light brown sugar

3 eggs, separated
½ cup evaporated milk
1½ teaspoons vinegar
½ teaspoon baking soda
½ teaspoon salt
1 teaspoon cinnamon
1 teaspoon ground cloves
1 teaspoon allspice
½ teaspoon nutmeg

Rinse raisins and currants and drain on paper towels. Cut pineapple, cherries, and citron into small pieces. In a bowl, combine fruits, nuts, and ½ cup flour. Cream butter in a large bowl. Blend in sugar. Beat in egg yolks, one at a time. In a small bowl, combine milk and vinegar. Add to butter mixture. In another bowl, sift together remaining 1½ cups flour, baking soda, and remaining 5 ingredients. Stir dry ingredients into butter mixture. Add fruit mixture. In a bowl, beat egg whites until stiff, but not dry. Fold into batter. Drop by teaspoonfuls onto a greased baking sheet. Bake at 325° for 20 to 25 minutes or until lightly browned. Cool on a wire rack. Yields 8 to 10 dozen cookies.

Jambalaya Bread Pudding

Pudding

1 (18-inch) loaf French bread	2 tablespoons vanilla
4 cups milk	1 teaspoon cinnamon
3 eggs, beaten	1 cup raisins
2 cups sugar	3 tablespoons butter

Sauce

1 stick butter	1 egg, beaten
1 cup sugar	¼ cup bourbon

Break bread into bite-size pieces in a large bowl. Cover with milk and soak 60 minutes. Mix well. Add egg and sugar. Stir in vanilla, cinnamon, and raisins. Melt butter in a 9X13X2 inch baking dish, tilting to coat all sides. Pour pudding into dish. Bake at 375° for 60 minutes. To prepare sauce, heat butter and sugar in the top of a double boiler. Slowly whisk in egg. Cool slightly. Add bourbon. Serve warm over pudding or in a sauceboat on the side. Yields 12 servings.

Sour Cream Pound Cake

Cake freezes well.

1½ sticks butter	½ teaspoon salt
1½ cups sugar	1 cup sour cream
2 eggs	1 teaspoon vanilla
2¼ cups all-purpose flour	1 teaspoon almond extract
1 teaspoon baking powder	

Cream butter and sugar in a large bowl. Mix in eggs, one at a time. Beat until fluffy. In a separate bowl, sift together flour, baking powder, and salt. Add alternately with sour cream to butter mixture. Add vanilla and almond extract. Beat at high speed with an electric mixer for 2 to 3 minutes or until fluffy. Pour into a greased and floured tube pan. Bake at 350° for 45 minutes or until a toothpick inserted in the center comes out clean. Yields 12 servings.

Orange Cream Cake

Cake
4 egg whites, room temperature
1/4 teaspoon cream of tartar
1 1/4 cups sugar, divided
6 egg yolks
3/4 cup orange juice, divided

1 cup all-purpose flour
1 teaspoon baking powder
1/2 teaspoon salt
1/3 cup water

Icing
2 cups heavy cream
3 tablespoons powdered sugar
2 tablespoons orange zest

oranges section or orange zest for
    garnish

In a large bowl, beat egg whites and cream of tartar, using an electric mixer at high speed, until soft peaks form. Gradually add 1/2 cup sugar, 2 tablespoons at a time, beating after each addition until completely dissolved. Do not scrape sides of bowl. Mixture should form stiff peaks. In a large bowl, beat egg yolks until thick and lemon-colored with an electric mixer at high speed. Gradually add 1/2 cup sugar, and continue to beat until pale yellow. Reduce to low speed and add 1/4 cup juice and next 3 ingredients. Beat until well mixed, scraping sides of bowl occasionally. Fold in egg white mixture just until blended. Line two 9-inch round cake pans with wax paper. Divide batter between pans. Bake at 325° for 40 minutes or until cake springs back when lightly touched. Cool in pans on wire racks for 10 minutes. Remove from pans and cool completely on racks. Prick holes all over cake layers with a fork. In a small saucepan, combine water and remaining 1/4 cup sugar. Bring to a boil and cook 3 minutes. Stir in remaining 1/2 cup orange juice. Drizzle evenly over layers and let stand 30 minutes. To prepare icing, beat cream and sugar in a small bowl, using an electric mixer at medium speed, until soft peaks form. Fold in zest. Place a cake layer on a serving platter. Spread with icing. Top with second layer. Frost top and sides of cake with remaining icing. Garnish with orange sections or zest. Refrigerate. Yields 14 servings.

Date Sticks

2 eggs
1 cup sugar
1 cup all-purpose flour

1 cup chopped pecans
1 cup chopped dates
powdered sugar

Beat eggs in a large bowl. Add sugar. Mix in flour until smooth. Fold in pecans and dates. Spread in a greased, shallow 9X13 inch pan. Bake at 350° for 20 minutes. While warm, cut into 3X1/2 inch sticks. Sticks will be soft and may not appear done. Roll in powdered sugar. Yields 32 sticks.

Colonial Chocolate Cake

Filling
1 (21-ounce) can cherry pie filling
2 tablespoons sugar

2 tablespoons kirsch

Cake
1¾ cups all-purpose flour
2 cups sugar
¾ cup cocoa
2 teaspoons baking soda
1 teaspoon baking powder
1 teaspoon salt

2 eggs
1 cup strong black coffee
1 cup buttermilk, or 1 cup milk plus
    1 tablespoon vinegar
½ cup vegetable oil
1 teaspoon vanilla

Icing
1½ cups heavy cream

¼ cup powdered sugar

Combine filling ingredients in a bowl. Chill several hours, or place in freezer while proceeding with recipe. Filling must be very cold to spread. To make cake, combine flour and next 5 ingredients in a large bowl. Add eggs and remaining 4 ingredients. Beat at medium speed with an electric mixer for 2 minutes. Batter will be thin. Divide between 2 well-greased and floured 9-inch cake pans. Bake at 350° for 35 to 40 minutes. Cool 2 minutes in pans. Remove from pans and cool completely. Prepare icing by beating cream and sugar until stiff. Assemble cake by placing a cake layer, up-side down, on a serving platter. Make a ring of icing, ½ inch high and 1 inch wide, on top of layer around outer edge. Spread about 1 cup of filling in center. Carefully place second layer on top, top-side up. Gently spread icing over entire cake. Fill center of top of cake with remaining filling. Chill at least 60 minutes before serving. Keep refrigerated. Yields 12 servings.

Pound Cake

2 sticks butter
3 cups sugar
6 eggs

3 cups all-purpose flour
1 cup heavy cream
1 teaspoon vanilla

Cream butter in a large bowl. Gradually mix in sugar. Beat in eggs, one at a time. Add flour and cream alternately. Blend well. Stir in vanilla. Pour into a greased and floured tube pan. Place in a cold oven. Turn oven to 325° and bake 1 hour, 15 minutes or until a toothpick inserted in the center comes out clean. Cool in pan 15 to 20 minutes. Cake will shrink as it cools. Yields 12 servings.

Brown Sugar Pound Cake

Cake freezes well.

½ cup coarsely chopped pecans
3 sticks butter, softened
2 cups packed brown sugar
1 cup granulated sugar
5 eggs

3 cups all-purpose flour
½ teaspoon baking powder
1 cup milk
1 teaspoon vanilla

Sprinkle pecans in a greased and floured Bundt pan or 10-inch tube pan. In a large bowl, cream butter and sugars. Mix in eggs, one at a time. In a small bowl, combine flour and baking powder. In another bowl, combine milk and vanilla. Add mixtures to butter mixture alternately. Pour into pan and bake at 325° for 1 hour, 30 minutes to 2 hours or until a toothpick inserted in the center comes out clean. Cool in pan 30 minutes. Yields 16 servings.

Carrot Cake

Cake
4 eggs
1½ cups vegetable oil
2 cups sugar
2 cups all-purpose flour
2 teaspoons baking soda

½ teaspoon salt
2 teaspoons cinnamon
1 cup chopped pecans
3 cups grated carrot

Icing
1 (8-ounce) package cream cheese,
   softened
1 stick butter, softened

1 (16-ounce) package powdered
   sugar
2 teaspoons vanilla
12 pecan halves for garnish

In a large bowl using an electric mixer, beat eggs 5 minutes or until lemon colored and fluffy. Blend in oil. Slowly beat in sugar. In a separate bowl, sift together flour and next 3 ingredients. Add nuts. Fold dry ingredients and carrot into batter. Pour batter into 3 greased and floured 8-inch cake pans, or two 9-inch pans. Bake at 350° for 35 minutes or until layers pull away from sides of pan. To prepare icing, blend cream cheese and butter in a large bowl until smooth. Slowly add sugar and blend well. Mix in vanilla. Spread between cooled cake layers and over top and sides of cake. Garnish with pecan halves. Yields 14 servings.

Apple Spice Cake

Cake

1 stick butter, softened
2 cups sugar
2 eggs
4 cups peeled and diced cooking
  apples
1 cup chopped pecans
½ cup raisins

2 cups all-purpose flour
2 teaspoons baking soda
½ teaspoon salt
2 teaspoons cinnamon
½ teaspoon nutmeg
½ teaspoon allspice

Caramel Icing

1½ cups packed light brown sugar
¼ teaspoon salt
½ cup milk

3 tablespoons butter
1 teaspoon vanilla
3 cups powdered sugar

Cream butter and sugar in a bowl. Beat in eggs and mix until thick and creamy. Fold in apples, pecans, and raisins. In a large bowl, combine flour and remaining 5 ingredients. Blend in butter mixture. Pour batter into a greased 9X13 inch pan. Bake at 325° for 60 minutes. To make icing, combine brown sugar, salt, and milk in a saucepan. Bring to a boil. Cook slowly 5 minutes or until slightly thickened. Remove from heat and beat in butter and vanilla. Cool slightly. Blend in powdered sugar. Spread over cake. Yields 12 servings.

Orange Fruit Cake

If more brandy is desired, every few days, pour ¼ cup brandy over cake.

2½ cups all-purpose flour, divided
1 cup crystallized orange zest
1 cup chopped dates
½ teaspoon baking soda
½ teaspoon cinnamon
½ teaspoon ground cloves
2 sticks butter

1½ cups sugar
3 eggs
½ teaspoon vanilla
½ cup orange juice
1 cup chopped pecans
1 cup chopped almonds
½ cup orange brandy or curaçao

Sprinkle ½ cup flour over zest and dates in a bowl. In a separate bowl, sift together remaining 2 cups flour, baking soda, cinnamon, and cloves. In a large bowl, cream butter and sugar. Mix in eggs, one at a time. Add vanilla. Add dry ingredients and juice, alternately, to butter mixture. Mix well. Stir in date mixture, pecans, and almonds. Spoon into a greased and floured tube pan, or two 9X5X3 inch loaf pans. Bake at 300° for 2 hours or until a toothpick inserted in the center comes out clean. Cool completely in pan. Pour brandy over cake. Wrap tightly and store in a cool place for up to several weeks. Yields 12 servings.

Mocha Macaroon Torte

1 stick butter, softened
1½ cups powdered sugar
4 egg yolks
2 tablespoons rum
2 tablespoons strong black coffee
1 teaspoon vanilla

⅓ cup sliced blanched almonds
2 cups heavy cream, divided
2 (3-ounce) packages ladyfingers,
  split
24 almond macaroons, crumbled

Cream butter and sugar until pale yellow in a large bowl. Beat in egg yolks and next 4 ingredients. Mix well. Whip 1 cup cream. Fold into butter mixture until just blended. Line bottom and sides of an 8-inch springform pan with ladyfingers. Pour half of butter mixture over top and cover with half macaroon crumbs. Add remaining butter mixture and top with remaining crumbs. Let stand 30 minutes. Cover with foil and refrigerate at least 24 hours. When ready to serve, whip remaining 1 cup cream and spread over top of torte. Yields 12 servings.

Bavarian Apple Torte

Crust
1 stick butter
⅓ cup sugar

½ teaspoon vanilla
1 cup all-purpose flour

Cream Layer
1 (8-ounce) package cream cheese,
  softened
¼ cup sugar

1 egg
½ teaspoon almond extract

Spiced Apples
½ cup sugar
½ teaspoon cinnamon
½ teaspoon allspice
4 cups peeled and sliced cooking
  apples

1 tablespoon lemon juice
¼ cup sliced almonds
1 tablespoon butter

Cream butter, sugar, and vanilla in a bowl. Blend in flour. Spread dough over the bottom and 1 inch up the sides of a 9-inch springform pan. To make cream layer, combine cream cheese and sugar in a bowl. Mix well. Blend in egg and extract. Pour over crust and bake at 400° for 10 minutes. Prepare spiced apples by combining sugar and next 4 ingredients in a bowl. Spoon apples over torte. Sprinkle almonds on top. Dot with butter. Bake at 400° for 25 minutes. After 10 minutes, cover with foil. Cool before removing sides of pan. Serve with hard sauce or sweetened heavy cream. Yields 10 servings.

Basic Pie Crust

½ cup less 1 tablespoon vegetable
   shortening
3 tablespoons boiling water

1 teaspoon milk
1¼ cups sifted flour
½ teaspoon salt

Beat shortening, water, and milk until smooth in a bowl. Add flour and salt. Blend well. Form into a ball and flatten to a 6-inch circle. Place between 2 sheets of lightly floured wax paper. Roll dough out to a 12-inch circle. Place in a pie pan and trim. For a baked pie crust, bake at 450° for 15 minutes. Yields one 9-inch pie crust.

Macaroon Graham Pecan Pie

3 eggs, room temperature
½ teaspoon baking powder
1 cup granulated sugar
11 graham cracker squares, crushed
1 cup chopped pecans

½ teaspoon almond extract
¾ teaspoon vanilla
1 cup heavy cream
3 tablespoons powdered sugar

Beat eggs and baking powder in a bowl until foamy. Slowly add granulated sugar and continue to beat until stiff. Carefully fold in cracker crumbs and pecans. Add almond extract and vanilla. Spread into a well-greased 10-inch pie pan. Bake at 350° for 30 minutes or until top of pie rises. Cool completely. Refrigerate at least 4 hours. When ready to serve, whip cream and powdered sugar until stiff. Spread over pie. Yields 10 servings.

Creole Pecan Pie

4 tablespoons butter, softened
½ cup sugar
3 eggs
½ cup cane syrup (no substitutions)
½ cup light corn syrup
1/16 teaspoon salt

1 teaspoon vanilla
1 cup chopped pecans
2 teaspoons orange zest
1 (9-inch) pie crust, unbaked
½ cup pecan halves
1 cup heavy cream, whipped

Cream butter and sugar in a bowl. Add eggs, one at a time, beating until light and fluffy. Add cane syrup and next 5 ingredients. Blend well. Pour into pie crust. Arrange pecan halves over top of pie. Bake at 350° for 45 minutes or until firm when gently shaken. Cool on a wire rack. Serve with whipped cream. Yields 8 servings.

Banana Cream Pie

½ cup granulated sugar
6 tablespoons all-purpose flour
¼ teaspoon salt
2¼ cups milk
1 egg
1 tablespoon butter

1 teaspoon vanilla
1 (9-inch) pie crust, baked and
   cooled
3 ripe bananas, sliced
1 cup heavy cream
1 tablespoon powdered sugar

Combine granulated sugar, flour, and salt in the top of a double boiler. Gradually stir in milk. Cook, stirring constantly with a whisk, over boiling water for 10 minutes or until thickened. Cover and cook 10 minutes, stirring occasionally. In a bowl, beat egg. Add a small amount of milk mixture and blend. Add back to double boiler and cook 2 minutes. Remove from heat and add butter and vanilla. Cool completely. Line pie crust with about half of banana slices. Pour half of milk mixture over bananas. Make a layer of remaining banana slices. Top with remaining milk mixture. Chill several hours. When ready to serve, whip cream and powdered sugar until stiff. Spread over pie. Yields 8 servings.

Deep Dish Apple Pie

Filling
8 cups peeled and sliced cooking
   apples
½ cup packed light brown sugar
2 tablespoons all-purpose flour

2 tablespoons water
1 teaspoon cinnamon
½ cup chopped pecans or walnuts

Topping
1 cup all-purpose flour
1 stick butter, softened

1½ cups packed dark brown sugar

Toss apples and next 4 ingredients. Place in a greased, round, 1½-quart casserole dish. Sprinkle with nuts. Blend all topping ingredients in a bowl and knead. Form into a ball. Roll out large enough to cover casserole dish. Place over filling. Bake at 350° for 60 minutes or until lightly browned. Yields 8 servings.

Blueberry Pie

4 cups fresh blueberries, or 1
   (16-ounce) bag frozen, divided
½ cup granulated sugar
½ cup packed brown sugar
2½ tablespoons all-purpose flour
1 tablespoon butter
1 tablespoon lemon juice

½ teaspoon cinnamon
⅛ teaspoon nutmeg
¼ teaspoon salt
1 (8-inch) pie crust, baked
1 cup heavy cream
1 teaspoon vanilla

Combine 2 cups blueberries and next 8 ingredients in a saucepan. Cook and stir over low heat until mixture comes to a boil. Simmer 10 minutes or until thickened. Cool. Stir in remaining 2 cups blueberries. Pour into pie crust and chill. When ready to serve, whip cream. Mix in vanilla and spread over pie. Yields 8 servings.

Caramel Nut Angel Pie

Meringue Pie Shell and Filling
2 egg whites
¼ teaspoon salt
¼ cup sugar
1½ cups finely chopped almonds or
   pecans

1 quart coffee-flavored ice cream,
   slightly softened
1 quart chocolate ice cream, slightly
   softened

Caramel Sauce
2 tablespoons butter
½ cup packed brown sugar
¼ cup half-and-half

½ teaspoon vanilla
2 tablespoons nuts

Beat egg whites and salt with an electric mixer on high speed until soft peaks form. Add sugar, 1 tablespoon at a time, beating 1 minute after each addition to form a stiff meringue. Fold in almonds. Spread meringue in a well-greased 9-inch pie pan, with sides extending over rim. Bake at 400° for 10 minutes or until lightly browned. Cool. Fill with ice creams. Cover tightly and freeze. To make sauce, melt butter in a saucepan. Stir in sugar and cook until dissolved. Slowly mix in half-and-half and cook 1 minute, stirring constantly. Mix in vanilla and nuts. Cool slightly. When ready to serve, drizzle over frozen pie. Yields 8 servings.

Praline Pumpkin Pie

Pie
1 (9-inch) pie crust, unbaked
4 tablespoons butter
½ cup granulated sugar
1 cup chopped pecans
1 (¼-ounce) envelope unflavored
  gelatin
½ cup cold water

¾ cup packed brown sugar
1 (16-ounce) can pumpkin
¼ cup milk
½ teaspoon salt
1 teaspoon cinnamon
¾ teaspoon nutmeg
1 cup heavy cream

Topping
½ cup heavy cream
½ teaspoon vanilla

2 tablespoons powdered sugar

Prick pie crust all over. Bake at 375° for 10 minutes or until lightly browned. In a skillet, cook and stir butter, granulated sugar, and pecans for 3 minutes or until golden. Spread out on foil, cool, and crumble. Sprinkle 1 cup of praline mixture over pie crust. Reserve remaining praline mix. In a saucepan, combine gelatin and water. Cook over low heat until dissolved. Remove from heat and add brown sugar. Blend in pumpkin and next 4 ingredients. Whip cream until stiff, but not dry. Fold into pumpkin mixture. Pour into pie crust and top with reserved praline mix. Refrigerate overnight. When ready to serve, prepare topping. Beat cream until stiff, gradually blending in vanilla and sugar. Place a dollop of topping on each serving. Yields 8 servings.

Fresh Lemon Pie

1½ cups graham cracker crumbs
6 tablespoons butter, melted
¼ cup sifted powdered sugar
1 teaspoon cinnamon
1 (14-ounce) can sweetened
  condensed milk

⅓ cup lemon juice
¼ teaspoon almond extract
1 cup heavy cream, whipped
2 tablespoons granulated sugar
¼ teaspoon vanilla
lemon slices

Combine cracker crumbs and next 3 ingredients in a bowl. Press into an 8-inch pie pan. Bake at 300° for 15 minutes. Cool. Combine milk, lemon juice, and almond extract in a small bowl. Pour into crust. Blend cream, granulated sugar, and vanilla. Spread over pie. Chill. Garnish with lemon slices and serve cold. Yields 8 servings.

Chocolate Meringue Pie

Crust
1¼ cups crushed buttery shortbread
    cookies

1 tablespoon sugar
6 tablespoons butter, melted

Filling
2 cups milk
3 tablespoons cocoa
1 cup sugar
⅓ cup all-purpose flour
¼ teaspoon salt
3 egg yolks, beaten

2 teaspoons vanilla
1 tablespoon butter
Meringue
3 egg whites
3 tablespoons sugar

Combine all crust ingredients in a small bowl. Pat into bottom and up sides of a 9-inch pie pan. Bake at 325° for 7 minutes. To make filling, scald milk in a saucepan. In a bowl, combine cocoa and next 3 ingredients. Gradually mix dry ingredients into milk, whisking until thick. Do not allow to boil. Add yolk and cook and stir 3 minutes. Add vanilla and butter and continue to cook 1 more minute. Pour filling into cooled pie shell. Prepare meringue by beating whites until soft peaks form. Gradually add sugar, 1 tablespoon at a time, beating until stiff. Spread meringue over pie, completely covering crust edges. Bake at 325° for 10 to 12 minutes or until lightly browned. Yields 8 servings.

Crépes

Recipe does not work with a crépe maker. To freeze, stack crépes with wax paper in-between each. Wrap tightly in plastic. Thaw to room temperature.

1 cup all-purpose flour
3 eggs
pinch of salt

1½ cups milk, divided
4 tablespoons butter

Place flour in a large bowl and make a well in center. Add eggs, salt, and ½ cup milk. Beat, starting from center, until batter is thick. Gradually beat in remaining 1 cup milk until batter is consistency of light cream, just coating a spoon. Refrigerate at least 2 hours, or preferably overnight. Stir well. If needed, add extra milk to achieve cream consistency. Melt butter in a 6-inch skillet. Pour butter into batter and stir well. Wipe pan with paper towels and heat until a drop of water bounces. Spoon in 1 tablespoon batter, or just enough to coat bottom of skillet. Turn when top looks dry, or cook only on one side. Stir batter frequently. Yields 16 to 20 (6-inch) crépes.

Cottage Peach Cobbler

Filling
2½ tablespoons all-purpose flour
1/16 teaspoon salt
1½ cups sugar
1 teaspoon cinnamon

12 large fresh peaches, sliced, or 3
   (16-ounce) cans sliced peaches,
   drained
4 tablespoons butter, melted
¼ teaspoon almond extract

Pastry
2 cups all-purpose flour
1 teaspoon salt
½ teaspoon baking powder

⅔ cup vegetable shortening
5 tablespoons butter, softened
4 tablespoons ice water

Garnish
3 cups heavy cream, whipped

1 pint fresh blueberries

Combine flour and next 3 ingredients in a large bowl. Add peaches, butter, and extract. To prepare pastry, combine flour, salt, and baking powder in a bowl. Cut in shortening and 1 tablespoon butter until mixture resembles coarse meal. Gradually add water and mix until dough holds together in a ball. Divide dough in half. Roll 1 half onto a floured surface or between 2 floured pieces of wax paper. Line sides and 1 inch around bottom of a lightly greased 9X13X2 inch baking dish with strips of dough. Pour peach filling into dish. Roll out remaining half of dough. Cut into ¾-inch wide strips. Place in a lattice or criss-cross design over filling. Melt remaining 4 tablespoons butter and drizzle over top. Bake at 375° for 45 minutes or until pastry is lightly browned. Garnish each serving with whipped cream and blueberries. Yields 14 servings.

Grand Marnier Crépes

2 sticks butter
1 cup powdered sugar
½ cup fresh orange juice

⅛ teaspoon cinnamon
¼ cup Grand Marnier, warmed
18 crépes (page 218)

Melt butter in a skillet. Add sugar and stir until dissolved. Add juice. Cook and stir over low heat until thickened. Stir in cinnamon. Add Grand Marnier and ignite, stirring until flame dies. Place crépes in skillet, one at a time, and fold into quarters. Serve with remaining sauce spooned over top. Yields 6 servings.

Crépes Suzette

1 (8-ounce) jar orange marmalade
12 crépes (page xxx)
4 tablespoons butter

¼ cup fresh orange juice
2 tablespoons brandy, warmed
1 tablespoon sugar

Place 1 tablespoon marmalade in center of each crépe. Fold into quarters. In a large skillet or chafing dish, melt butter. Add remaining marmalade and juice. Simmer until blended. Place crépes in orange sauce, arranging in an overlapping circle around skillet. Refrigerate up to several hours, or proceed. When ready to serve, add brandy and ignite. Spoon sauce over crépes and sprinkle sugar over top. Yields 6 servings.

Chocolate Cheesecake

Crust
1 (6-ounce) package zwieback toast, crushed into fine crumbs
2 tablespoons sugar

1½ teaspoons cinnamon
1 stick butter, melted

Filling
3 (8-ounce) packages cream cheese, softened
1 cup sugar
3 eggs

½ teaspoon vanilla
2 ounces German sweet chocolate, finely grated or chopped

Topping
2 cups sour cream
4 tablespoons sugar
½ teaspoon vanilla

1 ounce German sweet chocolate, finely grated

Combine all crust ingredients and mix well. Press into bottom and up sides of a 9-inch springform pan. To prepare filling, cream cheese until fluffy. Gradually add sugar and continue to cream. Add eggs, one at a time, beating after each addition. Add vanilla. Stir in chocolate. Spoon into crust. Bake at 375° for 20 minutes. Cheesecake will not be firm in center. Cool completely. Make topping by beating together sour cream, sugar, and vanilla. Spoon over cheesecake. Bake at 350° for 10 minutes. Cool and refrigerate overnight. Before serving, sprinkle chocolate over top. Yields 12 servings.

Classic Cream Puffs or Profiteroles

Puff Pastry

1 cup water	2 tablespoons sugar
4 tablespoons butter	½ teaspoon salt
1½ cups sifted flour	4 eggs, room temperature

Cream Puff Filling

2 cups milk	½ teaspoon salt
3 egg yolks	⅓ cup sifted flour
⅔ cup sugar	2 teaspoons vanilla
1 tablespoon butter, softened	2 teaspoons Grand Marnier

Profiterole Filling

2 cups heavy cream, whipped	1 teaspoon vanilla
2 tablespoons powdered sugar ·	

Fudge Sauce

4 tablespoons butter	6 squares semi-sweet chocolate
2¼ cups powdered sugar	½ teaspoon vanilla
⅔ cup evaporated milk	

Boil water in a saucepan. Add butter and stir until melted. Combine flour, sugar, and salt and add to water all at once. Mix thoroughly with a wooden spoon. Cook over medium heat for 4 minutes or until mixture leaves sides of pan and forms a soft dough. Cool 5 minutes. Add eggs, 1 at a time, beating well after each addition until pastry is smooth and shiny. Mound puffs on a lightly greased baking sheet, using a spoon or a pastry bag. Form either 2-inch cream puffs or 1-inch profiteroles. Leave 2 inches between each puff. Bake at 450° for 15 minutes. Reduce temperature to 325° and bake 20 minutes or until puffy and browned. Remove from oven and slit each puff horizontally. Turn off heat and return puffs to oven for 2 minutes, leaving door ajar, to dry out puffs. Cool on a wire rack. Store in an airtight container until ready to fill. To prepare cream puff filling, scald milk in the top of a double boiler. In a bowl, beat egg yolks until lemon colored. Add sugar and butter and blend until light and fluffy. Mix in salt and flour. Slowly whisk in milk. Return to double boiler and cook and stir 6 to 8 minutes or until creamy and thick. Add vanilla and Grand Marnier. Cool. Cover and refrigerate. Fill puffs with chilled mixture and drizzle with fudge sauce. If making profiteroles, prepare filling by combining whipped cream, sugar, and vanilla in a bowl. Fill profiteroles and stack in a pyramid on a serving platter. Drizzle with fudge sauce, serving remaining sauce on the side in a warmed sauceboat. To make fudge sauce, blend butter and sugar in the top of a double boiler. Add milk and chocolate. Cook 30 minutes. Do not allow to boil. Remove from heat and beat in vanilla. Thin, if necessary, with milk. Serve warm. Refrigerate any unused portion and reheat as needed. Yields 12 (2-inch) cream puffs or 24 (1-inch) profiteroles, 2 cups fudge sauce.

Orange Cheesecake

Crust
1¼ cups graham cracker crumbs
¼ cup sugar

4 tablespoons butter, melted

Filling
5 (8-ounce) packages cream cheese, softened
1¾ cups sugar
3 tablespoons all-purpose flour
1 tablespoon lemon zest

2 tablespoons orange zest
5 eggs
2 egg yolks
¼ cup heavy cream

Glaze
1 tablespoon lemon juice
1 tablespoon cornstarch

2 tablespoons cold water
¾ cup orange juice

Mix all crust ingredients in a small bowl. Press into bottom and up sides of a 9-inch springform pan. To make filling, cream cheese in a large bowl until fluffy. Combine sugar and flour. Blend into cheese. Add zests. Mix in eggs and yolks, one at a time. Stir in cream. Spoon mixture into crust. Bake at 500° for 10 minutes. Reduce temperature to 200° and bake 60 minutes. Cheesecake will not be firm in center. Cool. Combine all glaze ingredients in a saucepan. Cook and stir over low heat until thick. Spoon over cheesecake. Refrigerate overnight. Yields 12 to 16 servings.

Orange Crème Brûlée

3 cups light cream
⅔ cup packed brown sugar
¼ teaspoon salt

12 egg yolks
1 tablespoon orange extract
¾ cup packed light brown sugar

Scald cream with sugar and salt in the top of a double boiler. Whisk together yolks and extract until well blended. Gradually stir some cream mixture into yolk mixture, one tablespoon at a time. Add back into double boiler. Cook, stirring constantly, over very low heat. When mixture reaches the consistency of a thick cream sauce, pour into 8 custard cups or ramekins. Chill. On a greased piece of foil, form 8 thin circles of light brown sugar the size of top of custard cups. Bake at 300° for 10 minutes. Cool and peel from foil. Place on top of each custard 30 minutes before serving. Yields 8 servings.

Lemon Cheesecake

Crust
1 tablespoon butter

¼ cup graham cracker crumbs

Filling
3 (8-ounce) packages cream cheese,
   softened
1¼ cups sugar
3 eggs

1 egg yolk
2 tablespoons lemon juice
1 tablespoon lemon zest

Topping
2 cups sour cream
¼ cup sugar

1 teaspoon lemon juice

Use butter to grease bottom and sides of a 9-inch springform pan. Sprinkle cracker crumbs over all. To make filling, cream cheese until fluffy. Add sugar and continue to cream. Beat in eggs and yolk, one at a time. Add juice and mix well. Fold in zest. Spoon into pan. Bake at 350° for 20 minutes. Cool. Beat all topping ingredients until smooth. Spoon over filling. Bake at 350° for 10 minutes. Cool and refrigerate overnight. Yields 12 servings.

Chilled Lemon Soufflé

2 (¼-ounce) envelopes unflavored
   gelatin
½ cup water
6 eggs
1½ cups plus 2 teaspoons granulated
   sugar

⅔ cup fresh lemon juice
1 tablespoon lemon zest
2 cups heavy cream, divided
1 teaspoon vanilla
1 tablespoon powdered sugar

Sprinkle gelatin over water in a saucepan. Let soften 5 minutes. Heat until dissolved and cool. Beat eggs and granulated sugar in a bowl for 7 minutes or until very thick. Combine juice, zest, and gelatin mixture. Add to egg mixture. Blend thoroughly and freeze. Stir every 2 minutes for 6 to 8 minutes or until mixture thickens. Whip 1½ cups cream and vanilla. Fold into lemon mixture. Pour into a soufflé dish or individual dessert glasses. Refrigerate 2 to 3 hours. Whip remaining ½ cup cream and powdered sugar. Top soufflé with whipped cream before serving. Yields 12 servings.

Frozen Lemon Cream

1 cup milk
1 cup heavy cream
1 cup sugar
2 teaspoons lemon zest

3 tablespoons lemon juice
3 large lemons, halved lengthwise
lemon leaves or mint sprigs for
  garnish

Combine milk, cream, and sugar in a bowl. Mix until sugar dissolves. Pour into a shallow bowl and freeze until slightly thickened. Whisk in zest and juice. Refreeze 2 hours. Beat again thoroughly. Refreeze until solid. Scoop out pulp of lemon halves. Fill each half with frozen cream and garnish. Yields 6 servings.

French Cream

Suitable other fruits include blueberries, raspberries, grapes, or peaches.

1 cup heavy cream
1/3 cup sifted powdered sugar
1/2 cup sour cream
1/2 teaspoon lemon zest
1/4 cup Grand Marnier

4 cups strawberries or other fresh
  fruit
1 tablespoon grated sweet dark
  chocolate for garnish

Whip cream in a bowl. Fold in sugar, sour cream, and zest. Add Grand Marnier. Arrange strawberries in a serving bowl and top with cream mixture. Garnish with chocolate. Yields 8 servings.

Fresh Fig Mousse

1 cup fresh figs, peeled
3 tablespoons fresh lemon juice
1/2 cup powdered sugar

1 cup heavy cream, whipped
16 fig halves, peeled

Mash figs in a bowl with a fork. Add juice and sugar. Mix until all sugar is blended. Fold in cream. Freeze in 8 dessert cups for 3 hours or until firm. Top each with 2 fig halves and serve. Yields 8 servings.

Classic Caramel Custard

3 eggs
1 cup sugar, divided
2 cups half-and-half, scalded

½ teaspoon vanilla
⅛ teaspoon salt
1/16 teaspoon nutmeg, optional

Beat eggs and ½ cup sugar in a bowl. Slowly add half-and-half, whisking until well blended. Add vanilla and salt. Place 6 custard cups in 1 inch of warm water in a shallow pan. In a skillet, heat remaining ½ cup sugar for 10 minutes or until it dissolves and turns caramel-colored. Be careful not to burn. Pour a little caramel into each custard cup, reserving some for topping, and swirl before it hardens. Pour egg mixture over top and sprinkle with nutmeg. Bake at 325° for 60 minutes or until a knife inserted in the center comes out clean. Cool and refrigerate. When ready to serve, loosed edges with a thin knife and unmold onto plates. Drizzle remaining caramel over top. Yields 6 servings.

Mousse in a Minute

1 (12-ounce) package semi-sweet
   chocolate chips
¼ cup sugar
⅛ teaspoon salt
7 tablespoons strong coffee

4 egg yolks
1½ cups half-and-half
½ cup heavy cream
chocolate shavings

Place chocolate chips and next 4 ingredients in a blender. In a saucepan, bring half-and-half to a boil. Pour immediately into blender. Process on high speed for several minutes or until dark brown and smooth. Divide among 10 dessert cups. Chill several hours. When ready to serve, whip cream. Place a dollop on each mousse and sprinkle with chocolate shavings. Yields 10 servings.

For a slightly different flavor, use 3½ tablespoons strong coffee and 3½ table-spoons Kahlúa.

Chocolate Mousse

4 eggs, separated
4 ounces semi-sweet dark chocolate
1 tablespoon brandy

1 tablespoon water
½ cup heavy cream, whipped

Beat egg yolks until thick and creamy. In a saucepan, heat chocolate, brandy, and water over very low heat. Slowly stir into yolk. Beat egg whites until stiff. Fold into chocolate mixture with a metal spoon. Pour into pots de crème and refrigerate at least 4 hours. Top each serving with a dollop of whipped cream. Yields 4 servings.

Drambuie Flummery

4 egg yolks
¼ cup sugar
¼ cup Drambuie
1½ cups heavy cream, divided

2 egg whites
1 tablespoon slivered almonds
1 teaspoon butter

Beat yolks and sugar in the top of a double boiler until mixture thickens and increases in volume. Add Drambuie. Mixture will thicken and form soft peaks. In a bowl, whip 1 cup cream and egg whites until stiff peaks form. Gently fold into yolk mixture just until blended. Pour into champagne glasses or dessert dishes and refrigerate several hours. In a small saucepan, sauté almonds in butter until nicely browned. Drain. Whip remaining ½ cup cream. Top each dessert with a dollop of whipped cream and sprinkle with almonds. Yields 4 servings.

Bourbon On A Cloud

1 (¼-ounce) envelope unflavored
   gelatin
¾ cup sugar, divided
3 eggs, separated

¾ cup bourbon
1 cup heavy cream, whipped
2 teaspoons semi-sweet chocolate
   shavings

Combine gelatin and 6 tablespoons sugar. In a saucepan, lightly beat egg yolks and slowly add bourbon. Add gelatin mixture. Cook and stir over low heat until sauce coats a spoon. Cool. In a large bowl, beat egg whites until stiff, but not dry, gradually adding remaining 6 tablespoons sugar. Fold yolk mixture into whites. Reserving some for topping, fold whipped cream into egg mixture. Spoon into dessert dishes and refrigerate at least 6 hours. Top each with a dollop of whipped cream and sprinkle with chocolate shavings. Yields 8 servings.

Praline Sauce

¾ cup white corn syrup
1½ cups packed light brown sugar
4 tablespoons butter

1 (5⅓-ounce) can evaporated milk
¾ cup chopped pecans

Combine syrup, sugar, and butter in a saucepan. Bring to a boil, Remove from heat and cool. When lukewarm, stir in milk and pecans. Refrigerate. Yields 2½ cups.

Praline Parfait Sauce

Good over ice cream or layered in parfait glasses with ice cream and topped with whipped cream.

1½ cups dark corn syrup
½ cup packed dark brown sugar
4 teaspoons all-purpose flour
¼ teaspoon salt

2 tablespoons butter
1 cup water
1½ teaspoons vanilla
1 cup chopped pecans

Combine syrup and next 5 ingredients in a saucepan. Bring to a boil and cook 10 minutes. Remove from heat and add vanilla and pecans. Serve warm or cold. Yields 2 to 2½ cups.

Yum Yum Chocolate Sauce

Keeps in refrigerator for several weeks.

2 cups sugar
1 cup cocoa
1 cup milk

1 cup light corn syrup
2 tablespoons butter
1 teaspoon vanilla

Combine sugar and next 4 ingredients in a saucepan. Bring to a boil and cook 5 minutes. Add vanilla. Serve hot over ice cream or cake. Yields 3 cups.

Hot Chocolate Sauce

1 (8-ounce) package unsweetened
   chocolate
2 cups sugar
2 tablespoons corn syrup, light or
   dark

1 (13-ounce) can evaporated milk
2 teaspoons vanilla
½ teaspoon salt

Melt chocolate in the top of a double boiler. Gradually mix in sugar. Stir in syrup. Slowly add milk and mix until creamy. Remove from heat and stir in vanilla and salt. Yields 3 cups.

Hard Sauce

2 sticks butter, softened
1 (16-ounce) package powdered
   sugar

1 egg, separated
¼ cup whiskey or brandy

Cream butter and sugar in a bowl until smooth. In a separate bowl, beat egg yolk. Add to butter mixture. In another bowl, beat egg white until stiff and fold into butter mixture. Gradually fold in whiskey, mixing well between additions. Chill. Yields 2 cups.

Tangerine Ice

Reserve tangerine shells when squeezing juice. Use shells as serving containers for ice.

¾ cup light corn syrup
⅔ cup sugar
½ cup water
2 cups fresh tangerine or Louisiana
   satsuma juice

3 tablespoons fresh lemon juice
2 egg whites
1 tablespoon vodka, chilled,
   optional
slivered tangerine zest

Combine syrup, sugar, and water in a saucepan. Bring to a boil and cook 5 minutes. Cool 10 minutes. Add juices. Freeze in a shallow bowl until almost firm. Beat egg whites until soft peaks form. Transfer syrup mixture to a chilled bowl and beat until smooth. Fold in egg white. Freeze until firm. If mixture separates, beat again and return to freezer. Serve with a splash of vodka and sprinkle with zest. Yields 6 servings.

Meringue Nests with Raspberry Sauce

Nests
4 egg whites, room temperature
½ teaspoon cream of tartar
1 teaspoon vanilla

1 cup sugar
1 cup chopped pecans

Raspberry Sauce
2 tablespoons cornstarch
⅔ cup sugar

4 cups fresh raspberries, or 2
   (10-ounce) packages frozen
2 tablespoons fresh lemon juice

Beat egg whites until frothy. Add cream of tartar and vanilla. Beat until doubled. Continue to beat while adding sugar, 1 tablespoon at a time, until meringue is stiff and glossy. Fold in pecans. To make a nest, drop about 2 tablespoonfuls of meringue onto a baking sheet lined with brown paper. Hollow out center with back of spoon to form a nest. Repeat with remaining meringue. Bake at 250° for 50 minutes. Turn off oven, leaving nests for 10 minutes to dry out. Remove from oven and cool. Store in an airtight container. To make sauce, combine cornstarch and sugar in the top of a double boiler. Add raspberries and cook and stir until thickened and shiny. Add lemon juice. Chill. Serve nest with a scoop of vanilla ice cream and top with sauce. Yields eight (3½-inch) nests.

Louisiana Pecan Pralines

1 cup light brown sugar, not packed
1 cup granulated sugar
½ cup evaporated milk
2 tablespoons butter

2 tablespoons light corn syrup
1/16 teaspoon salt
1 teaspoon vanilla
1¾ cups pecan halves

Using a wooden spoon, combine brown sugar and next 5 ingredients in a saucepan. Cook 10 minutes or to soft ball stage. Test for doneness by dropping a drop of mixture into cold water. Drop should be soft when picked up with fingers. Remove from heat. Add vanilla and pecans. Beat 1 minute or until mixture starts to thicken. Drop by teaspoonfuls onto greased wax paper. Cool. Yields 2 dozen.

Notes and Other Recipes

EQUIVALENTS

Ingredient	Equivalent
3 medium apples	3 cups sliced apples
3 medium bananas	2½ cups sliced, 2 cups mashed banana
1 medium lemon	2 to 3 tablespoons juice and 2 teaspoons grated rind
1 medium lime................	1½ to 2 tablespoons juice
1 medium orange	⅓ cup juice and 2 tablespoons grated rind
4 medium peaches	2 cups sliced peaches
4 medium pears	2 cups sliced pears
1 quart strawberries	4 cups sliced strawberries
1 pound head cabbage	4½ cups shredded cabbage
1 pound carrots..............	3 cups shredded carrots
2 medium corn ears	1 cup whole kernel corn
1 large green pepper	1 cup diced green pepper
1 pound head lettuce	6¼ cups torn lettuce
8 ounces raw mushrooms	1 cup sliced cooked mushrooms
1 medium onion	½ cup chopped onion
3 medium white potatoes	2 cups cubed cooked or 1¾ cups mashed white potatoes
3 medium sweet potatoes	3 cups sliced sweet potatoes
8 slices cooked bacon	½ cup crumbled bacon
1 pound American or Cheddar cheese	4 to 5 cups shredded cheese
4 ounces cheese..............	1 cup shredded cheese
5 large whole eggs	1 cup eggs
6 to 7 large eggs..............	1 cup egg whites
11 to 12 large eggs............	1 cup egg yolks
1 cup quick-cooking oats	1¾ cups cooked oats
1 cup uncooked long grain rice .	3 to 4 cups cooked rice
1 cup pre-cooked rice..........	2 cups cooked rice
1 pound coffee	40 cups perked coffee
1 pound pitted dates	2 to 3 cups chopped dates
1 pound all-purpose flour	4 cups flour
1 pound granulated sugar	2 cups sugar
1 pound powdered sugar.......	3½ cups powdered sugar
1 pound brown sugar	2¼ cups firmly packed brown sugar
1 cup (4 ounces) uncooked macaroni	2¼ cups cooked macaroni
4 ounces uncooked noodles	2 cups cooked noodles
7 ounces uncooked spaghetti ..	4 cups cooked spaghetti
1 pound shelled nuts	4 cups chopped nuts

1 cup whipping cream .... 2 cups whipped cream
1 cup soft bread crumbs ...... 2 slices fresh bread
1 pound crab in shell .... ¼ to 1 cup flaked crab
1½ pounds fresh, unpeeled   2 cups cooked, peeled, deveined
   shrimp....................   shrimp
   1 pound fresh small shrimp .. 35 or more shrimp
   1 pound frèsh medium shrimp 26 to 35 shrimp
   1 pound fresh large shrimp... 21 to 25 shrimp
   1 pound fresh jumbo shrimp.. less than 20 shrimp
Crackers
   19 chocolate wafers .... 1 cup crumbs
   14 graham cracker squares... 1 cup fine crumbs
   28 saltines .... 1 cup finely crushed crumbs
   22 vanilla wafers .... 1 cup finely crushed crumbs

SUBSTITUTIONS

Recipe Ingredients	*Substitution*
1 cup sour or buttermilk	1 tablespoon vinegar or lemon juice plus sweet milk to make 1 cup
1 cup commercial sour cream ..	1 tablespoon lemon juice plus evaporated milk to equal 1 cup
1 cup yogurt	1 cup sour or buttermilk
1 whole egg	2 egg yolks plus 1 tablespoon water
1 tablespoon cornstarch	2 tablespoons all-purpose flour
1 teaspoon baking powder	½ teaspoon cream of tartar plus ¼ teaspoon soda
1 cup cake flour	1 cup all-purpose flour minus 2 tablespoons
1 cup self-rising flour	1 cup all-purpose flour plus 1 teaspoon baking powder and ½ teaspoon salt
1 cup honey	1¼ cups sugar plus ¼ cup liquid
1 ounce unsweetened chocolate	3 tablespoons cocoa plus 1 tablespoon butter or margarine
1 pound fresh mushrooms	6 ounces canned mushrooms
1 tablespoon fresh herbs	1 teaspoon ground or crushed dry herbs
1 teaspoon onion powder	2 teaspoons minced onion
1 clove fresh garlic	1 teaspoon garlic salt or ⅛ teaspoon garlic powder

MEASUREMENTS TO REMEMBER

3 teaspoons	=	1 tablespoon
4 tablespoons	=	¼ cup
8 tablespoons	=	½ cup
16 tablespoons	=	1 cup
5 tablespoons plus 1 teaspoon	=	⅓ cup
4 ounces	=	½ cup
8 ounces	=	1 cup
16 ounces	=	1 pound
1 ounce	=	2 tablespoons fat or liquid
2 cups fat	=	1 pound
2 cups	=	1 pint
1 pound butter	=	2 cups or 4 sticks
2 pints	=	1 quart
4 cups	=	1 quart

THE METRIC SYSTEM

2 cups	=	473 milliliters
1 cup	=	237 milliliters
¾ cup	=	177 milliliters
⅔ cup	=	157 milliliters
½ cup	=	118 milliliters
⅓ cup	=	79 milliliters
¼ cup	=	59 milliliters
1 tablespoon	=	15 milliliters
1 teaspoon	=	5 milliliters
1 fluid ounce	=	30 milliliters

How to Convert:

liters	x 2.1	= pints	kilograms	x 2.2	= pounds
liters	x 1.06	= quarts	grams	x .035	= ounces
cups	x .24	= liters	pounds	x .45	= kilograms
gallons	x 3.8	= liters	ounces	x 28	= grams

Temperatures:
250 degrees Fahrenheit = 121 degrees Celsius
300 degrees Fahrenheit = 149 degrees Celsius
350 degrees Fahrenheit = 177 degrees Celsius
400 degrees Fahrenheit = 205 degrees Celsius
450 degrees Fahrenheit = 232 degrees Celsius

Index

Index

Index

Index

Index

Index

Index